Varieties of European Subsidiarity

A Multidisciplinary Approach

EDITED BY

GÜNTER WALZENBACH & RALF ALLEWELDT

E-INTERNATIONAL RELATIONS PUBLISHING

E-International Relations
www.E-IR.info
Bristol, England
2021

ISBN 978-1-910814-57-4

Production: Michael Tang
Cover Image: frees/ilolab/Shutterstock

A catalogue record for this book is available from the British Library.

E-IR Edited Collections

Series Editor: Stephen McGlinchey
Books Editor: Bill Kakenmaster
Editorial assistance: Patterson Deppen, Kaiqing Su, Simon Hilditch, Alyssa Blakemore.

E-IR's Edited Collections are open access scholarly books presented in a format that preferences brevity and accessibility while retaining academic conventions. Each book is available in print and digital versions, and is published under a Creative Commons license. As E-International Relations is committed to open access in the fullest sense, free electronic versions of all of our books, including this one, are available on our website.

Find out more at: http://www.e-ir.info/publications

About E-International Relations

E-International Relations (E-IR) is the world's leading open access website for students and scholars of international politics, reaching over three million readers per year. In addition to our books, our daily publications feature expert articles, reviews and interviews – as well as student learning resources. The website is run by a non-profit organisation based in Bristol, England and staffed by an all-volunteer team of students and scholars.

http://www.e-ir.info

This book amply demonstrates the utility of political analysis for a fuller understanding of the concept of subsidiarity. It offers important insights for students of regional and global governance, particularly for those concerned with the future evolution and political legitimacy of European governance. The volume's organisation is exemplary, and the editors identify multiple sources of political authority with far-reaching consequences for supranational policy making. They do so without losing sight of the real-life stakeholders at national and local levels.

– Tsuneo Akaha. Professor Emeritus, Middlebury Institute of International Studies at Monterey, USA.

The editors of this volume reinvigorate the international debate on the role of subsidiarity in theory and practice. *Varieties of European Subsidiarity* moves beyond legal analysis with a multidisciplinary exploration of the principle in its many empirical manifestations. Despite the focus on EU policy, individual contributions also delve into comparative and international dimensions, offering valuable accounts of key topics in European governance. A rigorous, empirically informed, but critical and new contribution to an important field.

– Kostas A. Lavdas. Professor of European Politics, Panteion University, Athens, Greece.

Walzenbach and Alleweldt's *Varieties of European Subsidiarity* offers a state-of-the-art account of the complex and politically contested system of multi-level governance in Europe. Those with an interest in the shifting sites of political authority in Europe will greatly benefit from the book's multidisciplinary insights. It competently explores the legal foundation of the principle of subsidiarity and thoroughly examines practical applications in different policy areas and across EU member states.

– Oliver Schmidtke. Professor, Centre for Global Studies, University of Victoria, Canada.

The multidisciplinary perspective offered here nicely blends theoretical exploration with practical relevance and includes intriguing case studies as a must read for anyone interested in the workings of the European Union. This book will be an essential source for students and scholars in the Eastern Neighbourhood designing their own processes of decentralisation.

– Volodymyr Yemelyanov. Professor, Institute of Public Administration, Petro Mohyla Black Sea National University, Mykolayiv, Ukraine.

Abstract

Subsidiarity as a principle in favour of decentralised decision-making is a cornerstone of the very legal construction of the EU. Yet, the question of how decision-making powers should be distributed between the EU and the member states is not, or only to a minimal extent, answered in Article 5 (3) of the Treaty on European Union (TEU). This collection draws on social science disciplines to go beyond a purely legal analysis to provide clarity over this principle as applied. With the help of theoretical exploration and empirical case studies the contributors identify significant variation in the implementation of the subsidiarity concept. By tracing the precise location of political authority at different levels of European governance they examine the pressures for effective decision-making despite the changing policy preferences of governments.

Acknowledgements

We are most grateful to the authors of this volume who invested considerable time and effort to see its successful completion. What started out as a project of German-Italian cooperation soon reached beyond the confines of any specific country comparison. Rosa Mulé deserves our joint credit for getting the project off the ground and for being such a welcoming workshop host at the University of Bologna. While working on this book, the editors have benefitted from discussions on subsidiarity with students and colleagues from the University of the West of England, Bristol, the Brandenburg State Police University, Oranienburg, and the American University of Armenia, Yerevan. The argument advanced here has been further explored in a special issue on 'Spaces of Subsidiarity – Diverging Politics and Policies', published by *Commonwealth & Comparative Politics* as volume 57(2) in April 2019. Finally, without the support of Stephen McGlinchey and the E-International Relations editorial team this collection would have never become a finished product.

G.W. and R.A.

Bristol and Berlin, February 2021

About the editors

Günter Walzenbach is Senior Lecturer in European Politics at the University of the West of England, Bristol, and was Associate Professor of Political Science at the American University of Armenia, Yerevan. His research interests are in comparative political economy and multi-level governance.

Ralf Alleweldt is Professor of Constitutional and European Law at the Brandenburg State Police University, Oranienburg. His key research interests are in international human rights law, prevention of torture, refugee law, and constitutional justice.

Contributors

Hartmut Aden is Professor of European and German Public Law at the Berlin School of Economics and Law as well as Deputy Director of the Institute for Safety and Security Research.

Sian Affolter is a Doctoral Candidate at the Institute of European Law of the University of Fribourg, Switzerland. Her Ph.D. research focuses on European environmental and agricultural law.

Marco Balboni is Professor of European Union and International Law at the University of Bologna, where he is also the Coordinator of the Degree in International Relations and Diplomatic Affairs. His research interests include international and EU migration law, EU non-discrimination law and human rights.

Marco Borraccetti is Associate Professor in European Union Law at the University of Bologna. His research focuses on EU migration, human trafficking as well as refugee and asylum policy.

Maximilian Bossdorf is a Doctoral Candidate at the University of the West of England, Bristol, and a former Trade Commissioner of the Canadian Government in Germany. His PhD research explores public-private partnerships in European trade policy.

Jörg Michael Dostal is Associate Professor in the Graduate School of Public Administration, Seoul National University, South Korea. He is also Senior Research Fellow at the Centre for Syrian Studies, University of St Andrews.

Jörg Dürrschmidt is Professor of Sociology at the University of Applied Sciences Ludwigsburg, where he is the Co-Director of the Institute of Applied Research as well as the Co-Organiser of the International Summer School on Safe, Orderly and Regular Migration. He specialises in globalisation studies, migration and urban change.

Barrie B. F. Hebb is a Development Economist consulting with public and private agencies providing aid to vulnerable people in the context of natural and man-made disasters. His research interests focus on the impact of institutional failures on poor communities in transition economies.

Giuliana Laschi is Associate Professor and Jean Monnet Chair *ad personam* in Contemporary History and the History of European Integration at the University of Bologna. Her research focus is on the political history of the CAP and the external relations of the European Communities.

Thilo Marauhn is Professor of Public and International Law at the Justus Liebig University, Giessen, and Head of the Research Group on Public International Law at the Peace Research Institute Frankfurt.

Daniel Mengeler is a Research Assistant in the Department of Public and International Law at the Justus Liebig University, Giessen.

Rosa Mulé is Associate Professor of Political Science at the University of Bologna, where she teaches globalisation, states, and markets and the political economy of welfare systems. Her research focuses on comparative political economy.

Peter Rinderle is Privatdozent at the University of Tübingen. His research focuses on ethics, political philosophy and the philosophy of international law. He was previously Professor of Practical Philosophy at the Universities of Hamburg, Konstanz and Marburg.

Donatella M. Viola lectures International and European Union Politics at the University of Calabria and European Union Law at Mediterranea University. She is also an Associate Fellow at University College London. Her main research interests focus on European foreign policy, the European Parliament and national parliaments.

Contents

Introduction

Varieties of European Subsidiarity

GÜNTER WALZENBACH & RALF ALLEWELDT

The Treaty on European Union (TEU) offers a simple rule on the application of the idea of subsidiarity. Article 5 (3) TEU demands that in cases of joint competence between Brussels and the member states, responsibility of any kind should always be allocated to the lowest level possible: local, regional and national action should take priority in line with the criterion of operational efficiency. However, while this definition of subsidiarity provides guidance as a legal principle in favour of decentralised decision-making, it encounters many practical challenges when it comes to implementation. Fundamental questions related to state sovereignty, democratic participation, and political culture make drawing the line over which level of government should have, and does in fact have, decision-making authority in specific cases far more difficult. For this reason, political science and the sub-disciplines of public policy, political economy, political sociology and international relations augment the concept's relevance beyond its foundation in EU law.

To understand the implementation of subsidiarity in European public policy, this collection works with multiple disciplinary perspectives and identifies conceptual variation with the help of empirical case studies and case-specific evaluations. The variation observed in subsequent chapters depends in no small measure on whether subsidiarity concerns have their root cause in the interaction of different forms of political authority, the interpretation of legal doctrine, the need for effective decision-making or the changing nature of governmental preferences. This introduction further spells out why and how the distribution of competences in EU policy making matters. After our interpretation why this aspect was overlooked in the Brexit debate, we conclude with the Commission's latest review of subsidiarity mechanisms.

Sources of variation

From a normative point of view, a first source of variation in the subsidiarity concept is established by the organisational features of a good society. According to Robert Dahl (1990, 70), the demand for decentralisation to a core political unit where people share similar 'aims, feelings, outlooks and ways of doing things' is a fundamental expression of social existence. This is even more obvious if one adds references to a community sharing territorial space, language, and history. In the idea of federalism, for example, it is obvious that

> there must be several stages of 'democratic' governments, that 'the people' who are entitled to 'rule' at one stage are a subset of 'the people' who are entitled to 'rule' at a more inclusive stage, and that the rights and obligations of 'the people' at various stages are embodied in a system of mutual guarantees (Dahl 1990, 71–2).

The logical response to the public desire to have a say on matters of individual concern seems to be the organisation of government similar to a set of nested boxes. Whether the issue at hand is soil pollution, a sudden influx of migrants, the prevention of terrorist attacks or trade in endangered species, there is a general expectation of a coordinated response executed by legitimate political authority. Yet, effective decision-making in cases of individual importance will most likely engage stages of government that are less 'democratic' than others. Due to the complexity of policy problems, there is always an element of contingency when trying to find the most appropriate form of authority. As the process of European integration has repeatedly shown, it could be misleading to see the sovereign nation state as the single, all-purpose problem-solver. Instead, government actors across countries can form a range of associations depending on functional purpose and delegate authority further to administrative bodies.

This said, such behaviour should not lead to excess where a new constitutional arrangement is added with every new problem. Rather, in the spirit of good governance, use should be made of the prevailing task divisions despite a degree of mismatch in the competences held at different levels of a political system. Only at critical junctures, and after careful judgement, the conclusion might be reached that the disadvantages of an imperfect power distribution do outweigh the advantages of a small number of decision-making centres. In the meantime, subsidiarity serves as the pragmatic principle that allows for the regular balancing, adjustment and calibration that is needed in multi-level systems of the federal as well as quasi-federal type. It encompasses the classic set of normative recommendations made by Dahl (1990, 79) for the design of 'authority in a good society':

1. If a matter needs democratic association – choose smallest association that can deal with it satisfactorily.
2. If larger association is considered more satisfactory, consider its extra costs, including a possible increase in the sense of individual powerlessness.
3. The criterion of economy requires that the number of democratic associations in which you participate are few, even if this means that all are too large or too small for some matters.
4. The alternative to larger association may include not only smaller association but also autonomous decisions – for example through the market.

These recommendations are not identical with the legal definition given in Article 5 (3) of the Treaty on European Union (TEU). Here, fundamentally, the applied subsidiarity concept requires that the EU holds the power to legislate in a certain field, i.e. that member states have (voluntarily) transferred this power to the EU. If this is the case, then, according to EU law, two further criteria need to be fulfilled before Brussels can legislate in a certain field. First, a negative condition, in that the objectives of the proposed action cannot be sufficiently achieved by the member states on their own; and, secondly, a positive condition that these objectives can be better achieved at the level of the Union as a whole. In the precise wording of Article 5 (3) TEU:

> Under the principle of subsidiarity, in areas which do not fall within its exclusive competence, the Union shall act only if and in so far as the objectives of the proposed action cannot be sufficiently achieved by the Member States, either at central level or at regional and local level, but can rather, by reason of the scale or effects of the proposed action, be better achieved at Union level.

In this provision, the specific words 'the objectives of the proposed action' are most important. Only once these objectives are clearly defined, it will be possible to assess whether the member states, or indeed the EU, are in a better position to achieve them. Thus, whatever political actor determines the 'objectives' largely controls the application of the subsidiarity principle in a particular policy area.

Thus, the variation of the applied subsidiarity in legal terms depends crucially on how the EU determines the objectives of the proposed actions. Typically, general objectives are stated in relevant provisions of the EU treaties; and by definition, 'proposed actions' are those proposed by an EU institution. Moreover, the precise objectives of an action are usually given in the preamble of a legislative act, as proposed by the Commission, and, in line with the ordinary legislative procedure, amended and adopted by the Council and the European Parliament (see Articles 289 and 294 TFEU). Therefore, the power to set the objectives of legislative action always remains with the EU institutions as central authorities in policy making. As can be seen from the wording of Article 5 (3) TEU above, the subsidiarity rule refers only to the question as to who is best placed to achieve these objectives, as set by the EU. Furthermore, under Article 5 (3) TEU, the Union shall act only if the objectives of the proposed action can be 'better' achieved at EU level. This condition is closely connected to the previous legal reasoning. As long as the member states are not in a position to achieve the objectives of the 'proposed action', their only option is to turn to the Union.

A third source of variation in the applied subsidiarity concept follows from a focus on the substance of decision-making. On the one hand, decentralised decisions privilege local officials who hold detailed knowledge about the communities they represent. They are more likely to operate smaller programmes and implement policy measures within given resource limitations. They also have an opportunity to experiment more with policy ideas and identify what works well on a small scale. As a result, decision-making is more responsive to diverse local needs, creating a sense of autonomy and individual liberty among citizens.

Centralised decisions, on the other hand, consider the broader implications of a common problem. As large-scale projects serve multiple communities, implementation requires more resources and mechanisms of burden-sharing. Central authority has an advantage when spreading standardised best practices across jurisdictions and draws more easily on extended levels of technical expertise. It can also oversee the establishment of uniform legal rights across all subunits of a polity. Thus, by redistributing power resources among smaller jurisdictions equally, decision making by officials at central level can create a sense of fairness among citizens.

In theory, at least, higher levels of political authority have the means to achieve a redistribution among the subunits at lower levels. Reality, however, is more complicated as decisions are heavily influenced by the specific constellation of interests and attitudes among key stakeholders in any area of public policy. Conflicts over the location of decision-making within centralised and decentralised systems can be constructed as a dispute over the precise distributive results these produce (Stone 2012, 368). For example, a quasi-federal system such as the EU – due to its regulatory power – may consistently benefit a different set of people than what would be the case under purely state-centric arrangements. In the same way a federal government is more likely to engage in redistribution than subnational units on their own.

A final source of variation in the applied subsidiarity concept stems from the changing preferences of governments. In response to pressures from economic globalisation, for example, countries react differently through domestic policy changes and adaptations. Depending on the positioning in the global economy, public spending behaviour has often been reactive to the pressures created by economic liberalisation. If central government is unable to attract foreign investments, experiences a financial crisis or is forced to introduce austerity measures, the passing on of government responsibilities (and costs) to local and sub-national entities becomes an appealing strategy (Kahler and Lake 2003, 421). More generally, once subsidiarity is framed in reaction to the diversity and volatility of political preferences, the concern about the level of governance becomes secondary as they find 'naturally' their expression at lower or higher levels in line with individual cost-benefit calculations. As a result, there is a constant risk that demands for an upscaling of political decision making to European or international fora will spark a cultural backlash, thus strengthening local, regional and national identities requesting stronger political recognition.

Many factors have the potential to create changes in governmental preferences. Therefore, the substantive reaction in terms of institutional arrangements and regulatory competences will be equally varied. What matters for the analysis presented here is the extent to which new demands are accommodated through democratic procedures ensuring political accountability. It is no coincidence, therefore, that the working of the EU's early warning system (EWS) as regards subsidiarity breaches is the prime example in the theoretical contribution by Peter Rinderle in chapter one, as well as that of Thilo Marauhn and Daniel Mengeler in chapter two.

EU competences and policy making

The EU is a supranational organisation. This means, inter alia, that EU institutions like the Council, the European Parliament or the Commission are responsible for taking decisions and, if necessary, creating new legal rules which will be binding on EU member states. In institutional terms and as regards its competences in relations with member states, it tries to defend and maintain what has been achieved in terms of organisational power. The competence term is used here to indicate responsibility or authority on part of the EU in an area of public policy.

Paradoxically, its constitutional foundation is not too dissimilar to that of other international organisations. Member states have created the EU, and assigned certain competences to it, by concluding international treaties (TEU, TFEU). The EU can only act where it has been given authority by the member states to achieve objectives set out in the treaties; this is confirmed by the principle of conferral laid down in Article 5 (2) TEU. If, by contrast, an area of competence is not specifically listed in the treaties, it firmly rests in the hands of the member states. Thus, the EU officially acts only through a single, policy-specific empowerment, and EU law should protect the member states from a hollowing out of their authority. In terms of constitutional design, the member states represent the main political space, whereas the EU performs only secondary tasks delegated by national governments. In this general meaning, subsidiarity is a cornerstone of the very legal construction of the EU.

Once competences have been transferred to the Union, the Council, being the strongest legislative organ of the EU, may still decide not to make use of these competences. In this case, again, member states retain all the power for themselves. Since the Council is composed of representatives of the member states' governments, it is exactly these governments which are fully in control about the extent to which the EU makes use of its powers to legislate. Nobody can force member states' governments, sitting in the Council, to adopt a certain new EU legal act without a qualified majority. Without such approval given by the Council, no legal act can be validly adopted. Accordingly, in a strict legal sense, the matter is simple. If member states, out of subsidiarity concerns or for any other reason, do not want the EU to legislate in a certain field, they just should refrain from transferring this power to the EU. At least, they should oppose proposals in the Council to make use of this power.

Nevertheless, a fundamental dynamic occurs as in the current stage of European integration authority over policy is divided in most areas. In fact, the precise degree to which competences are divided, mixed and shared between the EU and the member states is not crystal clear. Therefore, the selection of chapters in sections two to four – on cohesion policy, social policy, the environment, the area of freedom, security and justice, immigration, as well as external relations and economic policy – try to come to terms with this general ambiguity. Substantive EU policy areas with exclusive competences other than trade policy – competition, customs, fisheries conservation and monetary policy – are not part of the investigation.

As regards policy implementation, the Union has preferred the legal tool of directives rather than regulations to foster the idea of subsidiarity. It is worthwhile to recall that, under Article 288 TFEU, a regulation shall have general application, be binding in its entirety and directly applicable in all member states. In other words, a regulation takes immediate and direct effect throughout Europe. A directive, by contrast, shall be binding on member states as to the result to be achieved, but shall leave to the national authorities the choice of form and methods. Accordingly, directives do not have immediate legal effect for citizens, but need to be transposed into the national law of member states within a certain time period. Both regulations and directives are usually adopted through the EU's ordinary legislative procedure as further specified in Article 294 TFEU. In general, they need the approval of a qualified majority in the Council together with the approval or silence of the European Parliament. Furthermore, in impact assessments, the European Commission provides justifications for EU actions, explains the need for harmonisation and explicitly considers subsidiarity concerns.

Despite this elaborate institutional design, critics, such as the former judge of the German constitutional court (*Bundesverfassungsgericht*), Dieter Grimm, consider the attempt to limit the transfer of competences to the EU with the help of subsidiarity mechanisms as a failure. For him, uncertainty continues as to whether policy areas are located inside or outside the sphere of EU power. In particular, he is concerned about the very few court cases adjudicating whether the principle has been breached or not (Grimm 2016, 194). While there is much less dispute over the usefulness of subsidiarity as a guiding principle for policy development in federal and quasi-federal systems (as highlighted in the case study by Maximilian Bossdorf on export and investment promotion agencies in chapter 14), it appears useless as a yardstick for decision-making when there is an actual conflict over the distribution of competences between member states and EU institutions (Grimm 2016, 23).

Once an act is legally adopted in the Council, the member states have confirmed – at least by qualified majority – that the EU is in a comparatively better position to achieve the stated objectives of legislation. In other words, member states want the EU to act. In such circumstances, it is logically difficult to argue that member states are still better placed to achieve the legislative objectives. Accordingly, there is hardly any room for successful legal challenges of adopted EU rules based on Article 5 (3) TEU. It is thus not surprising that the review process carried out by the European Court of Justice is very limited, and that the latter has never invalidated an existing EU law on grounds of subsidiarity (Craig and de Búrca 2015, 100). Once a government is outvoted in the Council, there is little chance to find redress in the court system.

Typically, the critique from the left and right of the political spectrum has identified a step-by-step depletion of member state competences due to the EU's overarching goal to establish and maintain a common market. Potentially, almost any member state norm or domestic piece of legislation can be interpreted as constituting a barrier to free market forces. For this reason, the interpretation of Article 5 (3) TEU – and the starting point of many contributions to this volume – may amount to a political and economic, rather than purely legal, question. The EU's functionalist logic of political integration with the help of integrated markets establishes a strong presumption that policy objectives can be 'better achieved' at the supranational level. The case of environmental policy, presented by Sian Affolter in chapter six, shows that this does even include politically motivated non-action by the EU itself.

Most of the time, EU actions envisage multiple objectives, and some of these may or may not require supranational measures. Given the challenging task to balance appropriately EU goals with those under the control of national authorities, a multidisciplinary approach suggests itself. The findings of individual chapters in this volume highlight that political and economic assessments sit not always comfortably with judicial procedures. The formulation and implementation of EU sectoral policies, as analysed in sections two and three of this volume, show the variety in which legal reasoning has dealt with complex market conditions and diverging political forces.

Another prominent critic, Claus Offe (2014, 67–8), identifies a 'deceptive' aspect in the 'subsidiarity tale' because of the 'fictitious nature of sovereignty claims' by the member states. For him, these stand in the way of a genuine revival of the Union's social dimension in response to the European financial crisis. The forces of economic liberalism have already undercut the capacity of nation states to regulate, protect, and intervene in social and political affairs in line with democratically established standards of rights and legal obligations. Regardless of the legal recognition of the subsidiarity principle, the factual balance that has been built over decades between the market and the state has shifted in favour of the former and challenges the conduct of democratic politics oriented towards social integration. Moreover, the lack of an independent EU budgetary authority or budget rights comparable to those of domestic legislative institutions prevents progress towards a European social security policy. As it stands, the EU does not control the necessary resources to conduct its own re-distributional policy (Offe 2016, 176–7).

Then, as Barrie Hebb argues by looking into the evolution of Canadian federalism in chapter 15, a purely legal definition of subsidiarity is less meaningful since each decision-making level must be able to raise adequate revenues to cover the expenses involved in carrying out the decisions it has the formal power and authority to make. Similarly, Rosa Mulé notes in chapter five the emptiness of the subsidiarity principle because eligibility for EU financial support has often been linked to strict conditions. Yet, she also sees the potential of innovative solutions as the proclamation of the European

Pillar of Social Rights (EPSR) asks for a more balanced approach to national and supranational activities in the social domain. Historically, the subsidiarity principle and attempts at European economic governance are not a contradiction in terms. Although EU cohesion policy might need to simplify expenditure rules in common funding arrangements, Giuliana Laschi is able to highlight in chapter four the truly transformative capacity of European institutions. Through the reform of financial allocations and funding access, the policy area has gradually morphed into one of the most important EU activities, now directing the highest percentage of budgetary resources.

Subsidiarity and Brexit

EU institutions are required to respect national identities while being further constrained by the principle of subsidiarity and the principle of proportionality. Why, then, did subsidiarity arguments not gain further prominence in the Brexit debate? Many, for example, saw immigration as a key issue around which the leave campaign did revolve. Indeed, as section three of this book and individual chapters by Marco Borraccetti, Ralf Alleweldt, Marco Balboni and Jörg Dürrschmidt indicate, subsidiarity has a major contribution to make to understand the EU's complex response in this specific policy area. Moreover, the chapters by Hartmut Aden and Günter Walzenbach in sections two and four extend the analysis to establish further linkages with other key policy aspects of Brexit, such as internal security cooperation and global trade negotiations.

From the subsidiarity angle, it is not surprising that individuals with exclusive British, English, Welsh or Scottish identities tend to be more Eurosceptic than individuals who embrace the notion of a 'nested identity'. Apparently, the number of people who claim to hold such a multiple English-British-European identity has declined since the formal introduction of the subsidiarity principle by the Maastricht Treaty (Taylor 2017, 49). Furthermore, without affinity to European subsidiarity, the devolution of Scotland, Wales and Northern Ireland was mainly interpreted as the hollowing out of the British state rather than as a step towards democratic reform and the successful accommodation of sub-nationalisms within the UK. Without a culturally embedded notion of subsidiarity, remain campaigners had a difficult stance to make a convincing argument for EU membership by bringing across the idea that Brussels does practise self-restraint in terms of power transfers from the member states.

Of course, in terms of substance, central elements of the subsidiarity concept are not alien to the UK's territorial power structure. In fact, standard arguments for devolution have emphasised opportunities for innovation, policy effectiveness and improved accountability once decisions are taken closer to those most affected by them. In the words of the Kilbrandon report (Royal Commission 1973, 165), those who hold transferred powers should

> have some measure of independence, permitting them to do things in their own ways which may not always have the support of the central government.

Similarly, the functional idea of a policy laboratory facilitating policy learning at the local level has been equally applied to devolved government in the UK. Whether this applies in the same way in a post-Brexit scenario is another question. If no appropriate balancing mechanism between the powers of central government and devolved entities is found, the break-up of the UK's territorial settlement could be a step closer (Bogdanor 2019).

The Brexit saga is an intriguing example of how government preferences can change. It also shows a continuing dilemma about the location of appropriate levels of decision-making. While the anticipated repatriation of EU competences should fulfil the promise 'that returning powers sit closer to the people of the United Kingdom than ever before', it is far less clear whether 'the outcome of the Brexit process will be a significant increase in the decision-making power of each devolved administration' (Greer 2018, 136). The fundamental question about the distribution of competences – equally relevant in the EU – is not going away. In fact, the analogy can be pushed further. Despite the absence of the subsidiarity debate in the UK, the emerging post-Brexit arrangements with Northern Ireland, Scotland and Wales may justify the 'quasi-federal' label usually reserved for the EU's system of multi-level governance.

Frequently, leading politicians of the centre-left and right did approach the UK-EU relationship in terms of red lines, opt-outs, and exceptions to defend national interests in negotiations with Brussels. In the British case, EU engagement was heavily contingent on the priorities of the domestic policy agenda and concerns about the precise way through which economic interdependence could compromise political sovereignty (Gifford 2010, 326). Against this background, it is less surprising that the British public never embraced the idea of Europe. Not only is there a lack of emotional empathy with the idea of integration, but there is also much less acceptance of the EU as a legitimate locus of decision-making with direct policy impact. Instead, popular stereotypes run down the argument according to which Brussels is 'meddling' with Britain's internal affairs.

Already for Margaret Thatcher the Maastricht Treaty and its federalist agenda augmented German power rather than contained it (Wellings 2010, 496).

Thus, the abstract principle of subsidiarity became part of the problem rather than a solution. The remnants of this theme continued to motivate hard-line Eurosceptics in the House of Commons from the early 1990s up to the aftermath of the Brexit vote in June 2016. In their view, a balance of power approach would be the only way forward to contain Germany's dominant role in the EU.

Is it possible, however, to tie the EU's principle of subsidiarity to a specific national interest? According to Paul Lever (2017, 95) former British ambassador in Berlin, 'Germans are proud of the F-word', whereas 'for many people in Britain, including many British Euro-parliamentarians, the workings of the EU seem alien and bizarre'. It seems, for example, no coincidence that many senior positions – including the Commission presidency – are held by officials who see EU politics as a 'natural extension' of the domestic political process. As power structures in Brussels resemble those in Germany, the EU appears to be 'familiar political territory' (Lever 2017, 98).

In contrast to the UK experience, the principle of subsidiarity has assumed greater importance in the domestic politics of Germany after unification. In particular, the state government of Bavaria argued in favour of stronger recognition when new *Länder* joined the federation in the 1990s. Such demands articulated at sub-national levels reached Brussels resulting in the principle's codification at Maastricht (Bulmer and Paterson 2019, 47). In turn, the German Basic Law (*Grundgesetz*) introduced a new Article 23 following a constitutional amendment:

> With a view to establishing a united Europe, the Federal Republic of Germany shall participate in the development of the European Union that is committed to democratic, social and federal principles, to the rule of law, and to the principle of subsidiarity, and that guarantees a level of protection of basic rights essentially comparable to that afforded by this Basic Law.

Despite the diverging development paths in the UK and Germany, Protocol no. 1 on the role of national parliaments in the EU and Protocol no. 2 on the application of the principles of subsidiarity and proportionality could have formed a useful corrective to any perceived or actual imbalance. Both Protocols are an integral part of the TEU and empower all national parliaments to submit opinions for further consideration by Brussels. Moreover, all national parliaments are entitled to initiate infringement proceedings with the European Court of Justice if they want to improve on the effectiveness of their control mechanisms (Article 5 TEU; Protocol no. 2, Article 8).

The Timmermans report

All said, subsidiarity must play an important role in the legislative procedure of the EU. Based on Article 5 (3) TEU, representatives of member states in the Council and their parliaments may defend national powers against an envisaged EU intrusion. European institutions – in particular, the Commission – are under pressure to justify why certain powers should be exercised by the EU at all. If they fail to convince governments about the need for EU action, and despite formal powers, a serious implementation deficit can arise.

In his State of the Union address of September 2017, then Commission President Jean-Claude Juncker set out his vision for the EU in 2025. He continued the debate launched in the White Paper on the Future of Europe and singled out one key option – 'to do less more efficiently'. While it makes sense for the EU to step up its work on certain issues, it equally should consider doing less in others; especially when it is unable to deliver on its own promises. As a result, a task force met under the leadership of the Commission's first Vice-President, Frans Timmermans, exploring a range of policy areas where activities could be either devolved or returned to the member states after thoroughly engaging with regional and local authorities.

The final report formed a collective effort overseen by three members of the European Committee of the Regions (CoR), three members from national parliaments, and one member of the European Commission. The European Parliament, entitled to nominate three members, preferred to not get involved. Overall, there were 41 national parliamentary chambers, 74 regional legislative assemblies as well as 280 regions and 80 000 local authorities entitled to contribute to the formal deliberations of the EU task force. Its mandate comprised three main objectives following on from the given guidance that 'the Commission must be big on the big things and act only where it can achieve better results than Member States acting alone' (European Commission 2018a):

- a better application of subsidiarity and proportionality in the work of EU institutions as related to the implementation of policies and legislation;
- the identification of policy areas where decision-making and policy implementation can be re-delegated or returned to the member states;
- and the search for ways to better involve regional and local authorities in the preparation and follow up of Union policies.

In its conclusion, the final report confirmed the added value of EU action when addressing new policy challenges in areas such as security, defence and migration, despite the need to intensify interventions as regards climate change (European Commission 2018b, 4). What is more, in recognition of resource limitations and efficiency criteria, priority was given to procedural changes in the interactions between Brussels and the member states rather than to the international dimension of policy areas. This relative neglect of the latter confirms the assessment of European foreign policy made by Jörg Michael Dostal in chapter 12.

The review of the principles of subsidiarity and proportionality focussed mainly on internal working arrangements to improve the EU's policy making process. To this end, it proposed the term 'active subsidiarity,' suggesting a common understanding among local and regional authorities (as well as national parliaments) to facilitate the genuine ownership of EU policies across governance levels. Essentially, the Timmermans report culminates in a new elaborate grid for a common administrative method by which all decision makers should assess subsidiarity and its proportional use. In other words, it constitutes a bureaucratic response to the desire to have a more systematic review of the two principles in draft legislation and cases of amendment. The model template, for example, focuses on the what, why and how of EU actions in 25 sub-questions concerning the legal foundations, formal com-petences, and procedural safeguards of EU actions (European Commission 2018b, 32–4).

The proposed reform steps include existing legislation as well as new policy initiatives undergoing closer scrutiny with the possibility of repeal. In fact, the final document recognised the common critique of EU legislation becoming too dense or complex as EU directives impose limits on decision-making spaces at state and sub-state level without the flexibility to accommodate national priorities. For the time being, however, the report confirmed the value-added deriving from all current EU policy areas. The extensive consultation process could not find substantive treaty competences where a definite re-delegation to the member states – 'in whole or in part' – would make sense.

Several proposals discussed by the task force were discarded as they would require a treaty change, for example, as regards modifications to the parlia-mentary control mechanisms of subsidiarity. However, as Donatella Viola highlights in chapter three, effective scrutiny may be achieved even without revised review mechanisms, if the multitude of actors in national and Euro-pean legislatures are willing and able to create synergies through dialogue and deliberation.

Easier to implement are reforms within the existing legislative process of the EU. The report points here to more targeted consultations with local and regional authorities. The CoR, for example has conducted over 200 citizen's dialogues on the future of Europe in all member states reaching out to over 30, 000 citizens. Furthermore, it suggests a revision of the Commission's 'Better Regulation Guidance' to engage more directly with sub-national entities when these have concerns about the impact of new legislation. Although legislative proposals by the Commission generally come with impact assessments exploring the costs and benefits of alternative policy options in the light of subsidiarity, these could have a stronger focus on territorial implications and a more explicit recognition of the EU's value-added.

What is the best way to ensure that common policies will be implemented across the Union to an adequate standard? The current system has led to a high level of legislative detail and prescription, especially when it comes to the substance of directives. This outcome reveals a fundamental trade-off. On the one hand, the creation of a level-playing field for the efficient working of the internal market requires compliance with Union legislation throughout all member states. On the other hand, detailed and prescriptive EU laws limit the flexibility of regional authorities and local actors. Of course, standard legal acts of the EU can be changed and improved to reduce the burden of the latter, but as the structure of this book suggests, this is best done on a case-by-case basis.

Conclusion

The question of how powers should be distributed between the EU and the member states is not, or only to a minimal extent, answered by Article 5 (3) TEU. This question is mainly decided in negotiations between member states on treaty amendments and in legislative deliberations between member states' governments in the Council. It is obviously an eminently political question that depends on regular feedback from local, regional and national actors. Fundamentally, it cannot be answered by applying legal rules alone. Instead, it requires an empirical investigation into the practical application of subsidiarity from the perspective of multiple disciplines.

References

Bogdanor, V. (2019). 'Post-Brexit Britain may need a Constitution – or face Disintegration'. *The Guardian*, 18 January. Available at: https://www. constitutionreformgroup.co.uk/the-guardian-post-brexit-britain-may-need-a-constitution-or-face-disintegration/

Bulmer, S. and W. E. Paterson (2019). *Germany and the European Union*. London: Red Globe Press.

Craig, P. and G. de Búrca (2015). *EU Law: Text, Cases and Materials*. 6th edition. Oxford: OUP.

Kahler, M. and D. A. Lake (2003). 'Globalization and Changing Patterns of Political Authority'. In M. Kahler and D. A. Lake (eds) *Governance in a Global Economy,* 412–38. Princeton and Oxford: Princeton University Press.

Dahl, R.A. (1990). *After the Revolution? Authority in a Good Society*. Revised edition. New Haven and London: Yale University Press.

European Commission (2018a). 'Future of Europe: President Juncker appoints Members to Task Force on Subsidiarity and Proportionality'. Press Release, 18 January. Available at: https://ec.europa.eu/commission/presscorner/detail/en/IP_18_341

European Commission (2018b). 'Active Subsidiarity: A New Way of Working'. Report of the Task Force on Subsidiarity, Proportionality and 'Doing Less More Efficiently'. 10 July. Available at: https://ec.europa.eu/commission/sites/beta-political/files/report-task-force-subsidiarity-proportionality-and-doing-less-more-efficiently_en.pdf

Gifford, C. (2010). 'The UK and the European Union: Dimensions of Sovereignty and the Problem of Eurosceptic Britishness', *Parliamentary Affairs* 63(2): 32–138.

Greer, A. (2018). 'Brexit and Devolution', *The Political Quarterly* 89(1): 134–8.

Grimm, D. (2016). *Europa ja - Aber welches?* München: C.H. Beck.

Lever, P. (2017). *Berlin Rules: Europe and the German Way*. London and New York: I.B. Tauris.

Offe, C. (2014). *Europe Entrapped*. Cambridge: Polity.

Offe, C. (2016). *Europa in der Falle*. Berlin: Suhrkamp.

Royal Commission on the Constitution (1973). *Kilbrandon Report: Devolution of Functions to Scotland and Wales*. London: HMSO.

Stone, D. (2012). *Policy Paradox: The Art of Political Decision Making*. 3rd edition. New York and London: Norton.

Taylor, G. (2017). *Understanding Brexit*. Bingley: Emerald.

Wellings, B. (2010) 'Losing the Peace: Euroscepticism and the Foundations of Contemporary English Nationalism', *Nations and Nationalism* 16(3): 488–505.

SECTION ONE

CONCEPT AND THEORY

1

The Political Philosophy of European Subsidiarity

PETER RINDERLE

Political philosophy is concerned with a systematic evaluation of the found-ations, the forms and ends of those practices and institutions which are called political because they constitute and influence the basic rules of human interaction within and between societies. Its central questions are (Simmons 2008, 1): who has a right to rule a particular community? How is the exercise of power to be conceived? What are the origins, the legitimate means and ends of political authority? What are the foundations and contents of social justice? These questions have received and still receive very different and highly controversial answers. Typically, many political conflicts which arise from different conceptions of how to legitimate and exercise power also appear within political philosophy. One of the main tasks of the discipline is to clarify these conflicts, and possibly, to contribute to their solution.

The principle of subsidiarity grows out of a long tradition of social and political thinking, and is still used in a variety of different national, regional and global settings. In recent times, it has received a prominent place within the European Union (EU). It gives a particular and controversial answer to the question of how to allocate and exercise authority between the centre and the members of a political community. Although there are several competing conceptions of subsidiarity 'with very different implications for the allocation of authority', its core idea consists in shifting the burden of proof to the central agency (Føllesdal 2013, 41; Føllesdal 2014). The right to make obligatory decisions should be allocated to the lower or smaller level of a community, unless there are good reasons to do otherwise. Although subsidiarity is compatible with a high degree of centralisation, its central tenet is the presumption that the best way to organise a community is to give its (individual or collective) members as much power as possible. To assess the idea of subsidiarity from a philosophical perspective, four questions need to be raised and answered: how to understand the term 'subsidiarity'; how to evaluate its key idea; how can the principle be put into practice; and how to understand its institutionalisation by the EU.

Clarifying concepts

To start with, the conceptual scheme in which the principle of subsidiarity is embedded needs clarification. What do people mean when they advocate an allocation of political authority in line with the principle, and what is the precise content of the underlying idea?

The concept of subsidiarity shares the fate of many political concepts such as 'democracy' or 'justice'. These concepts are essentially contested, and different people hold quite different conceptions of their meanings. However, the contestation and possible vagueness of a concept do not make it necessarily meaningless. One can note, for example, that many people attach a positive value to ideas such as democracy or justice. 'Democracy' is thus often used as the expression of an approval. Yet, the institutions people approve of may have very different shapes. Similarly, the concept of subsidiarity is frequently used to express a judgement of (positive) value although there is no clear meaning attached to it. One of the tasks of political philosophy is to separate questions of meaning and questions of value and show that a particular conception of democracy or subsidiarity is not, by itself, a sufficient reason for valuing these ideas.

As far as the concept of subsidiarity is concerned, the etymology of the word is of limited help. The term derives from the Latin word 'subsidium' which means 'support', 'assistance' or 'help', in particular by reserve troops used in case of a military necessity (Cahill 2017, 208; Donati 2009, 211). Abstracting from the particular origins of this term, one might say that the term subsidiarity refers to a relationship between two institutions, with one helping or supplementing the other in certain cases of necessity. Subsidiarity thus treats action at a hierarchically higher level as 'subsidiary' to an action at a lower level (Neuman 2013, 361).

How then are we supposed to allocate authority within a multi-level political order? By consulting the history of political thought, we might find some preliminary answers. The idea of subsidiarity – as it is still used in political discourse and practice today – was conceived in the tradition of Catholic social thought and was meant to structure and order the relation between a central authority and the members of a community. Accordingly, individuals and families were conceived as agents with inherent autonomy and dignity.

This assumption not only permits the limitation of the legitimate exercise of power, it also allows to derive two duties of political authority and, in the same manner, two varieties of subsidiarity: first, the negative duty not to interfere excessively in the lives of autonomous subjects, and secondly, a positive duty to support them to develop and exercise their capacities of self-determination. Thus, negative subsidiarity prohibits unnecessary action at a higher level, while positive subsidiarity prescribes action at the higher level when political subunits cannot achieve certain ends on their own (Føllesdal 1998, 195).

In this way, the core content of the contested concept of subsidiarity can be identified. In essence, subsidiarity privileges the part over the whole; it accords a certain space for exercising authority to the (individual or collective) members of a community; it introduces certain conditions to the centralisation of power; it distributes the burden of proof to the advantage of the lower level or the smaller units of a community; and it establishes 'a rebuttable presumption' for local decision-making 'unless good reasons exist for shifting it upward' (Jachtenfuchs and Krisch 2016, 6).

Power, however, also means responsibility. By limiting the central authority and empowering local agents, subsidiarity puts an emphasis on the responsibility of individual (or collective) members of a community. They are supposed to take their lives in their own hands. As a consequence, the state or any other central agency is relieved from the task of providing for the welfare of its citizens. In fact, by stressing the responsibility of the smaller unit, the advocates of subsidiarity may sometimes dispense with the solidarity of the whole community for its individual members:

> It is not by chance, many argue, that the so-called welfare state was a centralising state, because only at the national level could the interests of the disadvantaged receive sufficient weight to overcome the influence of local elites (Bird and Ebel 2007, 9).

Therefore, the idea of subsidiarity meant to protect and support the autonomy of local agents can create a conflictual relationship with the value of national solidarity and redistribution. Of course, this claim needs empirical confirmation as there are also indications to the contrary. The empowerment of the subunits of a community might be seen as the condition for the possibility of the implementation of social justice. Subsidiarity and solidarity therefore appear, in some cases, in a complementary relationship (see Donati 2009).

Remember, at this stage of the argument, that the main question concerns the allocation and use of political authority. A preliminary answer contains two elements. On the one hand, subsidiarity demands that power is allocated – as far as possible – to the single units of a community. It demands that power is used to further their particular interest in developing and exercising their capacities to self-determination; at least to the extent that this seems possible and expeditious. On the other hand, if there are any good reasons of efficiency speaking in favour of the centralisation of power, then subsidiarity cannot be used to defend a categorical stance on decentralisation. To put it in a nutshell, subsidiarity speaks – in a conditional and pragmatic manner – in favour of decentralisation for the allocation and use of authority. Thus, subsidiarity does not take any categorical or principled stance and cannot be used to justify a decentralised or federal distribution of political power. Indeed, proponents of a centralised world state as well as radical anarchists might defend their ideas with reference to the principle of subsidiarity.

Interestingly enough, the United States, with a system where vertical as well as horizontal checks and balances of the exercise of power are strongly implemented, 'has not made subsidiarity the measure of federalism' (Berm- ann 1994, 447). The idea of subsidiarity as developed in the hierarchical context of Catholic Europe 'is designed to soften hierarchy by vesting and protecting the powers of its lower levels'; by contrast, federalism is 'anti- hierarchical, based on convenant-based principles that see the proper political organisation as a matrix with larger and smaller arenas but not higher and lower' (Elazar 2001, 42).

With these findings in mind there are three problems of particular importance. The first of these concerns the units of communities (Føllesdal 1998, 192). Do we speak of the relation of a nation-state with individual citizens? Or do we conceive collective units as families, cities, regions or associations as the smaller entities to which political authority should be allocated (King 2014)? Maybe the 'smaller units' are the member states of a supranational organisation? Clearly, one needs to be aware that the principle of subsidiarity – depending on the unit of agency – can be applied in very different contexts.

A second difficulty has to do with the idea of political power. The concept of 'power' is a far-reaching umbrella which covers a broad variety of different mechanisms, means and measures of how to influence the actions of others. The power to make people act in a certain way, may rely on negative sanctions such as force or punishment, but it can also distribute positive incentives in the form of money or opportunities. Power can focus on a single individual, but may also aim at establishing and enforcing general rules for all members of a society. Hence the standard distinction between the exercise of legislative, executive and judicial powers. Although this categorisation is not without its own difficulties, the interpretation and application of the principle of subsidiarity needs a clear idea of what kind of power we are dealing with. Even if we assume that 'subsidiarity's central function must be its legislative one' (Bermann 1994, 367), different conceptions of subsidiarity might still be applied to the allocation of executive or judicial power (Føllesdal 2013; 2014).

These first two problems are hard enough, but comparatively easy to deal with – as will be shown below when looking at the institutional implementation of subsidiarity. The third problem goes straight to the heart of the matter. Its prime concern is the kind of *reasons* that can be invoked to centralise power. Subsidiarity does not oppose the centralisation of power categorically. Rather the central demand consists in allocating power to the smaller units unless there are good reasons to the contrary.

The obvious problem raised by this condition is the specific nature of these reasons (Jachtenfuchs and Krisch 2016, 7). What kind of consideration should be accepted as a good reason in order to regard the centralisation of power as legitimate? One might think here of very different candidates: maybe a central agency can solve a certain kind of political problem more efficiently; maybe it is necessary to produce a certain kind of public good? This answer, however, immediately raises further questions as regards the standard of 'efficiency' or the desirability of certain 'public goods'. Maybe the centralisation of power is better able to realise an idea of distributive justice or of political self-determination? Yet again, the very idea of justice and democracy are controversial. People do not agree on what these terms mean, and they might disagree on their respective value.

This third difficulty, thus, does not refer to problems of application or implementation only. As it touches on the very core of our idea, it points to a major obstacle of giving subsidiarity a clear and unambiguous meaning. There is always a lingering suspicion that might be invoked by very different people with different ideas in their mind – depending on the reasons for centralisation they accept. In short, subsidiarity might be used as a *passe-partout* for almost any idea on how to allocate and use political power. The principle therefore might well be a double-edged sword which can be used in different contexts for quite opposing aims. Someone might see overwhelming reasons to establish a central government, while someone else might see no reasons whatsoever for establishing political authority. One of the major difficulties for giving a substantive meaning to the principle of subsidiarity consists in answering precisely the question of who is to decide whether or not there are good reasons to centralise power in a given context. Unless there is a solid grasp of the kind of reasons invoked, it is not possible to use subsidiarity for affirming or rejecting any particular proposal. Such a grasp requires a look into the normative foundations of subsidiarity.

Providing foundations

The principle of subsidiarity establishes a presumption in favour of an allocation of authority to the smaller unit. Unless there are good reasons to the contrary, authority should be exercised at the most basic level. This presumption shifts the burden of proof to the higher levels of government. Decentralised government, in other words, is regarded as the baseline, and only centralisation stands in need of a particular justification. Is this a good answer to the question of how to allocate power? Are there any arguments for such a presumption? Even though the idea of subsidiarity means that there is not any particular reason for allocating power to the smaller unit, the question suggests itself whether there are any good reasons for postulating such an imperative.

The first and the most popular argument for the principle of subsidiarity is a concern for the liberty of individuals as well as for families and other social associations in the *negative* sense of an absence of external obstacles. By allocating political authority to the local level, subsidiarity may be regarded as a safeguard against tyranny and oppression. Central authorities, this moral argument contends, always develop a tendency of intervening excessively and illegitimately in the affairs of their subjects and thereby restricting their freedom. Distributing power on many shoulders is meant to prevent this development from happening.

A second, genuinely political consideration speaking in favour of the principle is the value of collective freedom in a *positive* sense of self-determination. Central government always develops a tendency of being dominated by experts or elites and thereby alienating its subjects from their own political culture. The establishment of a common political identity as well as the representation of a variety of different interests are much better facilitated by smaller units of government. Local bodies allow for a higher degree of participation, they give a voice to those affected by political decisions and can be regarded as a valuable source of political legitimacy (King 2014, 301–2).

A third argument is popular among political economists who are concerned with the efficient production of goods. Subsidiarity suggests allocating power by making use of efficiency criteria without addressing serious difficulties concerning the specification of the content of efficiency as well as the problem of who is to be the judge in cases of controversies on the best means for achieving it. On the assumption that these problems can be solved in a satisfactory manner, efficiency surely counts as a good argument for subsidiarity.

In addition to moral, political and economic defenses some authors also point to a particular advantage of subsidiarity in cultural matters. The distribution of power to local agents facilitates the development and preservation of cultural identity. Moreover, by fostering the existence of a plurality of cultural identities, subsidiarity makes a contribution to the development and preservation of cultural diversity within a political community (Bermann 1994, 341-2).

Do these considerations establish a good case for the principle of subsidiarity? Although the first, moral argument should be regarded as convincing, it still does not establish a very strong case. It is true, subsidiarity might be a safeguard for the liberty of individuals or other agents, but there could be other and possibly more effective means of protecting these liberties. Subsidiarity establishes only a presumption to allocate political authority to smaller units, but it does not take a principled stance as such to the detriment of other safeguards.

Matters are similar when turning to an assessment of the second, political argument. Subsidiarity might foster the identification of citizens, and it might increase the possibilities of participation as well as the representativeness of democratic institutions at a local level. Yet, subsidiarity only propagates decentralisation on certain conditions and might very well serve to legitimise the allocation of power to a central agency. Therefore, subsidiarity hardly can be regarded as a particularly strong defense of self-determination at the local level. Moreover, participation and representation at a merely local level might not adequately compensate for the deficit of the possibility of participation and representation at a higher, regional, national or global level. In other words, the allocation of power to smaller units might – if, for example, one takes account of conflicts between subsidiarity and solidarity – be regarded as an obstacle to the identification of members with their true community.

At first sight, the economic argument of efficiency (in the production of public goods) seems to make a strong case for subsidiarity. As everyone wants efficiency, efficiency might be regarded as a solid foundation for subsidiarity. And even more so, if it can be shown, that not only local public goods, but also global public goods (such as global climate protection or fresh water supplies) might benefit from adequate efforts of cooperation at the local level. Yet, there is a drawback to this consideration. Even if all agree on the value of having more goods, there is usually disagreement on the kinds of good we want more of; for example, thinking of the interests of developing countries, climate protection would also be contested. Furthermore, there is disagreement on the appropriate means for the efficient production of public goods. And in particular on the question, whether central government is able to realise higher efficiency gains than local authorities.

The argument around cultural identity and diversity does not fare much better. On the one hand, the term 'culture' is a notoriously elusive concept. It would be, for example, a capital mistake to assume without further elaboration a close tie between the preservation of cultural identity and the political autonomy of local units. On the other hand, it is far from clear that a particular allocation of power will be of great service to a specific cultural identity. There are good reasons to remain sceptical, in particular given the fact that subsidiarity permits the centralisation of power as soon as the case for a more efficient production of certain goods is convincingly established. Cultural matters, thus, do not always figure highly among subsidiarity considerations.

Two further moral objections against the principle of subsidiarity need to be considered. First, it might be criticised for granting too many liberties to local units in the government of their own affairs. If a particular community is given the authority to govern itself without external intervention or control from a central authority, the danger looms large that the unjust treatment of its own members cannot forcefully be counteracted. Certain conceptions of subsidiarity might thus be regarded as a possible threat to the basic rights of individuals (Føllesdal 1998, 202). Second, distributing political power to smaller units can also be seen as in tension with the moral values of distributive justice and democracy. If power is allocated to smaller units, general considerations about the just distribution of wealth, income or opportunities will necessarily have to be neglected or sacrificed entirely. The same holds true for the value of democracy. While subsidiarity may foster local participation and representation, this will inevitably reduce the possibility of effectively and legitimately influencing processes at some higher, collective level. For example, individual citizens assemble happily in the marketplace of their villages, but leave the more important decisions on national or global matters in the hands of elites and experts.

In short, there are principled reasons for and against the idea of allocating political authority to smaller, local units. The decisive matter, in the end, is a moral question: subsidiarity may protect as well as endanger the liberty of individuals. In protecting successfully the liberty of individuals subsidiarity will do a great service to justice, even if there remains a tension with other elements of justice such as social equality and democratic legitimacy. As far as the principle's foundations are concerned these reveal certain limits to the theoretical and normative perspectives of political philosophy. Indeed, subsidiarity is a phenomenon that cannot be approached solely from the distant perspective of an airplane flying above the often dire, dark and harsh realities of politics. Instead, the analytical 'devil' is hidden in the details of institutional implementation (Berman 1994, 366).

Implementing institutions

How is the subsidiarity principle made operational in practice? What kind of procedures and mechanisms does it entail? Ultimately, answers to these questions presuppose empirical investigations from a plurality of disciplinary perspectives as presented in the subsequent chapters of this book. They are beyond the reach of a purely philosophical investigation. However, this transition from a theoretical perspective to an empirical, real-world account needs to be accompanied by a set of general remarks.

Subsidiarity expresses the demand to allocate authority – unless there are reasons not to do so – to the smaller unit without specifying in detail the level of units and type of power it refers to. To investigate the institutional and procedural forms that subsidiarity takes in practice, two general questions suggest themselves: what are the units of political agency to which power is allocated, and what particular type of power is under use? As regards the smallest unit of collective agency, there are options on a spectrum ranging from the individual member of a community to the nation-state as a member of an international organisation (or even a world-state). On one end of the spectrum subsidiarity might take the individual as the smallest unit to which a maximum amount of power is allocated. A statist conception of subsidiarity, at the other end, might take a collective form of organisation such as the nation state as the smallest unit. Obviously, there are many more candidates for the most significant unit in between these extremes.

What then is the appropriate smallest unit? This depends on the theoretical foundation that is given to the principle. If we think – as has been claimed here – that individual liberties are of a particularly high value, some suspicion as regards statist conceptions of subsidiarity are in place. By contrast, if the principle should serve the protection of cultural identities and group diversity – as there are also good supporting reasons – implementation will prefer a statist or related form of collective conception of subsidiarity (see Cahill 2017). The economic efficiency argument cannot be used for a clear-cut defense of any of these propositions though. The pursuit of efficiency depends on context and circumstances with recent empirical research strongly supporting a polycentric approach best suited to produce certain kinds of public goods under tight budgetary constraints (see Ostrom 2012).

These considerations lead to the tentative conclusion that subsidiarity is to be used at different levels of governance. At the same time, individual liberties should be protected by interfering as little as is necessary. Certain powers need to be allocated to the individual as the smallest unit, but the development of cultural identities must not be forgotten. For that reason, the state or a similar unit on a more collective level such as a regional organisation becomes the appropriate entity for the allocation of certain powers. This multi-layered approach is further supported by considerations of economic efficiency best realised by the cooperation of a variety of political actors found at individual and local, collective and national as well as international and global levels.

Identifying a plurality of different levels or units as the subjects to which power is allocated, similarly assumes a plurality of different types of political power to be distributed. Power comes in many manifestations. It can force and punish, it can exert violence or impose taxes, but it can also produce public goods, distribute money and other resources. To this end, it employs language codes that manipulate or convince people. Without doing justice to these diverse means and mechanisms of political power, the legislative, executive and judicial branches of government need to be distinguished as the obvious context of this dimension of subsidiarity. While subsidiarity proposes the allocation of power to the smallest unit, it does not specify the type of power in question. Hence, it makes sense to acknowledge different conceptions – or varieties – of subsidiarity. One could, for example, assign a legislative power (for reasons of efficiency) to a central, supranational authority and, in the same way, distribute executive power (motivated by a concern for cultural identity) to a smaller, national or regional unit. In fact, the protection of the rights of individuals might be achieved best by reserving elements of judicial power to supranational or global institutions.

Looking at the relevance

As far as the institutional implementation of the idea of subsidiarity is concerned, the European context is certainly of particular relevance. Subsidiarity is one of the organising principles of a number of traditional nation states with a federal structure, and it also has become an important pillar of supranational organisation. Article 5 (3) of the Treaty on European Union (TEU) states:

> Under the principle of subsidiarity, in areas which do not fall within its exclusive competence, the Union shall act only and in so far as the objectives of the proposed action cannot be sufficiently achieved by the Member States, either at the central level or at regional and local level, but can rather, by reason of the scale or effects of the proposed actions, be better achieved at Union level.

With this principle, 'member states sought to defend against unwarranted centralisation and domination by Union authorities' (Føllesdal 2013, 50). This section, therefore, will take a look at the attempt to implement a review procedure to see whether the demands of subsidiarity have been sufficiently respected in legislative activities of the EU. The Early Warning Mechanism (EWM), as further elaborated in chapter three, enables the member states to issue a 'yellow card', if they suspect a breach of the subsidiarity principle.

This mechanism was first conceived in the 2002-2003 European Convention and subsequently codified in the 2009 Treaty of Lisbon (Article 12 and Protocol no. 2 on the application of the principles of subsidiarity and proportionality). It makes national parliaments the guardians of subsidiarity by giving them the right to monitor and intervene in European law-making. If a sufficient number of so-called 'reasoned opinions' from national parliaments are raised against a particular legislative proposal, the Commission has a duty to respond to these opinions (Cornell and Goldoni 2017; Kiiver 2012).

As far as the practical relevance of the EWM is concerned, one might make three observations. First, it is noteworthy that worries about a centralising bias of European legislation are addressed not by the separate power of the judicial branch, but by the legislative branches of the lower levels, i.e. the national parliaments of the member states (Cooper 2017, 24–5). The EWM thus functions primarily as a political instrument, with all the advantages and disadvantages this includes. Secondly, insofar as the Commission has only a duty to respond to the reasoned opinions of the national parliaments, it can defend a particular proposal without the need for withdrawal. Thus, the right of national parliaments to draw the 'yellow card' might be considered as a relatively weak and ineffective safeguard for the protection of subsidiarity (Cooper 2017, 26). A third observation underscores this second point. So far, since its introduction in 2009, the national parliaments have only shown three 'yellow cards' to a legislative proposal of the European Commission. In two cases, the Commission has upheld the proposals – without addressing the arguments of the reasoned opinions in detail. And in one other case (the Monti II regulation), it has withdrawn the proposal – for reasons, however, of political expediency and not out of a concern for a breach of subsidiarity.

It is, perhaps, too early to evaluate the EWM (see Cooper 2017; Fasone 2013; Føllesdal 2013, 50-5; Jachtenfuchs and Krisch 2016, 12–3; Kiiver 2012, 4). While there are a number of reasons for disappointment, there are also certain considerations that speak for a more optimistic appraisal. It is true, the EWM does not put a 'red card' in the hands of national parliaments. They do not have a genuine veto-right to stop legislation which might be detrimental to their rights. And while one might be sceptical about the real political influence of mere reasoned opinions and arguments, this procedure might still be seen as a valuable element in a deliberative conception of European democracy. The EWM does not only help to stimulate democratic debate between different levels of European governance, it does also help to bring about more coordination and deliberation between the national parliaments of the EU (Fasone 2013, 192–3).

Conclusion

David Miller (2003, 2) has defined political philosophy 'as an investigation into the nature, causes and effects of good and bad government'. If the legitimate or, for that matter, illegitimate exercise of government is distributed at several different levels – and this holds true for the European as well as global context – then political philosophy has to address the question of how we should evaluate this distribution of political competences. The core idea of subsidiarity is to allocate to and exercise political authority at the smallest level of a particular community, unless there are reasons to the contrary. Certainly, there might be controversies about the conclusiveness of those reasons to the contrary. The general idea of subsidiarity, however, remains intact – government at the lowest level is good government. From this follow several normative perspectives for further thinking. Subsidiarity can help to prevent the exercise of tyrannical power of the central government and protect a sphere of liberty in the smaller units of a community. It can, moreover, render a valuable service to the exercise of political self-determination of those smaller units of a community. With this emphasis on the liberty and self-responsibility of individual as well as collective members of a community, subsidiarity creates a tension with competing values such as equality or social solidarity. The more power is allocated to and exercised at the lower levels of a community, the less power, obviously, is available to remedy political problems which are of common concern for all members of a community.

The institutional implementation of the idea of subsidiarity raises two main questions. First, what levels of government are we referring to, and what are the units of agency to which political authority is allocated? Second, what particular kind of authority are we talking about, and which functions of government are allocated to its different levels? As far as the particular case of the EU is concerned, these questions have – leaving complications aside – a straightforward answer. Subsidiarity applies mainly to the distribution of legislative competence between the EU and its member states. The TEU allocates legislative authority – as far as it is possible and efficient – to the smaller units of the member states. The same Treaty has also implemented a formal procedure to review possible violations of the subsidiarity principle. Yet, it is contested whether the allocation of authority to the member states is respected in political practice, and it is the subject of intense debate whether the EWM can successfully fulfil its purpose. As it stands, the institutional implementation of subsidiarity in the European context is an important example for the practical relevance of political philosophy. However, the related political practice is equally relevant for the birth and development of theoretical ideas.

References

Bermann, G. A. (1994). 'Taking Subsidiarity Seriously: Federalism in the European Community and the United States', *Columbia Law Review* 94: 331–456.

Bird, R. M. and Ebel, R. D. (2007). 'Subsidiarity, Solidarity and Asymmetry: Aspects of the Problem'. In Bird, R. M. and R. D. Ebel (eds) *Fiscal Fragmentation in Decentralised Countries: Subsidiarity, Solidarity and Asymmetry*, 3-25. Cheltenham: Edward Elgar.

Cahill, M. (2017). 'Theorizing Subsidiarity: Towards an Onotology-sensitive Approach', *International Journal of Constitutional Law* 15(1): 201–24.

Cooper, I. (2017). 'Is the Early Warning Mechanism a Legal or a Political Procedure? Three Questions and a Typology'. In Cornell, A. J. and M. Goldoni (eds) *National and Regional Parliaments in the EU-Legislative Procedure Post-Lisbon. The Impact of the Early Warning Mechanism*, 17–49. Oxford and Portland: Hart.

Cornell, A. J. and Goldoni, M. (eds) (2017). *National and Regional Parliaments in the EU-Legislative Procedure Post-Lisbon. The Impact of the Early Warning Mechanism*. Oxford and Portland: Hart.

Donati, P. (2009). 'What Does "Subsidiarity" Mean? The Relational Perspective', *Journal of Markets & Morality* 12(2): 211–43.

Elazar, D. J. (2001). 'The United States and the European Union: Models for Their Epochs'. In Nicolaidis, K. and R. Howse (eds) *The Federal Vision. Legitimacy and Levels of Governance in the United States and the European Union*. 31–53. Oxford: Oxford University Press.

Fasone, C. (2013). 'Competing Concepts of Subsidiarity in the Early Warning System'. In Cartabia, M., Lupo, N. and A. Simoncini (eds) *Democracy and Subsidiarity in the EU. National Parliaments, Regions and Civil Society in the Decision-Making Process*, 157–95. Bologna: Il Mulino.

Føllesdal, A. (1998). 'Survey Article: Subsidiarity', *The Journal of Political Philosophy* 6(2): 190–218.

Føllesdal, A. (2013). 'The Principle of Subsidiarity as a Constitutional Principle in International Law', *Global Constitutionalism* 2(1): 37–62.

Føllesdal, A. (2014). 'Competing Conceptions of Subsidiarity'. In Fleming J. E. and J. T. Levy (eds) *Federalism and Subsidiarity. Nomos LV Yearbook of the American Society for Political and Legal Philosophy*, 214–30. New York: New York University Press.

Jachtenfuchs, M. and Krisch, N. (2016). 'Subsidiarity in Global Governance', *Law and Contemporary Problems* 79(1): 1–26.

Kiiver, P. (2012). *The Early-Warning System for the Principle of Subsidiarity: Constitutional Theory and Empirical Reality*. London: Routledge.

King, L. (2014). 'Cities, Subsidiarity, and Federalism'. In Fleming J. E. and J. T. Levy (eds) *Federalism and Subsidiarity. Nomos LV Yearbook of the American Society for Political and Legal Philosophy*, 291–331. New York: New York University Press.

Miller, D. (2003). *Political Philosophy. A Very Short Introduction*. Oxford: Oxford University Press.

Neuman, G. L. (2013). 'Subsidiarity'. In Shelton, D. (ed.) *The Oxford Handbook of International Human Rights Law*, 360–78. Oxford: Oxford University Press.

Ostrom, E. (2012). 'Nested Externalities and Polycentric Institutions: Must We Wait for Global Solutions to Climate Change Before Taking Actions at Other Scales?', *Economy Theory* 49: 353–69.

Simmons, A. J. (2008). *Political Philosophy*. New York: Oxford University Press.

2

The Subsidiarity Principle at the Interface of Law and Politics

THILO MARAUHN & DANIEL MENGELER

Subsidiarity, as a concept, is all over the place. It has attracted the attention of academia and practice, of philosophy and social science, and – last but not least – of lawyers. In the European Union, subsidiarity has moved beyond being a conceptual framework. It has become part of the law, nurtured by pertinent constitutional debates in federal systems. While federal systems in a strict sense and from a global perspective are the exception rather than the rule, they have conceptually become fairly influential as telling examples of multi-level governance (Chalmers, Davies and Monti 2014; Robbers 2017). Challenges of multi-level governance systems arise with regard to their prescriptive role, their enforcement capacity and their legal jurisdiction alike. However, as the European Union has been rightly described as a law-making entity, the focus in the following will be on the legislative branch only. The latter should be separated from the administrative and judicial branches of government as highlighted, for example, in the work of Montesquieu (1977).

This chapter will not address the question why the subsidiarity principle has become so important in the context of European integration. Rather, it will examine how the subsidiarity principle reflects the interface of law and politics in European Union law. To this end, this chapter will first consider the codification of the subsidiarity principle in the Treaty on European Union (TEU), and will then raise the question whether subsidiarity does not only operate between various levels of government but also between law and politics, meaning that the law is subsidiary to politics or *vice versa*. The chapter concludes by pointing to a form of dynamic interaction.

The codification of the subsidiarity principle in the Treaty on European Union (TEU)

Even though subsidiarity may be read broadly as addressing the complexities of the social fabric, this cannot be applied to governance structures in general without critical reflection and modification. Subsidiarity respects that there is a difference between the societal sphere and the governmental sphere. Federal systems refer to variations of subsidiarity when it comes to the separation of powers between various levels of government. And at the international level, there is a discourse about a division of labor between nation states and international organisations (Jackson 2002, 16–7). It is against this broad background that subsidiarity, especially when considering the debates of the 19th century, can be understood as defending the liberal sphere against excessive use of governmental powers (Schwarze 1992, 685).

This political, philosophical and historical setting has to be borne in mind when discussing the codification of the subsidiarity principle in the TEU. Preceding the Treaty of Maastricht, the debate included three options for framing the subsidiarity principle in the context of European Community (EC) and European Union law (see Schneider and Wagner 2012, 296–7):

1. a broad architectural principle ensuring multi-level governance even within the nation state;
2. a principle for the distribution of powers; and
3. a rule for the exercise of powers.

Eventually, Article 3 lit. b of the revised EC Treaty took up the third option. It may be argued that this detached the subsidiarity principle from its historical underpinnings and transformed it into a principle of efficiency. Understood in this way, law-making in the EC and EU was not to be an end in itself to achieve European integration.

The Treaty of Lisbon then built upon this in Article 5 (3) TEU with a much narrower definition than the broadly framed subsidiarity principle in the Treaty's preamble (see Schütze 2016, 252–3). The preamble, which expresses the resolution of EU member states

> to continue the process of creating an ever closer union among the peoples of Europe, in which decisions are taken as closely as possible to the citizen in accordance with the principle of subsidiarity,

respects the self-determination of peoples and aims for the EU to be citizen-friendly. This broad reading of the preamble mirrors itself in Article 39 (2) lit. a of the Treaty on the Functioning of the European Union (TFEU) referring to regional peculiarities and in Article 167 (1) TFEU respecting the 'national and regional diversity' of the member states. The narrow reading of Article 5 (3) TEU as a rule for the exercise of powers is itself closely linked to Article 5 (1) second sentence and Article 4 (2) first sentence TEU, respecting 'national identities' and 'fundamental structures' of member states without changing the distribution of powers as it emerges from the Treaties. The subsidiarity principle does not question the political (and legal) decision on the separation of competencies, but requires a twofold test for the exercise of a competence by the EU: a sufficiency test (permitting the EU to 'act only if and in so far as the objectives of the proposed action cannot be sufficiently achieved by the Member States') and a value-added test (whereby the EU's objectives can, 'by reason of the scale or effects of the proposed action, be better achieved at Union level'). As this requires a political-economic assessment, it illustrates that the subsidiarity principle serves a political rather than a legal purpose. Even more so, as this should be internalised by national parliaments being equipped with tools to ensure compliance with the principle as further spelled out in Article 12 lit. b TEU, Article 69 TFEU and Protocol No. 2 on the application of the principles of subsidiarity and proportionality (see annex to the TEU and the TFEU).

The political purpose of the subsidiarity principle becomes obvious via the just mentioned Protocol. This instrument, specifying the so-called early warning system, except for the criterion of efficiency lays down only procedural rules. The early warning system allows national parliaments to object to a Commission proposal within eight weeks of their publication, arguing that the proposal is in breach of the principle of subsidiarity.

The so-called 'yellow card' enables national parliaments to simply react to a Commission proposal. This is supplemented by the so-called 'orange card', which requires a review of the proposal if at least a simple majority of the votes allocated to national parliaments submits 'reasoned opinions'. If the Commission maintains the proposal, a majority in the European Parliament, or 55 per cent of the member states in the Council, can raise an objection (Geiger 2015, paragraphs 17–8).

Three features of the Protocol demonstrate that preference is given to political rather than judicial considerations: first, the early warning system defers the discussion of the principle of subsidiarity to national parliaments, not to a national court or the European Court of Justice (ECJ). A broad reading is given to the acts concerned by Article 3 of the Subsidiarity Protocol, which goes far beyond Commission proposals and includes, initiatives from a group of Member States, initiatives from the European Parliament, requests from the Court of Justice, recommendations from the European Central Bank and requests from the European Investment Bank for the adoption of a legislative act.

Likewise, the need to demonstrate compliance with the principle of subsidiarity according to Article 5 of the Protocol, stipulating that 'any draft legislative act should contain a detailed statement making it possible to appraise compliance with the principles of subsidiarity and proportionality', will stimulate pertinent political debates.

Second, the procedures foreseen by the Subsidiarity Protocol shift debates towards the political dimension and have an effect on the political discourse (Popelier and Vandenbruwaene 2011, 216–7). National parliaments will be able to live up to their political responsibility and can retain political momentum in the process of EU law-making. The dialogue stimulated by the 'yellow card' system clearly differs from judicial decision-making. Furthermore, the absence of specified criteria and the openness of the wording of Article 5 (3) TEU facilitates conflict management by consensus. In other words, Article 5 (3) TEU establishes a legal frame for conflict resolution in this particular way. Finally, reference to national parliaments may eventually lead to a stronger impact of their debates and deliberations on decision-making in the Council.

Third, so far, the ECJ has not applied strict scrutiny of the principle of subsidiarity. Leaving room for discretion and decision-making of EU organs allows political controversy between national parliaments and acting EU organs. Such controversy is not embedded in legal doctrine but opens up space for considerations of political expediency.

In essence, it can be argued that the codification of the principle of subsidiarity in the TEU as well as its operationalisation by EU organs and member states establishes a legal framework for political decision-making with regard to the exercise of competences. This raises an interesting question as to the relationship between the legal and political spheres: to what extent is the law as such subsidiary to political decision-making?

Subsidiarity of the law *vis-à-vis* political decision-making

The relationship between the law and political decision-making in a constitutional framework has been discussed from various angles. With the rise of the constitutional state, and with the recognition that constitutions include legal rules that can be taken up by a court of law, the relationship between political decision-making and the applicable legal and constitutional framework has become more complex. For this reason, it is necessary, first, to discuss this interaction in more general terms, before moving on to the interpretation and application of the law, and, finally, narrowing down considerations to the constitutional level.

To begin with, law and politics do not enjoy the same kind of relationships across all levels in a multi-level system of political decision-making and governance. The political dimension of public international law, for example, has often been debated, as has been the political dimension of constitutional law. It would be, however, an unacceptable simplification to argue that the global is largely subject to political considerations whereas the local is 'juridified'. The extent to which law and politics play a role at different levels of government varies – and their relationship cannot be read as a simple one-way street.

More generally, law and politics are considered to be mutually contingent. Law emerges from political decision-making and the political process normally channels the genesis of rules of law. Thus, politics serves as a foundation for the rule of law. Along these lines, law is never fully de-politicised – notwithstanding theoretical reflections and claims as, among others, emerging from Kelsen's (1967) pure theory of law. In fact, the law is much more limited than politics; in time, space, and scope. Not all matters of life – or politics – are subject to processes of legalisation and juridification. There is a moral, societal and political space outside the law. In short, law is not omnipresent.

However, there is a complex interplay between both 'systems' (Luhmann, 2017). This may be illustrated by separating two fields of analysis: the law's steering capacity and the law's capacity to organise and legitimise governance.

As to the steering capacity of law, political decision-makers use the law to control the behaviour of certain actors and certain parts of society. In doing so, political decision-makers also frame further political decisions. It may be argued that this interplay between political decisions and legal rules establishes a meta-regime of its own. Subsequent decisions at a lower level of abstraction have to be in accordance with the rules established by this meta-regime. Yet, this does not exclude changes of the meta-rules by political decisions which then themselves gain legal quality (*actus contrarius*). In this respect, a distinction can be made between amending the overarching legal framework and specifying existing legal rules. The significance or influence of politics on the law decreases with a higher degree of specification of legal rules. In turn, the rationalisation effect of law increases for subsequent political decisions. The precise relationship between politics and law cannot be determined without consideration of a particular context. Depending on the level of abstraction, it is subject to changing dynamics. Thus, politics and law interact in an alternate fashion.

This is shown clearly by the already mentioned capacity of law to organise and legitimise governance. Frequently, politics refers to legal rules set by its own process to achieve the necessary legitimacy. Accordingly, Popelier and Vandenbruwaene (2011, 205–6) describe the subsidiarity mechanism as a tool for legitimising EU laws. In normative terms, the law preserves a decision based on prior political consensus – even at the constitutional level. Politics within the framework of legal rules is legitimised by the law. Politics legitimises itself by means of self-imposed conditions that take a legal form. These self-binding mechanisms with formal and material constraints on politics increase the desired legitimacy effect (Elster 1993, 8–14; Popelier and Vandenbruwaene 2011, 205–6). Subsequent judicial control further reinforces this. Most importantly, in this perspective, the decision on self-commitment is a political act and is not legally prescribed.

Usually, enforcement of the law or the use of legal instruments is also within the boundaries of political opportunity. In other words, a strict relation of subsidiarity between the law and politics or *vice versa* does not exist. In many cases, the use of courts with final decision-making power will be a political decision in itself. Addressing an illegal situation is not an automatic process. In fact, there is the possibility of political instrumentalisation. For example, at EU level member states have a legal obligation to fulfil the convergence criteria of Economic and Monetary Union (EMU) to facilitate the implementation of the euro currency. In the case of Sweden, however, this goal has not been achieved mainly due to a lack of political will rather than due to a lack of actual ability (Chalmers, Davies and Monti 2014, 713–5). While this legal obligation could be enforced through the ECJ by skillfully employing legal arguments, such an attempt would still fail due to the political position taken by key domestic actors. The example shows the dependence of legal mechanisms on political behavior from two different angles. If objective law is not enforced, the legal system may counteract by granting claim rights, which enable individual actors to challenge such a violation in court. In other words, enforcement is not merely an end in itself, but also a political instrument.

In areas of legal interpretation and application, the interplay of law and politics can also be observed. Politics uses the legitimacy effect of law described above in battles of political opinion as an argumentative pattern. Potentially, this can also lead to the use of law as an instrument. Sometimes political decisions and political claims are declared to be identical in their content to alleged legal claims. Then political content forms the basis for the interpretation of law in order to develop arguments and reasoning as can be seen, for example, in the case of the German basic law (*Grundgesetz*) and related judgments of the Federal Constitutional Court (*Bundesverfassungsgericht*) (2016). In particular, political views have a great impact on legal interpretation in the field of constitutional law. For instance, theories on fundamental rights often serve as a vehicle for political beliefs. In the light of different theories, fundamental rights are seen differently and in accordance with political viewpoints. Fundamental rights are then further interpreted as democratic, social or liberal rights. As a consequence, the particular content of specific rights can vary.

The relationship between politics and law is highly relevant in constitutional law. This follows from the political function of many constitutional bodies. Constitutional law, for example, covers areas such as foreign policy where legal control is limited. At the same time, political control depends on constitutional conditions which, in general, favour political freedom and the ability to act politically. Political decisions of the executive branch, therefore, can only be judicially restrained to a limited extent. Despite the absence of clear-cut legal rules, political approval or rejection is, of course, still possible. In this sense, the law cannot answer every day-to-day question of political behaviour.

At the constitutional level, some standards reflect the relationship between law and politics with regard to legitimacy considerations as mentioned above. Several legal norms of the German basic law, for example, contain so-called 'policy objectives of the state' (*Staatszielbestimmungen*) to guarantee principles that define county-specific political arrangements as a social state or to ensure environmental protection (Robbers 2017, paragraphs 143–72). These policy objectives oblige political actors to achieve them with the help of political and legal instruments. At the same time, however, they are also instruments to provide legitimacy for the political decision-making process itself as this is done in accordance with existing constitutional norms. They provide a pattern of justification for decisions taken within the overall aim and purpose of a given constitutional frame.

In addition, the relationship between politics and law depends on the precise context at the constitutional level. In other words, there is no absolute subsidiarity from law to policy or *vice versa*; it rather varies according to the particular situation. Especially at the constitutional level an approach which strictly differentiates between law and politics cannot be upheld: law is always influenced by politics, and politics is always influenced by law.

Conclusion

Instead of absolute subsidiarity from law to policy or *vice versa*, there is considerable variation depending on the particular problem constellation. At the level of constitutional law, an approach which aims for a strict separation of law and politics is not convincing. Rather, there is a fairly consistent relationship of mutual interaction between both systems that cannot be qualified as a one-way street. Furthermore, the dynamic of this interplay is dependent on the social context. In legal terms, the subject-matter of regulation and the degree of detail with which a legal norm is expressed will have a major influence on the relationship between law and politics.

Therefore, law is never fully de-politicised. The use of legal instruments is often a political decision. The EU's early warning system shows this quite well. No doubt, the control of the exercise of competence on the basis of the principle of subsidiarity as set out in Article 5 (3) TEU increases political debate. The instruments of the 'yellow card' and 'orange card' facilitate and intensify political deliberations within representative fora. The involvement of national parliaments is done by procedurals rules, yet these do more than just guide the political discourse. They also create the very possibility of finding political solutions instead of legal ones. In sum, the principle of subsidiarity reminds us of the fact that law is not a hermetically sealed system cut off from society, but that it is always linked to other systems such as politics.

References

Chalmers, D., Davies, G. and G. Monti (2014). *European Union Law*. 3rd edition. Cambridge: Cambridge University Press.

Elster, J. (1993). 'Introduction'. In Elster, J. and R. Slagstad (eds) *Constitutionalism and Democracy*, 1–17. Cambridge: Cambridge University Press.

Federal Constitutional Court (2016). Judgment of the Second Senate of 03 May, 2 BvE 4/14 - paras. 1–139. Available at: http://www.bverfg.de/e/es20160503_2bve000414en.html

Geiger, R. (2015). 'Article 5 TEU'. In Geiger, R., Khan, D.-E. and M. Kotzur (eds) *European Union Treaties*. Munich: C. H. Beck.

Jackson, J. (2002). 'Sovereignty, Subsidiarity, and Separation of Powers: The High-Wire Balancing Act of Globalization'. In Kennedy, D. and J. Southwick (eds) *The Political Economy of International Trade Law: Essays in Honor of Rubert E. Hudec,* 13–31. Cambridge: Cambridge University Press.

Kelsen, H. (1967). *Pure Theory of Law.* Berkeley: University of California Press.

Luhmann, N. (2017). *Einführung in die Systemtheorie.* Heidelberg: Carl-Auer Verlag.

Montesquieu, C. de Secondat (1977). *'The Spirit of Laws'.* In Carrithers, D. W. (ed.) *Compendium of the First English Edition,* Berkeley and London: University of California Press.

Popelier, P. and W. Vandenbruwaene (2011). 'The Subsidiarity Mechanism as a Tool for Inter-level Dialogue in Belgium: On "Regional Blindness" and Cooperative Flaws'. *European Constitutional Law Review* 7: 204–28.

Robbers, G. (2017). *An Introduction to German Law.* 6th edition. Baden-Baden: Nomos.

Schneider, F. and A. Wagner (2012). 'Subsidiarity, Federalism, and Direct Democracy as Basic Elements of a Federal European Constitution: Some Ideas Using Constitutional Economics'. In Mudambi, R., Navarra, P. and G. Sobbrio (eds) *Rules and Reason: Perspectives on Constitutional Political Economy,* 289–311. Cambridge: Cambridge University Press.

Schütze, R. (2016). *European Constitutional Law,* 2nd edition. Cambridge: Cambridge University Press.

Schwarze, J. (1992). *European Administrative Law.* London: Sweet and Maxwell.

3

National Parliaments in the EU: Synergy Under the Subsidiarity Principle?

DONATELLA M. VIOLA

At its inception, the European integration project drew legitimacy from the so-called 'permissive consensus' granted by the people to their political elites (Lindberg and Scheingold 1970). Yet, over time, this has gradually turned into a 'constraining dissensus' (Hooghe and Marks 2009). Today, more than sixty years after the establishment of the Treaties of Rome, the European Union (EU) still appears as a remote, opaque and sometimes even threatening entity. As Charles Grant (2013) put it, 'EU institutions are geographically distant, hard to understand and often deal with obscure technicalities'. The EU legislative process lacks the basic rudiments of openness, transparency and legitimacy insofar as the Council of the European Union and the European Council hold their meetings behind closed doors and are unaccountable to the European Parliament (EP). In addition, despite nine subsequent electoral competitions at EU level, citizens hardly connect to their representatives sitting in the Brussels and Strasbourg arena. Against this gloomy picture, the idea of involving member state legislative chambers in EU decision-making has slowly emerged. The aim of this chapter is to trace the taken path by focusing on the new powers conferred to national legislators as watchdogs of subsidiarity.

The subsidiarity principle in the EU

Prior to proceeding with this investigation, it is worth recalling the origin, meaning and introduction of the subsidiarity principle. Stemming from Catholic social thought, the doctrine holds that nothing should be pursued by a large and complex organisation that may as well be carried out by a smaller and simpler entity. Thus, subsidiarity encourages a decentralised system. Later, this tenet was used to define the sharing of powers between several levels of authority in federal states with the purpose of ensuring a degree of independence for local authorities in relation to central government. Within the EU framework, the purpose of subsidiarity is to determine when supranational institutions are competent to legislate. More specifically, it aims to regulate the exercise of EU non-exclusive powers by ruling out its intervention when an issue can be dealt with effectively by member states at national, regional or local level. In conformity with subsidiarity, the EU may exercise its powers only if individual countries are unable to achieve satisfactorily the objectives of a proposed action which may instead be implemented successfully at supranational level. As Steiner (1994) has noticed, the notion is open to a wide range of interpretations, spanning from the view that it is an attempt to limit the EU's centralising drive to the opposite opinion that it represents a way for EU institutions to extend their reach. According to Evans and Zimmermann (2014, 223), 'the principle of subsidiarity is somewhat of a chameleon due to its ability to adapt to, and to inform scholarship across many disciplines'.

In February 1986, the Single European Act (SEA) implicitly introduced subsidiarity for the first time in the context of the European Community's (EC) environmental policy. Six years later, the Edinburgh European Council set out a global approach towards the application of this principle, which was formally enshrined in the Treaty on European Union (TEU), popularly known as the Maastricht Treaty. Subsequently in October 1997, the fifteen heads of state and government decided to annex to the Amsterdam Treaty a new, legally binding Protocol on the application of the principles of subsidiarity and proportionality.

Since then, the European Commission has been required to submit every year a report to the European Council, the Council of the European Union and the EP on the application of these principles in EU law-making. Given the close link between the subsidiarity control mechanism and the political dialogue between national parliaments and the EU, this document is deemed to be complementary to the Annual Report on relations with national parliaments. Finally, in December 2007, the Lisbon Treaty ensured full compliance with subsidiarity by clearly demarcating exclusive, shared and supporting competences between the EU and its member states. The new provisions set the potential as well as actual margin of action for national legislatures with the aim to enhance democratic accountability within the EU. Members of national parliaments (MPs) need to be informed directly and timely by EU institutions about new law proposals. As such, they have the opportunity to raise their concerns and exert their influence over European affairs.

The participation of national parliaments in European affairs

In the mid-1950s, member states' executive actors strengthened their hold on the EC decision-making process, often bypassing national legislatures which slowly became 'political outsiders' or even 'passive bystanders' (Crum and Fossum 2013). The European project, which involved the transfer of competences from national to supranational level, marked an unorthodox shift of legislative powers to member states' governments, acting collectively. The Council's dominance in the legislative sphere entailed a shrinking of the rights of national parliaments, casting a shadow over the democratic legitimacy of the European construct. As Pollak and Slominski maintained (2013, 144), like a 'crop duster', European integration contributed to diminish the role of national legislators, 'slowly but efficiently eroding national democracy'.

To counterbalance this loss of democratic oversight, political leaders eventually agreed to entrust the EP with greater decision-making powers, being the only directly elected EU institution. However, despite its new status of co-legislator in the post-Lisbon framework, the Strasbourg and Brussels assembly has not inherited all traditional parliamentary functions. It is still deprived of the right of legislative initiative, which remains virtually a monopoly of the European Commission. In addition, it does not enjoy the core prerogative of granting or withholding approval to government policy by issuing a motion of censure against the Council of the EU or the European Council. Furthermore, members of the EP (MEPs) are largely unknown, often invisible and widely unloved, highlighting the lack of a European *demos* and confirming that the question of the EU's democratic deficit has not yet been solved.

On the assumption that domestic legislators are closer to the people and have a better sense of their needs, the question has arisen on how to translate MPs' legitimate democratic competence in EU decision-making. While in the past there has been, to a certain extent, an antagonistic relationship between MPs and MEPs, the Strasbourg and Brussels assembly has become a strenuous supporter of close interparliamentary cooperation. In particular, with regard to the scrutiny of the executive, MEPs have called for the assistance of their counterparts in EU countries, trying to turn them into political allies. After all, the representatives of national parliaments and the EP have to deal with the same ministers either as members of governments or of the EU Council.

As a matter of fact, MPs can control the Council in an indirect and fragmented manner by asking their ministers to answer for decisions taken at EU level and, if dissatisfied, release a governing cabinet through a motion of censure.

In other words, national legislators could act as vehicles for 'the domestication and normalization of EU policy making within the democratic processes of the member states' (Kröger and Bellamy 2016, 131). In sum, MPs' direct involvement may enhance the transparency of the EU legislative process, narrow the gap between citizens and EU institutions, and defuse democratic deficit claims.

National parliaments on the European stage

From the outset, national parliaments carried out the task of ratifying the original Community Treaties, their successive revisions as well as all accession agreements. Beyond this competence, however, their role was often confined to rubber-stamping decisions reached by the heads of state and heads of government. Thus, MPs remained in the shadow, losing some of their legislative rights to the benefit of ministers represented collectively in the Council.

With the first direct elections to the EP in June 1979 and the gradual abolition of the dual mandate, representatives of national parliaments felt as if they had 'missed the European boat'. This disempowerment over European affairs went largely unnoticed in most member states, so that scholars referred to national legislators as latecomers, losers and victims of the European integration process (Maurer and Wessels 2001). It was necessary to wait until the signing of the SEA in February 1986 to awake national parliaments' interest in Community policies and institutions. As a result, European Affairs Committees were established in national legislative chambers whilst also initiating sporadic interparliamentary discussions.

Subsequently, in February 1992, a declaration on national parliaments was annexed to the Maastricht Treaty, making all EU law proposals available to them in 'good time for information and possible examination'. Another declaration established that the Conference of European Affairs Committees of the Parliaments in the European Union (COSAC), set up in November 1989, would gather twice a year to exchange experiences and best practices in the scrutiny of national government policies on EU issues. Such meetings would include a six-member EP delegation with two Vice-Presidents familiar with interparliamentary relations.

Five years later in Amsterdam, a Protocol was attached to the revised EU Treaty officially formalising all previous arrangements. Since then, the European Commission forwards all draft proposals to national legislative chambers, and the Council has to wait for six weeks after their transmission before putting them on the agenda. In February 2001, the Laeken Declaration on the future of the Union, annexed to the Treaty of Nice, stressed the need to investigate the role of national parliaments in the European framework. Almost a year later, the Constitutional Affairs Committee of the EP adopted a report on its relations with national parliaments, drafted by Giorgio Napolitano, listing a number of practical proposals. Accordingly, interparliamentary cooperation 'should be deliberative by nature, non-decisive with regard to the existing EU policy cycles and characterised by mutual recognition of parliaments and parliamentarians as mirrors of society' (Napolitano 2002). To address national legislators' concerns over the EU, it would be necessary to define better their powers *vis-à-vis* their respective national governments as well as their relations with EU institutions. Indeed, EU democratisation and parliamentarisation could be achieved through the broadening of EP legislative competences and the strengthening of domestic parliamentary control over governments. At any rate, cooperation is intensified between MPs and MEPs from corresponding committees in order to discuss matters of common concern.

National parliaments under the Lisbon Treaty

In December 2007, after nearly a decade of failed institutional reforms, the EU heads of state and government signed a new Treaty in Lisbon. They agreed to include a special reference to national parliaments in the main text rather than in Protocols and Declarations. According to the new Article 10 (2),

> Citizens are directly represented at Union level in the European Parliament. Member states are represented in the European Council by their Heads of State or Government and in the Council by their governments, themselves democratically accountable either to their national parliaments, or to their citizens.

Further provisions foresaw the involvement of national legislative assemblies to be implemented through domestic laws. In Germany and Italy, parliamentary interpretation went even beyond the terms of the Lisbon Treaty by granting member states' legislatures full rights of information, consultation and participation in EU decision-making.

Under the Lisbon framework, national parliaments receive all legislative drafts forwarded to the EP and to the Council as well as agendas and minutes of Council meetings. Most importantly, for the purpose of this chapter, MPs may review all legislative proposals in compliance with the subsidiarity principle. While the real impact of the new EU arrangements still depends on the willingness and determination of parliamentary actors, their symbolic value cannot be underestimated. As stated by the first permanent President of the European Council, Herman Van Rompuy (2012): 'maybe not formally speaking, but at least politically speaking, all national parliaments have become, in a way, European institutions'. In short, the Europeanisation of national parliaments follows a dynamic towards closer transnational cooperation. For this process to happen, legislative chambers rely on the technical expertise and administrative support of their internal organisational environment.

One of the most innovative tools of the Lisbon Treaty consists of the 'Early Warning Mechanism' (EWM). Originally advocated by former British prime minister Tony Blair, this mechanism invested members of national parliaments with the responsibility to monitor compliance of EU legislative acts with the principle of subsidiarity. In line with Protocol no. 2 to the Lisbon Treaty, domestic chambers can object to EU law proposals within eight weeks from their publication. For this purpose, they have to submit to the Presidents of the European Parliament, the Council and the Commission a reasoned opinion outlining why these are considered an unwarranted trespass on national sovereignty. Frequently, this tight timeframe has not been sufficient to examine complex law drafts and to exchange cross-country information. As shown in Table 1, national parliaments in the EU member states are entitled to two votes, one for each house in the classic bicameral system.

Table 1: National parliaments in EU member states *(table continues overleaf)*

Entry Year	Member State	Lower Chamber	Upper Chamber	Unicameral Parliament	Votes
1957	France	*Assemblée Nationale* (National Assembly)	*Sénat* (Senate)		1+1
1957	Germany	*Bundestag* (Federal Diet)	*Bundesrat* (Federal Council)		1+1
1957	Italy	*Camera dei Deputati* (Chamber of Deputies)	*Senato della Repubblica* (Senate of the Republic)		1+1
1957	Belgium	*Chambre des Représentants (Kamer van Volksvertegen- woordigers)* (House of Representatives)	*Sénat (Senaat)* (Senate)		1+1
1957	Netherlands	*Tweede Kamer* (Second Chamber)	*Eerste Kamer* (First Chamber)		1+1
1957	Luxembourg			*Chambre des Députés (Abgeordneten- kammer)* (Chamber of Deputies)	2

1973	United Kingdom*	**House of Commons**	**House of Lords**		1+1
1973	Ireland	**Dáil Éireann** Irish Lower Chamber of Oireachtas (Parliament)	**Seanad Éireann** (Irish Senate)		1+1
1973	Denmark			**Folketinget**	2
1981	Greece			**Vouli Ton Ellinon** (Hellenic Parliament)	2
1986	Spain	**Congreso de los Dipudatos** (Congress of Deputies)	**Senado** (Senate)		1+1
1986	Portugal			**Assembleia da República** (Assembly of Republic)	2
1995	Austria	**Nationalrat** (National Council)	**Bundesrat** (Federal Council)		1+1
1995	Finland			**Eduskunta**	2
1995	Sweden			**Riksdag**	2
2005	Malta			**Kamratad Deputati** (House of Representatives)	2
2005	Cyprus			**Voulī´tōn Antiprosṓpōn Temsilciler Meclisi** (House of Representatives)	2
2005	Slovenia	**Drzavni Zbor** (National Assembly)	**Drzavni Svet** (National Council)		1+1
2005	Estonia			**Riigikogu**	2
2005	Latvia			**Saeima**	2
2005	Lithuania			**Seimas**	2
2005	Czech Republic	**Poslanecka Snemovna** (Chamber of Deputies)	**Senat** (Senate)		1+1
2005	Slovakia			**Národná Rada** (National Council)	2
2005	Hungary			**Országgyülés** (National Assembly)	2
2005	Poland	**Sejm**	**Senat** (Senate)		1+1
2007	Bulgaria			**Narodno Sabranie** (National Assembly)	2
2007	Romania	**Camera Deputatilor** (Chamber of Deputies)	**Senatul** (Senate)		1+1
2013	Croatia			**Sabor**	2

* Up to the end of the Brexit transition period on 31 December 2020.

If at least one third of all member states' legislative assemblies submits a reasoned opinion identifying a breach of subsidiarity, a yellow card is issued. For all draft acts in the field of justice, this threshold is one fourth of national law makers. Under this procedure, the Commission has to reconsider the legislative proposal, but can maintain its original text, regardless of objections by national parliaments. By contrast, if the number of reasoned opinions reaches half of all the votes attributed to national chambers, an orange card is activated. In this case, the Commission has to review the draft and, if it still intends to proceed with its initial proposal, it must provide clear evidence of compliance with the subsidiarity principle. Only on this basis, may the Council and the EP decide whether the text goes ahead. In fact, each of the two EU institutions is entitled to block the proposal outright: the former by a majority of 55 per cent and the latter by a simple majority. In this way, national legislators have gained a degree of collective power in EU affairs since a majority of them, acting jointly, can trigger an early vote on any new proposal.

In fact, MPs can use these procedural mechanisms to comply more efficiently with their legislative, representative and deliberative functions (Cooper 2012). Even after the ratification of the Lisbon Treaty, representative institutions in the member states have tried to increase their influence over EU policy. In 2015, for example, an informal working group of MPs met in Brussels to review the Commission's annual work programme, discussing further extensions of the EWM.

While the orange card has never been initiated, the yellow card has been applied on three occasions. In May 2012, it was issued over the controversial 'Monti II regulation' dealing with domestic labour relations and the right to strike as part of the EU's economic freedoms. On this occasion, 12 out of 40 national chambers by way of 19 out of 54 allocated votes, agreed that the draft regulation was in violation of the principle of subsidiarity. In particular, rejection of this proposal came from countries such as Finland, Latvia and Sweden facing cross-border labour disputes. Their complaints received further support from Belgium, Denmark, France, Luxembourg, Malta, the Netherlands, Poland, Portugal, and the United Kingdom. Eventually, the European Commission withdrew its draft, but denying that a subsidiarity breach had occurred.

In October 2013, parliaments in Cyprus, Hungary, Ireland, Malta, the Netherlands, Romania, Slovenia, Sweden, and the United Kingdom, along with the French and Czech senates, drew a yellow card over the Commission's initiative to create an independent European public prosecution office. Despite the reasoned opinions forwarded by the above-mentioned chambers, the European Commission maintained its proposal, arguing that subsidiarity would allow for enhanced cooperation to tackle crimes.

In May 2016, a yellow card was triggered over the proposal for a revision of the directive on the posting of workers. Ten Central and Eastern European countries, notably Bulgaria, Croatia, Czech Republic, Estonia, Hungary, Latvia, Lithuania, Poland, Romania and Slovakia, were particularly concerned with this issue. Yet again, the Commission retained its original draft, claiming that it did not infringe subsidiarity since the posting of workers represented a truly transnational question.

The poor propensity to resort to the EWM may be connected to diverse factors rooted in domestic political tradition. These include the constitutional organisation of parliaments, their understanding of the legislative functions, the executive-legislative checks and balances as well as the government-opposition relationship. Moreover, the resonance given by media over specific affairs and its impact on public opinion may elicit national legislators' interest in EU draft legislation. The domestic subsidiarity check constitutes a key innovation to strengthen democratic accountability of the European legislative process. National parliaments have gained an opportunity to signal their disagreement with their own governments' stance on EU matters. As such, prior to striking deals in Brussels, parliamentary chambers, even the frequently ignored upper ones, are expected to be consulted (Brady, 2013).

EU scrutiny models in national parliaments

Since the ratification of the Lisbon Treaty in December 2009, national legislators have been faced with the challenge of playing a formal role in EU decision-making, which has posed both normative and empirical questions on how to exert such prerogatives. The response has been diverse across the EU, depending on a plurality of political, institutional and cultural factors as well as general approaches to European integration.

There is indeed no single model for the participation of national parliaments in EU affairs. Even within the same country, legislative chambers may act differently, such as the House of Commons and the House of Lords in the United Kingdom. With regard to EU decision- making, national assemblies may follow: a 'document-based system', which entails direct, in-depth examination of all legislative proposals; or a 'mandating or procedural system', where government ministers receive a precise mandate from a European Affairs Committee prior to Council meetings; or an 'informal influencer system' that engages in general parliamentary dialogue with executive actors on EU policy (Kiiver 2006). Furthermore, according to Hefftler et al. (2013), it is possible to distinguish seven types of parliamentary approaches to EU affairs:

1. The 'limited control' model where national law makers rarely monitor EU decision-making and accept a reserved domain for the executive in EU meetings.
2. The 'Europe as usual' model where national parliaments scrutinise EU legislation primarily through *ex ante* control pursued by specialised committees and with a truly minor involvement of the plenary.
3. The 'expertise' model which foresees an active involvement of European affairs committees especially to scrutinise the performance of their government at EU level.
4. The 'public forum' model which, in opposition to the expert model, puts emphasis on full plenary sessions and public deliberation on specific EU themes.
5. The 'government accountability' model where national parliaments exert an *ex post* control through plenary debate after Council meetings, focusing on the stance adopted by their prime minister.
6. The 'policy maker' model with national parliaments seeking, via debates at both committee and plenary levels, to influence their respective governments prior to Council meetings.
7. The 'full Europeanisation' model which involves a mix of expertise and publicity to prepare and de-brief Council meetings.

As shown in the above classification, member state legislative assemblies rarely address EU issues in their plenaries. In fact, most national chambers prefer delegating such a function to their EU affairs committees. This allows a confidential exchange of views between the executive and the legislative aimed at 'depoliticising' EU matters and building national consensus without risking to jeopardise the cabinet's image (Auel 2007). On the other hand, the poor involvement of plenaries in EU questions undermines the traditional debating function of national parliaments and contributes to their political marginalisation (Raunio 2009).

A multi-level parliamentary system?

Over the years, the question regarding national legislators' participation in EU policy making was occasionally raised. In February 2003, as a member of the Convention on the Future of Europe, former British Labour MP Gisela Stuart (2003) suggested to entrust member states' parliamentary chambers with the right to block EU draft legislation. According to the so-called 'red card mechanism', an equivalent of two-thirds of national parliaments, through their reasoned opinions, could oblige the European Commission to withdraw its proposal within a standard six-week period. The Lisbon Treaty failed to introduce this procedure but redefined the space of manoeuvre for MPs, thus challenging the blame game of undesirable laws coming from Brussels.

Full implementation of subsidiarity and, more generally, a greater role of national parliaments in the EU were amongst the key demands of the UK government to renegotiate EU membership (Cameron 2015). This *de facto* veto power was widely discussed but always dismissed. For example, the Chair of the EU Affairs Committee of the Italian Senate, Vannino Chiti, declared his opposition to this proposal which risked pre-empting the EP's legislative function. In his view, it would also contradict the general expectation of parliaments to contribute to the 'good functioning' of the Union. Instead, their actions should be constructive and complementary to that of EU institutions, highlighting critical issues related to specific law drafts (Chiti 2017).

In January 2014, at the meeting of COSAC Chairs in Athens, the Danish *Folketinget* put forward the proposal that national legislators, acting as guardians of subsidiarity, should be entitled to review EU draft laws and make direct requests to the European Commission within a ten-week deadline. Under the so-called 'green card' procedure, should one third of national chambers agree to introduce an amendment, the Commission would be obliged to take it into consideration. By contrast, should national parliaments fail to reach a common position within the set timeframe, the draft legislation would get an automatic green light (Folketinget 2014).

The willingness and individual capacity of MPs to engage in the monitoring of subsidiarity crucially depends on the scope for politicising EU issues in the domestic arena. Paradoxically, both Eurosceptics and Europhiles support a greater parliamentarisation of the Union based on efficient collaboration, common vision and joint commitment among key actors at several levels. As the Belgian liberal MEP Anne-Marie Neyts-Uyttebroeck stressed in 1997 (Napolitano 2002):

> The quality of relations between the European Parliament and the national parliaments is of fundamental importance for the overall democratic nature of the Union. If they became rivals democracy would definitely suffer. If, on the other hand, they recognise that they have a joint mission, democracy will win.

For this purpose, the Lisbon Treaty floated the idea of a European parliamentary system where MPs and MEPs would engage effectively and constructively over EU issues. Interparliamentary cooperation would allow the Strasbourg and Brussels assembly to adopt decisions on the basis of broad consensus and member state parliaments to transpose more swiftly European provisions into national law.

Conclusion

Over the past two decades, subsidiarity has become an important instrument to strengthen the role of national parliaments in the European architecture. By gradually becoming aware that the EU did matter after all, member state lawmakers realised that they should recover the lost ground. Under the Lisbon Treaty, MPs' original status in the EU has been therefore upgraded to subsidiarity watchdogs, competitive actors and policy shapers. However, as this chapter has shown, representative institutions at the domestic level have to fight to obtain the political space necessary for an effective scrutiny of EU matters; and even more so, if their ambition is to become the EU's 'virtual third chamber' (Cooper 2012). National legislators' chances to affect EU policy and to become real gatekeepers of European integration strongly rely on their intense cooperation and swift synergetic action.

The loss of popular consensus over the European project, culminating in the 2016 Brexit referendum, stems from a deep sense of alienation in the face of EU imposed political decisions that appear remote and uncontrollable. An antidote could be found in further Europeanisation of national parliaments and parliamentarisation of the EU. Certainly, all this cannot be reached without the backing of the subsidiarity principle, yet bearing in mind that it is not a magic wand capable of dissolving the EU's democratic deficit. The President of the European Commission, Ursula von der Leyen, has expressed her commitment to boost European democracy. For this purpose, she has promised to launch a two-year Conference on the Future of Europe, which would entail, among its priorities, a positive agenda for national parliaments based on subsidiarity and fruitful cooperation with EU institutions. At the same time, it is worth highlighting that these goals may be achieved even without further revised review mechanisms, as long as the multitude of actors in national and European legislatures are willing and able to create synergies through dialogue and deliberation.

References

Auel, K. (2007). 'Democratic Accountability and National Parliaments: Redefining the Impact of Parliamentary Scrutiny in EU Affairs'. *European Law Journal* 13(4): 487–504.

Brady, H. (2013). 'The EU's "Yellow Card" comes of Age: Subsidiarity Unbound?' *Insight*, 12 November. Brussels: Centre for European Reform. Available at: http://cer.eu/insights/eus-yellow-card-comes-age-subsidiarity-unbound

Cameron, D. (2015). 'A New Settlement for the United Kingdom in a Reformed European Union', Letter addressed by British Prime Minister David Cameron to EU President Donald Tusk, 10 November. Available at: https://assets.publishing.service.gov.uk/government/uploads/system/uploads/attachment_data/file/475679/Donald_Tusk_letter.pdf

Chiti, V. (2017) 'Speech at the Inter-parliamentary Meeting organised by the Constitutional Affairs Committee of the European Parliament', Brussels, 2 May. Secretariat Office: 14th Permanent Committee of the Italian Senate. Available at: https://www.europarl.europa.eu/ep-live/en/committees/video?event=20170502-1500-COMMITTEE-AFCO

Cooper, I. (2012). 'A "Virtual Third Chamber" for the European Union? National Parliaments after the Treaty of Lisbon'. *West European Politics* 35(3): 441–65.

Crum, B. and J. E. Fossum (eds) (2013). *Practices of Interparliamentary Coordination in International Politics: The European Union and Beyond.* Colchester: ECPR.

Evans, M. and A. Zimmermann (2014). 'Conclusions: Future Directions for Subsidiarity'. In Evans, M. and A. Zimmermann (eds) *Global Perspectives on Subsidiarity,* 221–3. Dordrecht: Springer.

Folketinget (2014). 'Twenty-three Recommendations to Strengthen the Role of National Parliaments in a Changing European Governance'. European Affairs Committee, Danish Parliament. Available at: http://renginiai.lrs.lt/renginiai/EventDocument/6fa11f98-fc15-4443-8f3f-9a9b26d34c97/Folketing_Twenty-three%20recommendations_EN.pdf

Grant, C. (2013). 'How to Reduce the EU's Democratic Deficit'. *The Guardian*, 10 July. Available at: https://www.theguardian.com/commentisfree/2013/jun/10/how-to-reduce-eu-democratic-deficit

Hefftler, C., V. Kreilinger, O. Rozenberg, and W. Wessels (2013). 'National Parliaments: Their Emerging Control over the European Council', 29 March. TEPSA and Notre Europe - Jacques Delors Institute. Available at: http://www.tepsa.eu/download/Policy%20Paper%20NEJDI-TEPSA%20NPEC%20study%20final.pdf

Hooghe, L. and G. Marks (2009). 'A Postfunctionalist Theory of European Integration: From Permissive Consensus to Constraining Dissensus'. *British Journal of Political Science* 39(1): 1–23.

Kiiver, P. (2006). *The National Parliaments in the European Union: A Critical View on EU Constitution-Building*. The Hague: Kluwer Law International.

Kröger, S. and R. Bellamy (2016). 'Beyond a Constraining Dissensus: The Role of National Parliaments in Domesticating and Normalising the Politicization of European Integration'. *Comparative European Politics* 14(2): 131–53.

Lindberg, L.N. and Scheingold, S.A. (1970). *Europe's Would-be Polity. Patterns of Change in the European Community.* Englewood Cliffs: Prentice Hall.

Maurer, A. and W. Wessels (eds) (2001). *National Parliaments on their Ways to Europe. Losers or Latecomers?* Baden-Baden: Nomos.

Napolitano, G. (2002) 'Report on Relations between the European Parliament and the National Parliaments in European Integration'. Committee on Constitutional Affairs A5-0023/2002. Available at: http://www.europarl.europa. eu/sides/getDoc.do?type=REPORT&reference=A5-2002-0023&language=EN

Pollak, J. and P. Slominski (2013). 'EU Parliaments After the Treaty of Lisbon: Towards a Parliamentary Field?'. In Crum, B. and J. E. Fossum (eds) *Practices of Interparliamentary Coordination in International Politics: The European Union and Beyond.* 143–60. Colchester: ECPR.

Raunio, T. (2009). 'National Parliaments and European Integration: What We Know and Agenda for Future Research'. *The Journal of Legislative Studies* 15(4): 317–34.

Steiner, J. (1994). 'Subsidiarity under the Maastricht Treaty'. In O'Keeffe, D. and P. M. Twomey (eds) *Legal Issues of the Maastricht Treaty.* London and New York: Chancery Law.

Stuart, G. (2003). 'The Early Warning Mechanism – Putting it into Practice'. *The European Convention*, Contribution 233, CONV 540/03, 6 February. Available at: http://european-convention.europa.eu/pdf/reg/en/03/cv00/ cv00540.en03.pdf

Van Rompuy, H. (2012). 'Speech delivered to the Interparliamentary Committee meeting on the European Semester for Economic Policy Coordination'. EUCO 31/12, 27 February. Brussels: European Council. Available at: https://www.consilium.europa.eu/media/26439/128208.pdf

SECTION TWO

POLICIES

4

Subsidiarity and the History of European Integration

GIULIANA LASCHI

Since its very beginning, and after the dreadful experiences with two world wars, the main aim of European integration has always been to improve the quality of life for European citizens. The original six founding states of the European Economic Community (EEC) tried to achieve a unified Europe through a piecemeal, step-by-step process. They did not create a federation, as some political movements had asked for, but came together through a particular entity that was intergovernmental and supranational at the same time. In this way, nation states were not replaced, but instead sustained by a new form of community. This general idea was first proposed by Jean Monnet and Robert Schuman, in 1952, when establishing the European Coal and Steel Community (ECSC). It brought about a nascent form of subsidiarity, as European integration fundamentally required action at the national level as well as at the community level. Subsequently, further actions taken at local and regional level introduced another important location for the use of subsidiarity instruments. As regards the latter, regional and cohesion policy stands out (Piattoni and Polverari 2016). Both policies attempt to bring European citizens closer to new institutional arrangements, while offering a choice as to the level of governance at which problem-solving is supposed to occur.

Functionalist integration

A functionalist integration process has been designed to achieve prosperity and peace for the Community and the whole European continent. Accordingly, the first declared goal of the Treaty of Rome, signed in 1957, was to improve the quality of life for European citizens. Starting with an approach of gradual integration in a few selected economic sectors of strategic importance, the process kept evolving with an increasing scope for policy making and extended membership through enlargement. This also entailed the signing of a range of international agreements with 'third countries' outside the existing borders of the Union. Consequently, over the last six decades, the Community has been able to deepen the degree of integration among its member states by expanding a set of own competences and working towards the objective of social as well as political integration among the peoples of Europe (Azoulai 2014).

The economic domain has been used as a driver for cooperation among member states, further paving the way for political integration. For the same reason, the role of citizens and their representatives in EU decision-making has been a key issue. In the early days of European integration, represen-tation occurred mainly through membership in trade unions, expert bodies and industry associations. Yet, common institutions such as the European Commission and the European Parliament (to a lesser degree the Council) have regularly tried to expand the role of citizens and to find ways to represent them in a more inclusive way. Despite numerous reforms aimed at increasing participation and engagement, the perceived gap between European citizens and EU institutions has been widening during the last two decades of the past century. Paradoxically, this relative disengagement reached its peak in 1992, exactly when the Treaty on European Union (TEU) formalised the concept of European citizenship. With TEU ratification, a wave of disaffection and scepticism grew, best captured in the notion of a 'democratic deficit' within European institutions. Eventually, the general dissatisfaction became most evident through the rejection of the EU Constitutional Treaty by the French and Dutch electorate in 2002. In addition, a further blow to the already precarious relationship between EU institutions and citizens occurred in the aftermath of the global financial crisis in 2008 with austerity having severe repercussions in the societies of the member states.

Subsidiarity as solidarity

Already with the Treaty of Rome, the idea of reducing regional imbalances in economic and social performance had become a top priority for European governing bodies as well as for the governments of the member states. The legal founding act also contained the principle of economic solidarity as further guidance for the choices of the Community. In fact, long before the debate concerning UK budget contributions and the global financial crisis, solidarity considerations had led to common policy positions. By the 1960s, it was clear that solidarity necessarily implied subsidiarity, as the Community aimed for higher levels of development across its membership.

The path towards the implementation of a regional policy in combination with a direct involvement of sub-national authorities in the European decision-making process had already been laid out in the Treaty establishing the European Community. The latter stated in Article 130 (a) that 'the Community shall aim at reducing the disparities between the levels of development of the various regions'. Therefore, the focus on particular governance mechanisms can be traced back to the role of regional authorities, local citizens and a range of stakeholders operating in specific territorial settings (Cartabia et al. 2013). These actors held a privileged position in assessing whether Community action should be taken as a matter of priority.

In 1952 after the establishment of the ECSC, and with further countries joining the Community, important actions were taken by the member states as well as their common institutions. These served the purpose to establish mechanisms that would ensure a path towards economic and social convergence. An early initiative towards policy harmonisation had been undertaken at regional level in 1965, when the Commission presented a communication on the subject matter. Although a policy document without any legal effect, it allowed the Commission to set out its own opinion on the specific issue. Such communications are usually addressed to the Council of the EU and to the European Parliament. This document was a follow-up to officially sponsored expert studies suggesting that a harmonious development path had to consider the sharp economic differences between European regions. There, the Commission proposed a comprehensive European strategy aiming to address regional imbalances through the creation of 'growth poles' in less developed areas; further calling on member states to set up regional development programmes that would include such centres. Finally, in 1968, reports produced for more than a decade by expert circles led to the creation of a specific Commission Directorate-General for Regional Policy. Its mandate was to ensure a permanent improvement in the quality of life for European citizens, thus effectively institutionalising the regional dimension in the context of European integration. Until the early 1970s, however, the European Investment Bank and the European Social Fund (partially joint up with ECSC resources to support workforce re-deployment) remained the only financial mechanisms through which the European Community had an actual impact at regional level.

The 1972 Paris Summit of heads of state and government marked the true turning point towards an institutionalisation of regional policy and the recognition of sub-national authorities for the harmonious development of the Community as a whole. From then on, European regional policy should reflect an innovative process carrying vital importance for the member states. Firstly, the summit formalised the first enlargement of the European Community by admitting Denmark, Ireland and the United Kingdom, three new member states that would play a major role in the long-term development of the policy area. Secondly, the summit approved a future steps programme by which the Council committed itself to find a solution for the observed socio-economic imbalances. In the enlarged Community it would be the task of this inter-governmental body to coordinate regional policies at national level and to do so with the help of a newly established financial support fund.

For this reason, it is important to note the contribution of the United Kingdom for the decision to create a genuine regional policy. On the one hand, the new member state had economically depressed areas and hence advocated intervention with targeted policies for particular regions. In addition, a regional fund could be used as a bargaining chip to address dissatisfaction with low financial returns from the EU budget. On the other hand, the British national interest became a vehicle for strengthened subsidiarity concerns in the EEC. The 1973 Thomson Report, for example, advanced the idea that major regional imbalances are found in agricultural areas as well as those under-going industrialisation. As both types of locations continued to experience high levels of unemployment, the report concluded that while 'the objective of continuous expansion set in the Treaty has been achieved, its balanced and harmonious nature has not been achieved' (European Commission 1973).

Subsequently, the European Regional Development Fund (ERDF), establis-hed in 1975, aimed to guarantee the financial strength considered necessary for the achievement of social and economic convergence (Baun and Marek 2014, 11–16). The ERDF was the first true investment mechanism dedicated to the achievement of regional cohesion through subsidiarity. Ultimately, it would correct the existing imbalances and promote the required economic and social adjustments among the recipient entities. To this end, it was first necessary to reduce the disproportionate strength of the EEC agricultural sector. The Common Agricultural Policy (CAP) still absorbed up to 80 per cent of the Community budget. Therefore, the Commission tried to foster balanced industrial change in Europe. It also tried to address the challenges this strategy posed for individual citizens as well as the larger society, particularly as regards the problem of structural unemployment in Southern Europe.

In the early years, the ERDF primarily relied on pre-selected national projects considered worthwhile of European funding. The applications by member states were further limited to an annual funding cycle. Although priority was given to reducing regional disparities, the national interest bias in fund allocation followed from a still dominant inter-governmental paradigm. In the 1970s, the Commission was not seen as the implementer of Community-level policy, but as a promoter of coordination among established national policies. The relative dominance of domestic governments in regional policy upset the balance with subsidiarity considerations and produced inefficiencies in ERDF allocations. Accordingly, the 1974 Paris Summit highlighted economic distortions leading to a remarkable report authored by the then Belgian Prime Minister, Leo Tindemans. The European Council had issued an instruction to draw up a document that could revive the European project in times of economic crisis and potential threats of disintegration. A convinced federalist, Tindemans consulted not only European institutions, but also engaged with key representatives of political and economic organisations, the leadership of trade unions and local interest groups as well as cultural and intellectual elites. His recommendations were published on the 29th of December 1975 and presented to the Luxembourg European Council on the 2nd of April 1976. The Tindemans Report stands out with its call for a strong, properly resourced regional policy better suited to address the economic problems facing the Community. In particular, the report stressed the link between subsidiarity and the common good (Tindemans 1976, 12):

> Our peoples wish European Union to embody and promote the development of our society corresponding to their expectations, to provide a new authority to compensate for the reduced power of national structures and to introduce reforms and controls which often cannot be implemented at state level, to give an organic form to the existing solidarity of our economies, our finances and our social life. Europe can and must identify itself with the concerted and better controlled pursuit of the common good with economic resources being reoriented towards the collective interest, a reduction in regional and social inequalities, decentralisation and participation in decision-making. We will then have created a new type of society, a more democratic Europe with a greater sense of solidarity and humanity.

The report further suggested practical solutions to the observed dilemma such as closer attention to Community objectives, a better coordination of policy instruments and, most importantly, a stronger role for the Commission. Above all, the reform of regional policy had to be on the top of the agenda of European leaders and institutions. This was the imperative that came out of the deepening regional imbalances and a fast-changing economic environment due to the oil crisis. The Nixon declaration of dollar non-convertibility had generated a major financial crisis, breaking the exchange rate rules established in 1944 at Bretton Woods. Key European currencies started to fluctuate freely without any benchmarks in place. In combination with an indiscriminate rise in oil prices, the entire European economy came close to collapse. In addition, given an ongoing discussion on Economic and Monetary Union (EMU), a correct functioning of the EEC was considered essential. In fact, in 1970, the Werner plan for Economic and Monetary Union was published, following a decision by the heads of state and government during the 1969 European Summit in The Hague. Its aim was the gradual adoption of a single currency within ten years, even though the financial crisis led to a *de facto* suspension of such blueprints. Therefore, Tindemans (1976, 25–6) concluded:

> The common policies referred to in this chapter are the very essence of European Union. They give substance to the solidarity which binds our economies and our currencies. They give expression to the desire to enable all regions and all social classes to share the common prosperity and share power. ... All in all they offer us the instruments which make it possible to strive for new growth in a more just, more humane society.

The politics of reform

A first step towards reform was made in 1978, and again five years later, through modifications in the ERDF regulation. By 1984, substantial changes had entered into force suggesting a more community-centred approach. This included a significantly higher percentage of budgetary resources allocated to the ERDF, strengthened discretionary powers for the Commission in project selection, and an increase in the overall amount of eligible expenditure. Following on from the revived commitment of key political actors, a new trend in regional policy had emerged. Arguably, three interrelated events stand out to explain the heightened importance of improved policy implementation in this area: the first direct elections to the European Parliament in 1979, the enlargement of the European Community to Southern Europe, and the adoption of a strategy leading to the single market programme. The latter aims at the abolition of internal borders and other regulatory obstacles between the member states to guarantee the free movement of goods, services, capital and labour.

The reinforced legitimacy of the European Parliament paved the way for the further institutionalisation of an informal gathering that comprised elected representatives at local and regional levels. In previous years, this Intergroup had only operated within an informal setting allowing representatives of sub-national authorities to meet their counterparts in Commission and Parliament. The Intergroup consisted of 19 members of the European Parliament who previously held institutional roles at local or regional level. It maintained an ongoing dialogue in the form of hearings with local authorities giving them an opportunity to put forward requests, make proposals, and highlight priority areas for sub-national development. In practice, the Intergroup became an advisory body to the European Parliament in matters concerning urban areas, making a useful contribution to the EEC's subsidiarity goal. In addition, for the best part of the 1980s, the admission of Greece, Spain and Portugal spread disparity in Community economic performance as measured in Gross Domestic Product (GDP) figures. The percentage of people living in depressed areas had doubled, putting the European Commission under immediate pressure to reform the functioning of all three structural funds (Evans 2005).

Finally, the 1985 Single European Act (SEA) resolved the question about an appropriate legal basis for the conduct of regional policy by introducing in its Article 23 a new title V to part three of the EEC Treaty. The new legislation formally recognised the policy area, stating as its main aims the promotion of an 'overall harmonious development' of the Community and the strengthening of 'economic and social cohesion', particularly by 'reducing disparities between the various regions and the backwardness of the least-favoured regions'. The political declaration included in the SEA, and strongly endorsed by the Commission under its President, Jacques Delors, affirmed that regional disparities needed to be identified and recognised as a major hindering factor for the realisation of the common market. Consequently, deepening economic integration could not do without stronger efforts to achieve regional cohesion (Molle 2007, 6). For this purpose, the SEA identified key policy instruments such as the ERDF, the European Agricultural Guidance and Guarantee Fund (Guidance Section) and the European Social Fund; all three, in combination, better known as the structural funds.

The Maastricht Treaty

In 1992, the Maastricht Treaty initiated a second reform step in cohesion policy, albeit with a narrower scope. It attempted to enhance the role of citizens in the Union, specifically through the establishment of a formal European citizenship. This included a modification of the management capacity in regional policy by improving the relationship of European institutions with the general population and a stronger involvement of sub-national levels of government. Moreover, the new Treaty brought about a fundamental change in the European integration process by promoting EMU together with the core goal of economic and social cohesion. At Maastricht, cohesion policy acquired a level of relevance equal to the internal market or EMU itself. The legal text introduced a special cohesion fund to co-finance infrastructure projects in the less developed member states and to give support in fulfilment of EMU convergence criteria. The latter refers to a set of economic criteria in terms of limits to budget deficits and public debt that EU member states must fulfil before entering the third stage of EMU and adopting the euro as their currency. Furthermore, the Commission recognised a key role for cohesion policy through the doubling of resources in the second financial package published under the Delors Presidency, thus accounting for one-third of the entire EU budget. In this way, the Commission intended to continue the reform of the EU budget that started with the publication of its first financial package in 1987.

A second major innovation of the Maastricht Treaty was a modified institutional organisation, reinforcing subsidiarity. Article 198 TEU prescribed the creation of a Committee of the Regions (CoR) as a new entity composed of local and regional representatives from each member state acquiring an advisory role in the EU policy-making process. The CoR held the right to express its own opinions not only when called upon by Council or Commission, but as often as it deemed appropriate. Similarly, the envisaged Economic and Social Committee with representatives from the social partners would further upgrade cohesion policy. Whenever the latter is consulted by EU institutions, the former would also be entitled to issue an opinion. Their shared organisational structure further ensured a strong link between regional and cohesion policy. In fact, the Committee of the Regions and the Economic and Social Committee share the same building, thus operating in close physical proximity and through mutual consultation.

Yet, the most important innovation of the Maastricht Treaty was the formal recognition of the subsidiarity principle in Article 5(3) with the objective to provide clarity in the division of competences between the EU and the national or sub-national level of government (Estella de Noriega 2002). The principle promised a new approach to the management and implementation of EU actions in most policy areas. It assumed that by shifting decision-making power to the level of government closest to the citizens, a better outcome could be achieved in terms of efficiency considerations or actual results of the intervention:

> Under the principle of subsidiarity, in areas which do not fall within its exclusive competence, the Union shall act only if and in so far as the objectives of the proposed action cannot be sufficiently achieved by the Member States, either at central level or at regional and local level, but can rather, by reason of the scale or effects of the proposed action, be better achieved at Union level.

The institutional reforms introduced at Maastricht served later as a basis for the development of the Lisbon Strategy. Accordingly, the EU was supposed to become the most dynamic and competitive knowledge-based economy in the world, build around sustainable economic growth and the respect for the environment, creating more and better jobs, while at the same time working towards greater social cohesion. To this end, national governments would join forces to promote an investment-friendly climate that benefits the market entry of innovative small and medium-sized companies (SMEs). This revised strategy had become indispensable due to the fundamental changes in the geopolitical landscape following the implosion of the Soviet Union and the fall of the Berlin wall. With the end of the Cold War, several of the newly independent states in Central and Eastern Europe aimed for EU membership. After the 2004/2007 enlargement round, and the admission of twelve new member states, further changes to cohesion policy and its financial instruments were necessary (Baun and Marek 2008). These had the purpose to allow for adaptations to the changing policy making context, and to enable governments to catch up with the European average of GDP and employment rates.

Responding to crisis

Despite important variation, sub-national administrations have from the outset supported European efforts to strengthen subsidiarity. With the help of key policy instruments devoted to enhancing economic and social cohesion, regional and local authorities have been able to play a major role in addressing the needs of citizens across territorial divisions. With a similar objective in mind, the Commission and the European Parliament did also devote increasing attention and resources to maintain links with local communities.

More recently, the global financial crisis has reconfirmed the prominent role of regional actors. In fact, their role has become more pronounced as European integration is challenged by the consequences of austerity policies with severe repercussions for national social systems (Faucheur 2014). Eurosceptic movements and parties have grown, relying in their propaganda heavily on a local sub-culture that exposes nationalist and xenophobic sentiments. In response, the European Commission developed strategic priorities that should guide the Union out of the political, economic and social crisis. Once more, emphasis is on economic recovery, civic engagement and participation, as well as sustainability. Due to its transformative capacity, cohesion policy ranks high on the Commission agenda (Bachtler et al. 2017). It is now supplemented by a European Strategic Investment Fund that enables sub-national authorities to spark further growth. In collaboration with local and regional actors, Brussels has issued new guidelines that allow the combination of different funding arrangements for the realisation of a more inclusive economic recovery. While complex administrative procedures and a lack of professionalism in public services may still hinder progress in some European regions, the idea of embracing innovative financial instruments is gradually gaining momentum.

Conclusion

The short history of cohesion policy and the related reform of financial allocations show the transformative capacity of European institutions. Since the earlier state-centric approach that left only a marginal role for Brussels, the policy area has morphed into one of the most important Commission activities, directing the highest percentage of EU budgetary resources. The principle of subsidiarity occupies an important political space in the power division between European authorities. Through policy adaptations reflected in buzzwords, such as transparency and accountability, financial democratisation and funding access, the EU has mounted an effective response to economic crises. In the past decades, regional and local authorities have moved to the forefront of innovation, exploring solutions to European-wide challenges.

References

Azoulai, L. (ed.) (2014). *The Question of Competence in the European Union.* New York: Oxford University Press.

Bachtler, J., Berkowitz, P., Hardy, S. and T. Muravska (eds) (2017). *EU Cohesion Policy: Reassessing Performance and Direction.* Abingdon and New York: Routledge.

Baun, M. and D. Marek (eds) (2008). *EU Cohesion Policy after Enlargement.* Basingstoke and New York: Palgrave Macmillan.

Baun, M. and D. Marek (eds) (2014) *Cohesion Policy in the European Union.* Basingstoke and New York: Palgrave Macmillan.

Cartabia, M., Lupo, N. and A. Simoncini (eds) (2013). *Democracy and Subsidiarity in the EU: National Parliaments, Regions and Civil Society in the Decision-Making Process.* Bologna: Il Mulino.

Estella de Noriega, A. (2002). *The EU Principle of Subsidiarity and its Critique.* Oxford and New York: Oxford University Press.

European Commission (1973). *Report on the Regional Problems in the Enlarged Community*. COM (73) 550 final. Brussels: Commission of the European Communities.

Evans, A. (2005). *EU Regional Policy*. Richmond: Richmond Law & Tax.

Faucheur, P. (2014). 'Cohesion Policy Facing the Crisis: What Effects for the EU's Regions?' *Policy Paper,* 123, 15 January. Paris: Notre Europe – Jaques Delors Institute. Available at: http://www.institutdelors.eu/wp-content/uploads/2018/01/cohesionpolicyandcrisis-faucheur-ne-jdi-jan15.pdf?pdf=ok

Molle, W. (2007). *European Cohesion Policy*. London and New York: Routledge.

Piattoni, S. and L. Polverari (2016). 'Introduction'. In Piattoni, S. and L. Polverari (eds) *Handbook on Cohesion Policy in the European Union*. 1–16. Cheltenham and Northampton: Edward Elgar.

Tindemans, L. (1976). 'European Union. Report by Mr. Leo Tindemans, Prime Minister of Belgium, to the European Council', *Bulletin of the European Communities*, Supplement 1/76, Brussels: Commission of the European Communities. Available at: http://aei.pitt.edu/942/1/political_tindemans_report.pdf

5

Subsidiarity and Social Europe

ROSA MULÉ

Social policy is concerned with instruments, processes and activities designed to intervene in the operations of markets to provide social protection and social welfare. A central issue in social policy has been how to protect vulnerable groups consisting of individuals excluded from work due to age, sickness or family responsibilities. In the current stage of economic development there are various reasons why social policy should take on a supranational character. The most pressing reason follows from economic competition between countries. Unless there are supranational regulations in place, countries may try to shed the costs of social protection to increase their international competitiveness.

European integration can be viewed as a process of market-making with Economic and Monetary Union leaving the market-correcting functions of social policy at the national level. Therefore, the functioning of social protection at European and national level is characterised by an asymmetric structure (Scharpf 2010). Under the principle of subsidiarity, social policy remains within the competence of the member states, whereas economic policy has shifted significantly towards the European level. The principle recognises that action in the social policy domain is the responsibility of member states, but within a framework of common objectives. In other words, member states are not free to pick and choose whatever suits the preferences of their policy makers or voters. As a consequence, the development of a supranational social policy has been slow and cumbersome.

Varieties of social policy

Radically different welfare state programmes and institutions of political economy are a key hindrance to the development of a genuine European social policy. In social policy, national governments have come to set different dividing lines between what states are supposed to do and what should be left in the hands of private actors, the family, or the market. Only Scandinavian welfare states provide universal and high-quality social services, while in Southern Europe private provision dominates. In all countries and regions, citizens have come to base their life plans on the continuation of existing models. Any attempt to replace these with different European solutions would mobilize fierce domestic opposition. As Hall and Soskice put it, 'institutions of a nation's political economy are inextricably bound up with its history' (2001, 13). Hence, there is no single system of political economy throughout the member states of the European Union.

Due to path dependence – the notion that past choices affect the set of available policy options for policy makers – national social policies are deeply ingrained in existing institutions. Instead of a single social policy system there is considerable diversity among member states. The observable variety of capitalism means that in some countries economic policy making is more coordinated, while in others it is less institutionalised, and more market driven (Hall and Soskice 2001). Hence, governments acting within a specific political economy develop distinct strategies to cope with coordination problems in their interaction with public and private actors.

The United Kingdom, for example, fits the model of liberal market economies where firms coordinate their activities through competitive market arrangements. In this environment, firms organise their relationship with employees by relying on highly competitive markets driven by the demand and supply for goods and services. On the other hand, a coordinated market economy in the case of Germany gives preference to public modes of coordination. Firms align activities with actors, such as trade unions and banks, by relying on collaborative structures. In this classification Southern Europe adheres to a third model. The PIGS (Portugal, Italy, Greece, and Spain) champion mixed modes of governmental interaction, as there is a range of public as well as private owned businesses. Overall, and given further variation in the industrial relations and collective bargaining systems of the member states, a uniform impact on social policy would be extremely unlikely.

In addition, individual EU member states have enacted social policy programmes that provide general institutional advantages as well as immediate benefits to their domestic employers. The aim is to develop synergies with macroeconomic policy. Through the provision of unemployment benefits connected with economic downturns, personal sickness or disability, government policy enables workers to reject jobs unrelated to their individual skill set. In this way, official intervention supports the investment employers have made in upgrading the qualifications of their workforce.

Against this background, it is not surprising that varieties of capitalism correspond with variation in welfare state provision. The latter entails qualitatively different arrangements in the relationship between market, state and family. In some countries, governments intervene more deeply and effectively in market operations to protect vulnerable people, whereas in others, market activities appear as the better providers of social services.

Accordingly, the liberal welfare state of the United Kingdom embodies individualism and the primacy of market decision-making, also typical for the liberal market economy. By contrast, the conservative welfare state resembles most the corporatist model in Germany, where social policy emerges from an alliance of business groups, trade unions and public officials. Again, private sector strategies in the German welfare state seem to work best with the particular features of a coordinated market system. Similarly, a third type of welfare state, the social-democratic model of the Nordic countries, offers a country specific fusion of generous state provision with new opportunities for work (Esping-Andersen 1990). In sum, path-dependent trajectories constitute serious obstacles to a progressive European social agenda. Most notably, efforts to move away from the status quo have almost exclusively been confined to labour market policies, while the formulation of a European social safety net has frequently lagged behind.

Economic motives

The observed bias is partly due to the historical background of European integration. In the 1950s and 60s, profits, production and the competitive position of national economies topped the political agenda. Only from the 1970s onwards did social policy gradually become a relevant issue due to social dumping practices. The latter occur when a member state significantly cuts the social security contributions of employers to reduce the price of its exports. While this increases a country's competitiveness, it does so at the expense of its competitors on European markets. Already in 1972, the Paris conference called for measures to reduce social and regional inequalities, and the Social Action Programme two years later recognised an independent role for the Community in this policy area. Yet, by the 1980s, the complexities of intergovernmental bargaining and the unanimity requirement in the Council of Ministers continued to create serious difficulties for further social integration.

Subsequently, failures of market integration to achieve social inclusion convinced the EU Council to promote social policy further. The 1989 Charter of Fundamental Social Rights acknowledged positive interactions between social and economic policy, in that social protection is a contributing factor to better economic performance. A significant step towards the evolution of an EU social agenda was taken at the Lisbon European Council in March 2000. The member states adopted a long-term strategic goal proclaiming to aim for the most competitive and dynamic knowledge-based economy in combination with greater social cohesion. At the time, the number of people living in poverty and social exclusion throughout the Union was considered unacceptable. Already in 1998, over 60 million EU citizens were at risk of falling into poverty. The Lisbon Summit thus represented a remarkable turning point for the European social agenda. It advanced a new open method of coordination (OMC), whereby the Council of Ministers agrees first on policy objectives, a set of guidelines and quantitative as well as qualitative indicators before member states proceed with their application. To this end, governments also formulate national action plans subject to a European process of peer review.

In line with the subsidiarity principle, this process recognises that action in the field of social policy is the responsibility of national governments, but within a framework of common objectives. Article 137 (4) of the Nice Treaty stated that the provisions of the Community shall not affect the right of member states to define the fundamental principles of their social security systems. The OMC is a 'soft' instrument that has no binding power. It is nation state 'friendly' because the locus of political control over social security policy remains firmly in the hands of governments. Hence, more integration does not necessarily imply more supra-nationalism (Fabbrini and Puetter 2016). The OMC is specifically designed to help member states develop their own policies, reflecting on individual constellations. As Ferrera et al. (2002, 227) put it, as a process that can 'create trust and cooperative orientations among participants'. Nevertheless, social objectives were considered a secondary concern. So much so that in 2004 a high-level group, chaired by former Dutch Prime Minister Wim Kok, argued that fulfilment of the social objectives would result from progress in economic growth and employment policies. Primacy was still given to job creation.

The Kok report assumed that higher employment rates would automatically lead to the achievement of social objectives and poverty reduction. Yet, in the following years a correlation of this kind did not show up in the data. One potential explanation is that labour market reforms increase the incentive to take up employment by making the alternative less attractive. Indeed, there have been reductions in the level of social protection and a tightening of the conditions under which benefits are paid. This means that the rise in employment rates is achieved through an increase in the number of low paid workers, thus raising doubts about a central assumption of the Lisbon agenda – that employment growth will ensure social inclusion.

The global financial crisis

The economic downturn caused by the global financial crisis posed new threats and challenges to the European social agenda and its inclusion policy. An unprecedented influx of migrants and a rise in long-term unemployment nourished populist movements. This led some analysts to conclude that the Eurozone crisis had pushed social Europe towards a dead end (Lechevalier and Wielgohs 2015). Indeed, many scholars agree that the global financial crisis has brought institutions of social protection to a critical juncture. This theoretical concept captures a moment of uncertainty when political agency can play a more decisive role in triggering institutional change (Capoccia 2015, 148). Once a window for radical reorganisation opens, institutional gridlock is easier to overcome. Accordingly, historical-institutionalism traces a model of organisational development marked by long periods of stability occasionally interrupted by exogenous forces. Such forces may prompt dramatic changes and produce structural fluidity as they overcome the usual stickiness of institutions. Applied to social policy this means that major reforms are likely to occur in the aftermath of a global financial crisis. For Glassner and Keune (2012, 368), the crisis had undeniably aggravated the asymmetry between EU market reforms for the sake of labour cost competitiveness, on the one hand, and for the efforts to strengthen the 'social dimension', on the other.

No doubt, the global financial crisis of 2007/08 had an enormous impact on national social policies. While the particular critical juncture did create hardship, it also gave way to new opportunities. At the end of the decade, Commission President Manuel Barroso launched a new Europe 2020 agenda to move his organisation away from austerity policies to a stronger concern with people's welfare. Since then, the EU has adopted explicit targets covering main dimensions of economic and social development and convinced many scholars of a reinvigorated European social policy.

Another phase of policy making began under the leadership of Commission President Jean-Claude Juncker. In 2015, he firmly placed 'social Europe' among Brussels' top priorities. His administration suggested a re-launch of Europe built on issues of social protection, inclusion and access to basic services, as well as lifelong learning and gender equality. The Commission presented the European Pillar of Social Rights (EPSR) in 2017 with the ambition to build a fairer EU through a strengthened social dimension. The EPSR sets out twenty key principles and rights to support fair and well-functioning labour markets and welfare systems. These principles are structured around three main categories. The first category addresses issues of equal opportunities and access to the labour market, including education, training and life-long learning, gender equality as well as equal opportunities regardless of racial or ethnic origin, religion or belief, disability, age or sexual orientation. The second category deals with fair working conditions, stressing the fact that workers have the right to fair wages that provide for a decent standard of living. They also have the right to fair and equal treatment in terms of working conditions, regardless of the type and duration of the employment relationship. Finally, the third category focuses on social protection and inclusion by underlining the importance of a minimum income. Everyone who is lacking adequate resources has a right to minimum income benefits, ensuring a life in dignity at all its stages with effective access to enabling goods and services. In the words of Jean-Claude Juncker (European Commission 2017):

> I have been seeking to put social priorities at the heart of Europe's work, where they belong. With the European Pillar of Social Rights and the first set of initiatives that accompany it, we are delivering on our promises and we are opening a new chapter. We want to write this chapter together: member states, EU institutions, the social partners and civil society all have to take on their responsibility. I would like to see the Pillar endorsed at the highest political level before the end of this year.

The EPSR reaffirms citizens' rights already present in the EU and complements them to come to terms with new realities, such as long-term unemployment, work-life balance, multi-ethnic societies, global economic and financial integration. It lays out rights and protective measures European workers are entitled to through existing EU law, such as non-discrimination and equal pay. Initially, the proclamation applies to the euro area, but remains open to all member states. In line with subsidiarity considerations, the centre of gravity for action rests with the member states, but EU legislation will set minimum standards and, in selected areas, attempt to harmonise citizens' rights across Europe.

Recalibration

With the social dimension back at centre stage in EU policy making, questions of Europeanisation have come to the fore. Europeanisation identifies the changes within a member state whose motivating logic is directly linked to EU decision-making. This approach suggests that EU membership with its own political and economic dynamics triggers processes of policy elaboration, norm diffusion and institutionalisation that influence domestic policies as well as national political and administrative structures.

However, the predominance of the subsidiarity principle in social policy and a general absence of hard laws in the form of welfare state related European directives lead some scholars to conclude that EU influence in national social policy is weak. Moreover, many of the European guidelines do not appear in domestic reform trajectories.

This description can be challenged, as the conventional top-down approach is not appropriate for understanding social policy reforms. Since national and European levels are increasingly interwoven, the integration process influences social policy reforms in indirect and informal ways. Hence, the question is not if the EU matters, but when and how. Answering this question implies an exploration of mechanisms, of inputs, and of incentives, through which the EU system affects domestic policy makers (Graziano et al. 2011).

One way in which the EU shapes domestic social policy reforms is by advocating a new narrative. For example, the EU introduced a new discourse on 'recalibrating' welfare programmes towards more active and service-oriented policies (Laruffa 2015). Accordingly, social policy should be recast as a 'social investment' that strengthens the competitive standing of capital and labour on global markets. Investments in training and skills are crucial to adapt to a changing work environment. At the same time, there is an intense debate about how a social investment programme can be put into practice. Not everyone agrees with Hemerijck (2012) that welfare states have successfully stepped onto an investment path. Instead, a real paradigm change away from neoliberal understandings would require a strong push from 'below', from actors such as European social movements, trade unions and grass-roots organisations. Sceptics maintain that the EU's recent social investment policy does not present a break from the past, as it is still subordinated to economic considerations. In this view, it 'will fail to provide a sufficient answer to the current economic crisis and its deeper social and political aspects' (Laruffa 2015, 216).

The recalibration discourse has triggered a variety of domestic reforms to alter the traditional configuration of social policy. Comparative analysis indicates that this activity reflects particular strategies inside the member states to mobilise resources from Brussels for policy formulation and implementation. The EU initiatives constitute a set of constraints and opportunities for national policy makers that can be formal or informal as well as binding or non-binding. They allow domestic actors to use the EU system to strengthen their own legitimacy, to develop their power-base and to expand their overall room for manoeuvre.

Short-time work schemes in Italy

Trade unions, employers and governments sought jointly to mitigate the social consequences of the global financial crisis. Hence, executive actors assigned to collective agreements the function of an 'implementation mechanism' for crisis-specific social policy measures (Glassner and Keune 2012). Short-time work schemes (STW), for example, aim at preventing workers from losing their jobs and, thus, preserve human capital by reducing the number of working hours during periods of low demand. They are a device to reduce the negative effects of an economic recession on employment levels. As these wage subsidies are financed from public funds, they are a type of unemployment benefit. The respective schemes vary widely in terms of eligibility conditions, duration of support, coverage rate, compensation amount, and sources of financing. Specific company agreements for STWs are widespread in countries with multi-employer bargaining. The latter refers to constellations in which several small- to medium-sized employers in one industry join an association to negotiate with one or more labour organisations representing their employees. They work together to develop positions on themes associated with employer and employee relations such as wages, employment benefits, working hours, as well as the general terms and conditions of employment. In the case of Italy, this link between subsidiarity and STW implementation is particularly well established.

The 2009 State-Region Accord shifted the administrative responsibility for STW schemes from central to regional governments. Until then, the central government was solely responsible for the unemployment benefit system. After the Accord, the sources of funding for STW were split between national and regional governments in a ratio of 70 to 30 per cent. In 2011, the regional funding was raised further to 40 per cent. In addition, the Accord established that most of the regional STW resources would come from the European Structural Funds (ESF).

The territorial division in financial responsibility is best explained by ESF management rules. For the European Commission, this means that benefits financed through the ESF and tied to workers' participation also need to be systematically monitored and evaluated. Consistent with ESF rules, Article 2 of the Accord posits that regional governments implement active labour market policies, while central agencies pay for social security contributions and, in large part, for income maintenance.

The weighting in funding arrangements between regional and central governments has important implications for the subsidiarity principle. According to the Brussels rule book, ESF are meant to promote and implement an active labour market policy. Hence, their use amounts to a first move in the direction of an 'activation turn', which rests on improvements to the education system aiming for better training and a consolidation of the available skills. Although activation is not an entirely new notion in the Italian system, the suggested conditionality for beneficiaries has never been mandatory.

Therefore, between 1990 and 2005, the Italian spending profile in active labour market policies was one of the lowest in Europe (Bonoli 2012). Typically, unemployment benefit schemes were only conceived as passive measures. Now resources from the ESF are made available following a tripartite regional agreement among trade unions, employers and local government. This is in marked contrast to ordinary social shock absorbers schemes, which the Italian central government previously funded without any formal agreement among regional social partners. Such schemes were introduced after World War II in response to economic crises. They were considered special measures to extend the coverage of income protection schemes to many segments of the business sector and its workforce in order to maintain employment and to protect human capital. Thus, the implementation of the Commission's conditionality requirement represented an important novelty. It meant the redirection of labour policy measures from the mere provision of substitute income to welfare-to-work assistance with the ultimate aim to bring the unemployed back into work and out of state support (Mulé 2016). As part of the policy change in the wake of the global financial crisis, the EU effectively managed to circumvent the principle of subsidiarity through ESF conditionality rules.

Conclusion

Social protection at national and European level, as mentioned in the introduction to this chapter, functions within an asymmetric structure. This asymmetry is coupled with the principle of subsidiarity, demanding action at the lowest level of government to safeguard national sovereignty. Yet, as EU financial support is linked to conditionality, subsidiarity becomes a rather empty principle. In the words of Barbier (2015, 40), 'what happens is that practically no limit can be put to the gradual spill-over of economic law into the social domain'. For this reason, the 2017 EPSR has been widely welcomed. It puts the social dimension back to centre stage, emphasising the responsibilities of member states and taking subsidiarity seriously. Only the future implementation of the EPSR will show whether the principle is equally applicable in all member states, irrespective of their need for financial support. So far, not all policies related to the European social agenda have been smooth sailing. The principle of subsidiarity interferes with asymmetric policy structures and top-down conditionality. Therefore, it is vital that the European Commission finds new imaginative solutions for a more balanced interaction between national and supranational activities in the social domain.

References

Barbier, J. C. (2015). 'The State of Social Europe'. In Lechevalier, A. and J. Wielgohs (eds) *Social Europe: A Dead End,* 27–48. Copenhagen: Djøf Publishing.

Bonoli, G. (2012). 'Active Labour Market Policy and Social Investment: A Changing Relationship'. In Morel, N., Palier, B. and J. Palme (eds) *Towards a Social Investment Welfare State? Ideas, Policies and Challenges*, 181–204. Bristol: The Policy Press.

Capoccia, G. (2015). 'Critical Junctures and Institutional Change'. In Mahoney, J. and K. Thelen (eds) *Advances in Comparative–Historical Analysis*, 147-79. Cambridge: Cambridge University Press.

European Commission (2017). Press Release, 26 April. Available at: http://europa.eu/rapid/press-release_IP-17-1007_en.htm

Esping-Andersen, G. (1990). *Three Worlds of Welfare Capitalism*. Cambridge: Polity.

Fabbrini, S. and U. Puetter (2016). 'Integration without Supranationalisation: Studying the Lead Roles of the European Council and the Council in Post-Lisbon EU Politics', *Journal of European Integration*, 38(5): 481–95.

Ferrera, M., Matsaganis, M. and S. Sacchi (2002). 'Open Coordination Against Poverty: The New EU "Social Inclusion Process" ', *Journal of European Social Policy* 12 (3): 227–39.

Glassner, V. and M. Keune (2012). 'The Crisis and Social Policy: The Role of Collective Agreements'. *International Labour Review* 151(4): 351–75.

Graziano, P., Jacquot, S. and B. Palier (eds) (2011). *The EU and the Domestic Politics of Welfare State Reforms.* Basingstoke: Palgrave Macmillan.

Hall, P. and D. Soskice (eds) (2001). *Varieties of Capitalism*. Oxford: Oxford University Press.

Hemerijck, A. (2012). 'Two or Three Waves of Welfare State Transformation?'. In Morel N., Palier B. and Palme J. (eds) *Towards a Social Investment Welfare State? Ideas, Policies and Challenges.* 191–205. Bristol: Policy Press.

Laruffa, F. (2015). 'Social Investment: Towards a More Social Europe?'. In Lechevalier, A. and J. Wielgohs (eds) *Social Europe: A Dead End.* 215-36. Copenhagen: Djøf Publishing.

Lechevalier, A. and J. Wielgohs (eds) (2015). *Social Europe: A Dead End*. Copenhagen: Djøf Publishing.

Mulé, R. (2016). 'Coping with the Global Financial Crisis: The Regional Political Economy of Social Shock Absorbers in Italy'. *Regional & Federal Studies* 26(3): 359–79.

Scharpf, F. W. (2010). 'The Asymmetry of European Integration, or Why the EU cannot be a Social Market Economy'. *Socio-Economic Review* 8(2): 211–50.

6

The Subsidiarity Principle in EU Environmental Law

SIAN AFFOLTER

According to the Seventh Environment Action Program of the EU, 'many environmental trends in the Union continue to be a cause for concern', and in order to live well in the future, it is now necessary to take urgent and concerted action (European Parliament and Council 2013, annex point 6). On the one hand, this is due to insufficient implementation of existing EU legislation. On the other hand, the question arises whether the necessary legislation exists at all. When looking at recent developments in EU environmental law, it can be noted that the principle of subsidiarity has become an increasingly debated subject matter, explaining why action cannot be taken at Union level. This chapter discusses the role played by the principle of subsidiarity in the field of environmental law and illustrates key points by looking at EU legislation where the subsidiarity principle mattered in the adoption of law. At times, as this chapter will show, the principle is falsely used to explain the EU's inactivity in environmental affairs. To make this point, the basis of EU competence to take action in the field of environmental law is set out. Then, the principle of subsidiarity will be explored in general as well as more specific terms of environmental law. This serves as the basis for the analysis of two examples. First, it will be shown that EU legislation on soil protection – which was rejected by the member states – would have been in line with the principle of subsidiarity. Second, an amendment to the directive on the deliberate release of genetically modified organisms (GMOs) which re-nationalised the authorisation procedure will be analysed as regards subsidiarity. Finally, a conclusion is drawn, arguing that the principle of subsidiarity in its legal sense is sometimes used as an 'excuse' for the Union's (politically motivated) inactivity.

It is important to note that acts of EU environmental law can be motivated by different objectives. First of all, there is the genuine aim to protect the environment. Yet, there is also the aim to realise the goals of the internal market, which can be strongly influenced by environmental policy concerns. In the case of the latter, especially product- or production-related regulation often includes elements of environmental policy. For this reason, two different cases are chosen below: one as a legislative act based solely on environmental protection, and one, as a product-related piece of legislation, with strong components of environmental policy.

EU competences

According to the principle of conferral, established in Article 5 (1) of the Treaty on European Union (TEU), the EU may only take action if the treaties – and thus the member states – have granted the power to do so to the Union. For the practical working of subsidiarity, it is decisive whether the competence granted to the EU by the relevant provisions is of an exclusive or non-exclusive nature. Only in the case of non-exclusive competences does the subsidiarity principle come into play (see Streinz 2012, note 21). As environmental protection constitutes a cross-sectional task to be pursued in all EU policy fields, relevant measures can be issued in many different areas and, hence, with diverse foundations of competence. This is not least because of Article 11 of the Treaty on the Functioning of the European Union (TFEU) stating that requirements of environmental protection are to be integrated into the definition and implementation of Union policies and activities. The next section will focus on the two main bases of EU competence regarding environmental protection, Article 192 and Article 114 TFEU.

Article 192 TFEU

What action is to be taken to achieve the objectives of European environmental policy rests with a decision by the Council and the European Parliament. The objectives themselves are listed in Article 191 TFEU and include the preservation, protection and improvement of the quality of the environment, the protection of human health, the prudent and rational utilisation of natural resources and the promotion of measures to deal with regional or global environmental problems at an international level. Indeed, the EU competence in the field of environmental policy is defined by these policy objectives. Due to the wide remit of the list and the broad under-standing of the term 'environment', the Union's competence to take action is rather extensive (Epiney 2019, 105). Furthermore, as the policy area is not mentioned in the list of EU exclusive competences contained in Article 3 TEU, the Union's competence deriving from Article 192 TFEU must be of a non-exclusive nature and the subsidiarity principle is, therefore, of relevance.

Article 114 TFEU

Environmental measures can be based on Article 114 TFEU, if their primary aim is related to the objective of realising the internal market. This rule serves as the basis of EU competence to adopt measures for the approximation of national provisions which envisage the establishment or the functioning of the internal market. Therefore, it is possible that environmental measures follow from Article 114 TFEU if they, for example, constitute a product- or production-related regulation, further characterised by certain considerations related to environmental protection. As does Article 192 TFEU, Article 114 TFEU confers a non-exclusive competence to the Union. Thus, the subsidiarity principle is of importance in the field of environmental policy independent of the basis of competence for the concerned regulation. However, the objective of the regulation may still have an influence on the principle's implementation.

The principle of subsidiarity and environmental law

As mentioned above, the existence of a competence does not necessarily imply an EU right to jump into action. In fact, this is where the principle of subsidiarity matters. It does not contain any indication as to the limits of a certain competence, but instead limits the use of such competences (Kadelbach 2015, note 30). According to Article 5 (3) TEU, when non-exclusive competences are concerned, the EU:

> shall act only if and in so far as the objectives of the proposed action cannot be sufficiently achieved by the Member States ... but can rather, by reason of the scale or effects of the proposed action, be better achieved at Union level.

Two main aspects can be deduced from the wording of Article 5 (3) TEU. First, the need to examine before any action is taken whether its objective can be *sufficiently* achieved by the member states. This is the so-called negative criterion (see Kadelbach 2015, note 35). And second, in the sense of a positive criterion, the objective of action must be *better* achievable at Union level by reason of scale or effects. The principle of subsidiarity, thus, combines a Union perspective with that of the member states (Epiney 2019, 139). The negative criterion can be fulfilled due to objective reasons, i.e. a member state is unable to achieve the objective in question. Yet, this can also be due to subjective reasons: one or several member states would be able to achieve the objective, but do not take the necessary action. The positive criterion, by contrast, is examined in terms of quantity or quality. In the first case, the objective can be better achieved by reason of its quantitative extent, e.g. when the objective is the fighting of global or cross-border environmental hazards. An example for the case of the objective being better achievable at EU level due to its qualitative extent would be when the objective interacts with other objectives of the Union (such as the realisation of the internal market).

The subsidiarity principle and measures of environmental law

In the following, these general remarks shall be specified with regard to measures of environmental law, as set out by Epiney (2019, 140–3). As has been pointed out, environmental policy measures can be based on different objectives when examining questions of EU competence. The focus might be on particular aspects of environmental protection as well as on the aim of realising the internal market, thus the objective of market integration. If the primary aim of a measure is the latter, the criterion of not sufficiently achieving the objective at the member-state level is fulfilled whenever national measures lawfully impede the goal of market integration. Similarly, in the case of the main objective being derived from Article 191 TFEU, this criterion is typically fulfilled because of a broad understanding of the objectives listed in Article 191 TFEU. Therefore, it is sufficient for the negative criterion to be fulfilled if an environmental problem exists in one or more member states without being addressed adequately by the respective authorities. However, the existence of different – yet in terms of results equivalent – solutions by individual member states would imply that the objective of a measure is sufficiently achieved at national level.

Moreover, the criterion of the EU being able to better achieve the objective will frequently be fulfilled. For example, in the case of the realisation of the single market, the objective would be clearly contradicted if different national regulations continued to apply. Also, as regards measures orientated towards the achievement of genuine environmental protection, a respective policy objective is often better achieved at Union level, since this is the case as soon as the EU measures, overall, lead to an improvement of environmental quality.

As a consequence, the question whether the objective is better achieved at the level of the EU by reason of the scale or the effects of the proposed action becomes the decisive consideration. It must be assessed, if the objective to be achieved (or the identified environmental problem) is of such a comprehensive nature that action at EU level must be regarded as necessary. This appears to be the case in two situations: first, the proposed action addresses an environmental problem with cross-border effects suggesting large-scale, co-ordinated action. Then the question of maintaining or ameliorating environmental quality is not just relevant at national or regional level, but concerns many, if not all, member states. Second, the proposed action refers to the objective of market integration. Then, the necessity to adopt measures at EU level regularly derives from the operation of the internal market and the related guarantees of the 'four fundamental freedoms' and undistorted competition (see the European Court of Justice 2001, paragraph 32; 2002, paragraph 182; and rather clearly 2016, paragraph 150). To a certain extent, measures such as product- or production-related regulations can often also be qualified as environmental measures. However, the extensive character (or scale) of the action which calls for EU-wide measures does follow from the goal of market integration rather than an objective of environmental policy as such.

In sum, the application of the criteria identified above suggests that the setting of product- or production-related measures at EU level will, as a rule, conform to the subsidiarity principle. This is due to their important implications for the practical working of the internal market. As far as measures of genuine environmental policy are concerned, it has to be assessed on a case-by-case basis whether the EU is able to better achieve the objective of the proposed action given either its scale or effects. Presumably, this will often be the case since interdependent ecosystems turn seemingly local environmental problems into cross-border challenges. Thus, only in exceptional circumstances will the principle of subsidiarity constitute an opposing factor to EU action taken in the field of environmental policy. For that matter, it can also be found that the jurisprudence of the European Court of Justice (2001, paragraph 30–4; 2002 paragraph 180–5; 2011, paragraph 176–80) generally seems to grant the Union's organs a rather large scope in this regard. Nevertheless, it is of particular importance when it comes to the concrete design of policy measures which should allow for the taking into account of local specificities.

Selected environmental measures

Proposed soil framework directive

In 2006, the Commission presented a proposal for a directive establishing a framework for the protection of soil (European Commission 2006). The objective of this directive, as stated in its recital 8, was to establish a common strategy for the protection and sustainable use of soil. The proposed directive, however, was never adopted and eventually withdrawn by the Commission in May 2014 (European Commission 2014, 3).

The proposal foresaw an obligation on part of the member states to identify risk areas of soil erosion due to water or wind, decline of organic matter, compaction, salinisation and landslides. It granted member states a timeframe of five years to do so once the EU legislation had come into force (Article 6). In addition, the Soil Framework Directive would have expected member states to draw up a programme of measures, including risk reduction targets, measures for reaching those targets, a timetable for the implementation of measures as well as an estimate of the allocation of private or public funding (Article 8). It furthermore would have obliged member states to identify contaminated sites and to establish a national remediation strategy on the basis of an inventory of such sites. A proposed Article 12 also requested soil status reports be made available to the competent authority and the other party whenever a site on which potentially polluting activity has taken place was being sold. Finally, a proposed Article 16 would have established a far-reaching obligation for member states to make information available and largely increased their reporting duties (Petersen 2008, 149).

One of the main reasons for the rejection of the Soil Framework Directive by many member states was an alleged breach of the subsidiarity principle (Petersen 2008, 149). This claim can be assessed by drawing on the negative and positive criterion embedded in the legal codification of the principle.

As regards the former, the objective of the proposed action – the protection of soil and the preservation of its functions – was not met by several EU countries (Scheil 2007, 180). The desired objective was thus not *sufficiently* achieved at domestic level. Yet, whether it could be *better* achieved at the Union level due to the scale or effects of the proposed action was widely debated. As stated above, this is the case when the environmental problem addressed by the action has cross-border effects and calls for large-scale or co-ordinated action or when EU action is necessary to guarantee the fundamental freedoms and undistorted competition.

In the example of the Soil Framework Directive, both elements would have been present. Although the soil protection issue has a strong local component, trans-boundary effects cannot be denied. It is noteworthy that soil plays an important role in the context of climate change. It is the largest natural storage of carbon on a global scale, making its preservation an essential goal (Heuser 2007, 121; Klein 2007, 12). Therefore, the importance of healthy soils for the mitigation of climate change is more than evident. Moreover, the protection of soils greatly influences the protection and preservation of other resources such as biodiversity and groundwater, which in turn also have clear cross-border effects. While the protection of these resources is also envisaged by other, more specialised, EU instruments, this does not preclude common action in the field of soil protection.

Arguably, the proposal of a Soil Framework Directive would have complied with the principle of subsidiarity. In general, the principle does not stand in the way of EU action in the field of soil protection. In other words, the claim of the member states that the proposed legislative act was incompatible with the subsidiarity principle appears to have been without legal foundation. Most likely, the raised concerns were brought forward to prevent the adoption of a politically undesired regulation.

Amended GMO directive

In April 2015, the EU regime for GMOs changed with Directive 2015/412/EU amending Directive 2001/18/EG on the deliberate release of such organisms. The modified legislation introduced new possibilities for member states to restrict or prohibit the commercial cultivation of GMOs in their territory. Originally, the regime regarding the deliberate release of GMOs was characterised by the EU's attempt to centralise regulation in order to prevent the distortion of competition and to guarantee a uniform protection of the environment (see Christoforou 2004, 641; Salvi 2016, 202–4). However, some member states raised complaints to articulate their preference for a final say on GMO cultivation. This led to said amendment which indeed re-nationalises the competence to decide whether GMOs can be cultivated in a certain territory (see Geelhoed 2016, 20–1; Martínez 2015, 86).

More precisely, Directive 2015/412/EU introduced the possibility to restrict or prohibit the cultivation of GMOs at two different stages of the procedure: first, member states can demand that the geographical scope of the written consent or authorisation is amended so not to affect their territory; or second, they can adopt measures restricting or prohibiting the cultivation of GMOs, if the authorisation does cover their territory (Article 26b (1) and (3) Directive 2001/18/EC). These measures must be in conformity with EU law, reasoned, proportional, non-discriminatory, and based on compelling grounds. Article 26b (3) provides a non-exhaustive list to this end, stating environmental policy objectives first. Yet, any national measures must not stand in conflict with environmental risk assessments carried out by the European Food Safety Authority (EFSA) prior to the authorisation of GMOs (Art. 26b (3)). As a consequence, member states cannot rely on arguments in direct contrast to the facts established by the EFSA.

The directive's recitals and the preparatory work of the Commission show that, among other factors, subsidiarity concerns were relied upon to explain the amendment (recital 6 and 8 Directive 2015/412; European Commission 2010, 8). But does subsidiarity necessarily ask for a re-nationalisation in the case of GMOs? Further examination is required to determine whether the pre-amendment regime was indeed in conformity with the principle.

Again, the two criteria set out above are relevant. In a first step, the objective of the measure – the regulation of the authorisation procedure for GMOs at EU level – is to be determined. According to Article 1 Directive 2001/18/EC the main objective of the EU's GMO regime is 'to approximate the laws, regulations and administrative provisions of the Member States and to protect human health and the environment'. This applies whether GMOs are placed on the market or deliberately released into the environment for other purposes. Furthermore, as this directive is based on Article 114 TFEU, it was also adopted with the aim of a functioning internal market in mind. Clearly, the negative subsidiarity criterion (a member state not sufficiently meeting the objective) is fulfilled as diverging regulations for domestic GMO authorisation can or did lead to restrictions of the fundamental freedoms in the internal market.

As regards the second criterion (the objective is better achieved at EU level due to scale or effects of the action) the main objective of the GMO regime can only be achieved if regulation takes place at the EU level, making EU action a necessity. Thus, the positive subsidiarity criterion can also be considered as fulfilled. In sum, the regulation of the authorisation procedure at EU level conforms to the principle of subsidiarity. In fact, the normative density of the regulation leaves little discretion to national authorities.

At the same time, the GMO regime demands from the EU to ensure the protection of the environment. This can be derived from numerous legal sources. On the one hand, the acts of the EU secondary law in question set forth the protection of the environment as an aim. On the other hand, this can already be derived from the EU obligation to strive for a high standard of environmental quality when issuing regulations on the basis of Article 114 TFEU, as foreseen by Article 114 (3) TFEU. For this reason, the objective of the protection of the environment is to be duly incorporated into the acts under examination here. In the present case, this was done originally, inter alia, by obliging the EFSA to network and to consult with national authorities while carrying out environmental risk assessments. The EU also granted the member states a possibility to opt-out, if new information on risks of GMOs for human health or the environment became available. Nevertheless, member states claimed that this was insufficient – or the risk assessments not sufficiently executed – which then constituted one of the reasons for the adoption of an amended GMO regime (see Geelhoed 2016, 24–8; Salvi 2016, 203). Arguably, re-nationalising parts of the regime's authorisation procedure is beneficial to the environment as a whole, as it can be expected that certain member states will issue extensive restrictions or bans of GMOs. Yet, this runs counter to the measure's other – probably even primary – objective of realising the internal market. Thus, the answer to the question which level is better able to achieve the dual objective of the measure must point in the direction of the EU. The objective of the realisation of the internal market can only be achieved at a centralised level, and the objective of the protection of the environment can be duly incorporated in the framework of the regulation.

In other words, placing the regulation on GMO authorisation at Union level must be considered in line with the subsidiarity principle. The re-nationalisation resulting from the adoption of Directive 2015/412/EU seems to be driven by other political reasons. As stated above, product- or production-related regulations will most often be in line with the principle of subsidiarity, as their main objective is primarily related to the realisation of the single market. The objective of the protection of the environment must then be achieved by designing EU regulations in an adequate way.

Conclusion

The principle of subsidiarity in EU environmental law suggests a distinction between actions aiming for genuine environmental protection and actions aiming primarily at market integration, but also containing elements of environmental policy. The chapter has shown that these actions can rely on different EU competences. In the first case, the action will generally rely on Article 192 TFEU; whereas it is Article 114 TFEU in the second. It can be concluded that measures based on Article 114 TFEU will most often conform to subsidiarity, as the principle's negative and positive criterion will be fulfilled. For actions following Article 192 TFEU, it must be assessed on a case-by-case basis if due to the scale or the effects of the action, it is to be expected that the EU is able to better achieve the objective of the action. This is the case whenever the action addresses an environmental problem which has cross-border effects calling for large-scale or co-ordinated action. The two examples presented here confirm the general remarks. The proposal for a Soil Framework Directive, as an act based on Article 192 TFEU, would have been in conformity with the principle as all its criteria were met: not all member states protect soil in a sufficient manner and respective cross-border effects as well as the role of soil in the fight against climate change suggest the Union to be much better placed to achieve the objective. Similarly, the analysis of the amended GMO Directive, as an act based on Article 114 TFEU, showed that the changes to the authorisation procedure did not constitute a necessity deriving from the principle of subsidiarity. In fact, locating the GMO regime at EU level has to be seen in conformity with the principle. Given the main objective of the measure – the approximation of laws – this is impossible to achieve at national level and puts the EU in the 'better' position. Even if the subsidiarity test is carried out with regard to the internal market objective, environmental protection must, however, be duly incorporated into the relevant EU law.

From a legal point of view, claims that measures of EU environmental law breach the subsidiarity principle are frequently unfounded, as the limits set by the principle for EU action appear quite wide. However, as environmental protection is a main goal of EU law, supranational action must also consider local and regional problem constellations. This can be done, for example, by giving a large leeway to member states in terms of policy implementation, by providing mechanisms that recognise local and regional specificities, or by granting extensive opt-out provisions. Of course, the conclusion that subsidiarity breaches often appear legally unfounded does not preclude the EU from non-action or re-nationalisation of certain competences for political reasons. At times it does, however, appear that the principle of subsidiarity in its legal sense is used as an excuse for the Union's (politically motivated) inactivity.

References

Christoforou, T. (2004). 'The Regulation of Genetically Modified Organisms in the European Union: The Interplay of Science, Law and Politics.' *Common Market Law Review* 41: 637–709.

European Commission (2006). Proposal for a Directive of the European Parliament and of the Council establishing a Framework for the Protection of Soil and amending Directive 2004/35/EC, COM (2006) 232 final.

European Commission (2010). Proposal for a Regulation of the European Parliament and of the Council amending Directive 2001/18/EC as regards the Possibility for the Member States to restrict or prohibit the Cultivation of GMOs in their Territory, COM (2010) 375 final.

European Commission (2014). Withdrawal of obsolete Commission Proposals: List of Proposals withdrawn, *Official Journal of the European Union,* 21 May, C 153, 3.

European Court of Justice (2001). *Judgment of 9 October,* C-377/98 - Netherlands v. Parliament and Council. Available at: https://eur-lex.europa. eu/legal-content/EN/TXT/?uri=CELEX:61998CJ0377

European Court of Justice (2002). *Judgment of 10 December,* C-491/01 - British American Tobacco (Investments) and Imperial Tobacco. Available at: https://eur-lex.europa.eu/legal-content/EN/TXT/?uri=CELEX:62001CJ0491

European Court of Justice (2011). *Judgment of 12 May,* C-176/09 - Luxembourg v. Parliament and Council. Available at: https://eur-lex.europa. eu/legal-content/EN/TXT/?uri=CELEX%3A62009CJ0176

European Court of Justice (2016). *Judgment of 4 May,* C-477/14 - Pillbox 38 Ltd v. The Secretary of State for Health, Available at: https://eur-lex.europa. eu/legal-content/EN/TXT/?qid=1598354521064&uri=CELEX:62014CA0477

European Parliament and Council (2013). Decision No. 1386/2013/EU of the European Parliament and of the Council of 20 November 2013 on a General Union Environment Action Programme to 2020 'Living well, within the limits of our planet', *Official Journal of the European Union,* 28 December 2013, L 353, 171.

Epiney, A. (2019). *Umweltrecht der Europäischen Union.* 4th edition. Baden-Baden: Nomos.

Geelhoed, M. (2016). 'Divided in Diversity: Reforming the EU's GMO Regime.' In Armstrong, K. A. (ed.) *Cambridge Yearbook of European Legal Studies,* 20-44. Cambridge: Cambridge University Press.

Heuser, I. L. (2007). 'Überlegungen zur Gestaltung des EU-Bodenschutzrechts – Teil 2: EU-Bodenschutz de lege ferenda'. *Zeitschrift für Umweltrecht* 18: 113-22.

Kadelbach, S. (2015). 'Kommentar zu Art. 5 EUV.' In Groeben, H. von der, Schwarze, J. and A. Hatje (eds) *Europäisches Unionsrecht Kommentar.* 7th edition. Baden-Baden: Nomos.

Klein, U. (2007). 'Europäisches Bodenschutzrecht – Auf dem Weg zu einer Bodenschutzrahmenrichtlinie'. *Zeitschrift für Europäisches Umwelt- und Planungsrecht* 5: 2-12.

Martínez, J. (2015). 'Die Renationalisierung von Kompetenzen der EU – die grüne Gentechnik als primärrechtlicher Sündenfall oder Befreiungsschlag?' In Hendler, R., Ibler, M. and J. Martínez (eds) *Herausforderungen an die Kompetenzordnung der EU: Symposium zum 80. Geburtstag von V. Götz,* 81-95, Berlin: Duncker & Humblot.

Petersen, M. (2008). 'European Soil Protection Law after the Setback of December 2007 – Existing Law and Outlook.' *European Energy and Environmental Law Review* 17: 146–55.

Salvi, L. (2016). 'The EU Regulatory Framework on GMOs and the Shift of Powers towards Member States: An Easy Way Out of the Regulatory Impasse?' *European Food and Feed Law Review* 11: 201–10.

Scheil, S. (2007). 'Zweiter Entwurf zur europäischen Bodenschutzstrategie – Chance für ein hohes Schutzniveau zulasten der Subsidiarität.' *Natur und Recht* 29: 176–81.

Streinz, R. (2012). 'Kommentar zu Art. 5 EUV.' In Streinz, R. (ed.) *EUV/AEUV Kommentar.* 2nd edition. München: C.H. Beck.

7

EU Policy on Internal Security and the Subsidiarity Principle

HARTMUT ADEN

The principle of subsidiarity is of particular relevance when the role of the EU in policy and law-making is contested. This chapter builds upon the hypothesis that the situation is ambiguous for internal security: on the one hand, national sovereignty still plays an important role in this field, at least in the official discourse of certain actors in the member states. On the other hand, policy makers and security agencies more frequently recognise the necessity of effective coordination and cooperation in dealing with transnational threats; especially those related to international terrorism. Article 5 (3) of the Treaty on European Union (TEU) defines the requirements as follows:

> Under the principle of subsidiarity, in areas which do not fall within its exclusive competence, the Union shall act only if and insofar as the objectives of the proposed action cannot be sufficiently achieved by the Member States, either at central level or at regional and local level, but can rather, by reason of the scale or effects of the proposed action, be better achieved at Union level.

As internal security was considered by most European politicians as a core element of national sovereignty for many years, the institutions of the European Communities that were the predecessors of the current European Union only played a minor role in this field. With the Treaty of Maastricht, internal security shifted into the realm of official EU policy, albeit in the intergovernmental third pillar. Only since 2009, with the Treaty of Lisbon, have major parts of internal security become full EU policies. Nevertheless, some member states are still hesitant to get involved in more intensive cooperation (Aden 2015; 2018).

Today, the application of the subsidiarity principle to internal security under the Treaty of Lisbon is rather clear. The Treaty on the Functioning of the EU (TFEU) explicitly defines that the EU and the member states share legislative power over the area of freedom, security and justice (AFSJ) (Article 4 (2j) TFEU). For internal security, as far as it falls under the AFSJ, this means that the EU has the authority to legislate where security can be improved through coordination and cooperation among the member states' security agencies – but not for security issues that are of an entirely regional or local nature. Nevertheless, concerns persist that the EU initiatives might go further than necessary. The TFEU therefore attributes the role of watchdog to national parliaments in order to make sure that the EU only regulates AFSJ issues that member states cannot sufficiently address or provide security for on their own (Monar 2014, 201).

> National Parliaments ensure that the proposals and legislative initiatives submitted under Chapters 4 and 5 comply with the principle of subsidiarity, in accordance with the arrangements laid down by the Protocol on the application of the principles of subsidiarity and proportionality (Article 69 TFEU).

The AFSJ includes major, though not all, elements of internal security. While the EU now has legislative powers for trans-border aspects of policing and criminal justice, cooperation between secret services does not fall under the EU's authority completely. Thus far, the initiatives for secret service coordination are not part of the AFSJ, rather of foreign policy. Consequently, the EU Intelligence Analysis Centre (INTCEN) that was first established in 1999 as Joint Situation Centre (SitCen/JSC), became part of the EU's External Action Service in 2012.

This chapter asks from a trans-disciplinary legal and political science perspective: what is the relevance of subsidiarity for EU internal security policy? What is the relationship between subsidiarity, sovereignty and the logics of a policy area that is, for a major part, characterised by reactions to security incidents such as natural disasters or terrorist attacks? And finally: is subsidiarity only a political and legal concept, or is it also a relevant issue for the administrative practice of cooperation among security agencies in Europe?

Sovereignty and the monopoly of legitimate force

Analysing the role of subsidiarity for the EU's internal security policy must take specific tensions between claims for sovereignty and subsidiarity into account. These theoretical and empirical concepts sometimes conflict and sometimes converge. Both may be mobilised in order to support the position of policy makers who fear loss of political influence and power. While the appeal to sovereignty is mostly motivated by the wish to maintain power within nation states, the subsidiarity principle may result in either political decisions being made at the European level, or, at national or sub-national levels (van Kersbergen and Verbeek 2004, 144–5).

Even if privatisation has become an issue of internal security over the past decades, this policy area is still very closely connected to the nation state. In EU member states, police forces and secret services are public administrations often belonging to states or sub-national public authorities such as regions or cities. For policing, an important aspect of the public authorities' power is related to the state's monopoly to exert legitimate force. In the early 20th century, Max Weber (1980, 30) underlined the value of this state function, arguing that this is a key factor in discerning the modern states from feudalism where public security tasks were sold to private actors who bought the right to take money for providing protection or simply controlling the passage of travellers and goods. By contrast, modern rule of law style nation states with institutions that are bound to human rights and have to respect legal rules are much better positioned to provide security impartially.

Most political systems are multi-layered and have a well-established distribution of security tasks between different polity levels, such as local authorities, regions, and the central state. Therefore, most states have several police forces and secret services. States where police forces are primarily organised at the local level have a higher number of police forces, for example the United States of America.

If EU member states are still hesitant to transfer internal security tasks to the EU, this is often related to the questions if and to which extent the EU is evolving towards a state-like polity. Empirically, EU authority covers a broad range of policy areas, and the EU's institutions fulfil similar functions as national governments, parliaments, and courts. Therefore, over the past decades, the EU has made clear steps towards becoming a state-like polity, empirically rather than in a normative perspective. Defenders of the nation state have sustained political pressure in order to avoid the EU becoming a state. In this respect, the transfer of internal security powers to the EU is highly symbolic, as centralised police forces with executive rights would make the EU even more similar to a state. Therefore, using subsidiarity arguments to avoid internal security powers to be transferred to the EU is closely linked to the protection of national sovereignty and to euro-scepticism: both arguments are often used in the political discourse to prevent the EU from becoming more state-like. In this respect, the British opt-out from major parts of EU internal security policy (Tekin 2012, 186–95), that may now be interpreted as a kind of anticipated 'mini-Brexit', is highly symptomatic.

Europeanisation of policing and the perception of threats

The practical implementation of the subsidiarity principle for internal security is closely linked to the Europeanisation of this policy area. The analytical usefulness of the term Europeanisation has been intensively debated over the past two decades (see Goetz and Meyer-Sahling 2008). In this chapter, it is used as an analytical framework, including the perspectives that member states' policies are influenced by decisions taken at EU level and that decision-making processes and responsibilities have been transferred to centralised institutions in the EU. The perspective of subsidiarity, applied to police agencies and secret services as to other branches of public administration (see van Kersbergen and Verbeek 2004, 151; Craig 2012), is closely related to the question of how centralised or decentralised internal security institutions are and should be. How far should their work be bound to harmonised European standards?

Centralisation processes of internal security institutions have already been going on for a long time. However, centralisation is no continuous process. Sometimes centralisation and de-centralisation even take place in parallel (Aden 1998, 41-121). While the growing importance of transnational and global interconnections in business and everyday life have triggered centralisation of security structures, shortcomings in local security have sometimes led to re-decentralisation of policing. For example, a specific cybercrime unit associated to Europol was recently established, whilst the deployment of patrol officers whom are known by citizens has been a relevant issue in many local communities for a number of years. This form of (re-) decentralisation is in response to studies which have demonstrated that citizens feel safer if they regularly see police officers in the streets – ideally patrol officers whom the citizens know personally. These empirical examples demonstrate that the ideas behind the principle of subsidiarity may be helpful to answer the normative question of what role the European Union should play in internal security and how far Europeanisation should go. Security problems that are rather local or regional can be better solved at decentralised levels, while security problems with trans-border or even global implications require some degree of centralised coordination and cooperation.

De facto, despite the persisting importance of state sovereignty over internal security in the official discourse, this policy area is already considerably Europeanised. The institutional setting that has been established at EU level for facilitating trans-border policing is closely related to threats of internal security perceived in the relevant period of time (Bigo 1996, 258-66). A core element of Europeanised policing in the sense of centralised coordination is Europol, the EU agency for cooperation in criminal investigations, based at The Hague in the Netherlands. In the 1990s, Europol was established for combating international drug trafficking and organised crime, both perceived at that time as major threats for internal security. The international dimensions of these kinds of crime establish – in the perspective of subsidiarity – the relevance of coordination at EU level and beyond. However, combating international drug trafficking and other forms of organised crime by international coordination has not been very effective thus far. Illegal markets that allow criminals to make money will attract new criminals when others have been stopped and arrested by the police. Alternative policy measures avoiding illegal markets would therefore probably be more effective. Thus, these examples show that the subsidiarity principle does not prevent policy makers and security agencies from following strategies that are ineffective.

Over time, EU coordination in the field of internal security has been extended to a number of other threats, from counterfeiting the Euro to international terrorism and cybercrime. As these threats could hardly be dealt with effectively solely at a member state's level, the subsidiarity principle clearly supports the establishment of a European coordination infrastructure. In recent years, EU policy makers have opted for harmonising this coordination infrastructure by transferring them into EU agencies. Europol was attributed the status of an official EU agency in 2009. Since its establishment, this agency has been part of the broader EU system, but it enjoys a relevant degree of autonomy. EU Regulation 2016/794 highlights Europol's support function:

> Europol shall support and strengthen action by the competent authorities of the Member States and their mutual cooperation in preventing and combating serious crime affecting two or more Member States, terrorism and forms of crime which affect a common interest covered by a Union policy ... (Article 3 (1)).

Even under the binding Europol Regulation that has replaced the former 'third pillar' legal instruments, the member states make use of Europol's support on a mostly voluntary basis. In this respect, subsidiarity and national sovereignty still play an important role.

Horizontal coordination among the member states' police agencies is another interesting pattern that is related to subsidiarity: the liaison officers that police agencies of member states send to Europol are a core element of this function. One of their tasks is to organise information-sharing between Europol and the police agencies from their home countries. This is an element of vertical, but mostly non-hierarchical cooperation (Aden 2015). Beyond this task, they also exchange information related to investigation cases directly with the liaison officers from other member states. Therefore, liaison officers play an important role in horizontal cooperation among the member states' police agencies. In the perspective of the subsidiarity principle, the relevant internal security tasks remain within the member states' responsibility. The EU provides a platform for coordination among them.

Similarly, other elements of a support infrastructure have been established at EU level, leaving discretion to the member states as to how to use them. The centralised databases introduced for internal security cooperation over the past decades can be classified as centralised administrative structures delivering services for the member states' administrations (Aden 2018, 986– 8; Boehm 2012, 259–319). The member states are obliged to establish a central unit that filters data relevant for trans-border cooperation and enters it into the databases. The most important database of this type is the Schengen Information System (SIS) established in the 1990s. The member states' law enforcement and immigration authorities enter data into this database, especially information related to wanted criminals or stolen goods. The SIS information may also be related to the refusal of entry for individuals – mostly in connection with the implementation of a restrictive immigration policy. The SIS is linked to national police information systems. This means that police checks in any Schengen country can lead to a 'hit', indicating that a person or good is sought by a police agency somewhere in Europe, or that immigration authorities have decided to refuse entry to said person. Further proceedings, i.e. extradition, will then have to be managed on a bilateral basis by the police agencies and the judicial authorities of both countries.

In 2012, the management of the 'second generation' SIS and other AFSJ databases was attributed to a then newly created separate EU agency: eu-LISA, the EU Agency for the Operational Management of Large-Scale IT Systems in the area of freedom, security and justice, located in Tallinn (Estonia – headquarters), Strasbourg (France – IT infrastructure) und Sankt Johann (Austria). So far, beyond the SIS, eu-LISA manages the fingerprint database Eurodac and the Visa Information System (VIS) (Balzacq and Léonard 2013, 133; Aden 2015). With the newly established Entry-/Exit-System and the European Travel Information and Authorisation System (ETIAS), EU databases will in the future cover additional data on people travelling to Europe. Here again, in the perspective of subsidiarity and national sovereignty, no essential power has been transferred to the EU, yet a centralised support infrastructure for the member states' law enforcement agencies has been established at EU level.

However, the establishment of EU agencies means that Brussels is expanding its administrative capacities and therefore opens opportunities to later transfer additional tasks to the EU level. With numerous proposals for additional coordination instruments, the European Commission is seeking to gain influence and power in a policy area still dominated by the member states. One example is the interoperability proposal presented by the Commission in 2017. In the past, each policing and migration database was separate and had its specific access rules. The Commission's interoperability proposal includes a common search portal for all databases, which may facilitate the use of EU databases but will also lead to challenging problems in the perspective of privacy, purpose limitation, and data quality management (Aden 2018, 988).

Other EU agencies for internal security follow a similar logic of respecting subsidiarity and national sovereignty. Frontex, the highly contested European Border and Coast Guard Agency, organises joint operations mostly carried out by border and coast guard forces delegated by member states. EU Regulation 2016/1624 which now governs the agency's work, defines Frontex as an institution that shares responsibilities with relevant member states administrations:

> The European Border and Coast Guard Agency ... and the national authorities of Member States which are responsible for border management, including coast guards to the extent that they carry out border control tasks, shall constitute the European Border and Coast Guard (Article 3 (1)).

Centralised administrative structures for police cooperation in the EU, as of yet, have only limited vertical-hierarchical top-down power enabling them to force the member states' security agencies to cooperate. The centralised administrative capacities established at EU level rather offer services which member states are principally free to make use of. The limited administrative and operational capabilities at EU level contribute to the result that, *de facto*, intergovernmental coordination and voluntary cooperation among the member states' security agencies remain the dominant modes of governance in this policy field (Monar 2014, 202). Thus, the member states still have broad discretion in decision-making in the area of trans-border internal security cooperation, and the subsidiarity principle is rarely mobilised to prevent the EU from further coordination.

The now circa 40 Police and Customs Cooperation Centres (PCCC) established in the border regions between the Schengen countries since the 1990s (Gruszczak 2016) are another interesting case in the perspective of subsidiarity. They have been established by bi- or multilateral agreements concluded between the neighbouring countries cooperating within these centres. EU institutions are usually not involved. Police and customs administrations from neighbouring countries share an office building within the border region in order to coordinate over trans-border cases. Due to the daily work which occurs in the same building, the PCCCs can be classified as a particularly strong variation of network-based horizontal administrative cooperation. In the perspective of subsidiarity, operational decision-making in the PCCCs is mostly decentralised.

Serious threats such as international terrorism trigger the question if – again in a subsidiarity perspective – the member states should transfer more powers to centralised coordination units for police work and secret services to make coordination more effective. Almost ritually, after major terrorist attacks, the EU ministers of the interior meet and promise to intensify cooperation. However, in the end, only limited policing power has been transferred to the EU so far (Aden 2015; 2018). Taking the subsidiarity principle seriously would probably require transferring more binding coordination power to the EU in order to react effectively to transnational threats – and even establishing EU internal security institutions with more executive powers.

The European Public Prosecutor's Office

As of now, Eurojust is the most established instrument of criminal justice coordination in the EU. Representatives from the member states' criminal justice systems exchange information and coordinate their work related to criminal investigation. Similar to Europol, the EU has established an infrastructure for coordination without forcing the member states to use it. Therefore, in the perspective of subsidiarity, the establishment of Eurojust has been mostly uncontested.

This changed with the following step. The Treaty of Lisbon made possible the establishment of a European Public Prosecutor's Office (EPPO) derived 'from Eurojust' – an idea which some actors had already been promoting for many years (Giuffrida 2017).

> In order to combat crimes affecting the financial interests of the Union, the Council, by means of regulations adopted in accordance with a special legislative procedure, may establish a European Public Prosecutor's Office from Eurojust. The Council shall act unanimously after obtaining the consent of the European Parliament' (Article 86 (1) TFEU).

The EPPO's authority will be, at the beginning, limited to the protection of the Union's financial interests, thus it will mainly cover cases of fraud related to the EU budget. From a subsidiarity perspective, it seems clear that a more uniform treatment of these cases could be better managed and coordinated by a European body for criminal investigation than by a single member states' criminal justice system.

The establishment of the EPPO as a new institution can be conceived of as a transfer of new powers to the EU. The Treaty of Lisbon opened the path to establishing the EPPO via a unanimous decision in the Council – not by a majority vote in the Ordinary Legislative Procedure. This is one example of a case in which the Treaty of Lisbon makes it possible to transfer powers to the EU without a treaty change. Article 86 also establishes the possibility of settling for enhanced cooperation among a number of member states if unanimity is not reached.

In July 2013, the European Commission proposed a regulation in pursuance of the EPPO's establishment. This proposal was intensively debated not only in the Justice and Home Affairs Council and in the European Parliament, but also by a number of member states' parliaments questioning the conformity of the proposal with the principle of subsidiarity. The relationship between the EPPO and national law enforcement authorities was particularly contested in this perspective (Lohse 2015, 177). The Commission proposed that most of the EPPO's investigative work should be done by the national law enforcement institutions – with a quasi-subordination of the member states' criminal investigation units under the EPPO:

> The designated European Delegated Prosecutor may either undertake the investigation measures on his/her own or instruct the competent law enforcement authorities in the Member State where he/she is located. The authorities shall comply with the instructions of the European Delegated Prosecutor and execute the investigation measures assigned to them (European Commission 2013, 23; Article 18 (1)).

During the discussion in the Council, the member states' governments maintained the idea of opting for a multi-level structure, attributing major investigation tasks to European Delegated Prosecutors who may also exercise as national prosecutors. But they softened the rules concerning the quasi-subordination of national criminal justice institutions to the Delegated Prosecutors. In 2017, Council Regulation 2017/1939 implementing enhanced cooperation in the establishment of the European Public Prosecutor's Office was passed. Twenty member states opted for enhanced cooperation, thus exceeding the minimum of nine member states required by Article 86 (1) TFEU. Whereas the United Kingdom, Ireland and Denmark never intended to join the EPPO due to their broad opt-out for JHA issues (Tekin 2012), other member states hesitated to join the initiative for various political reasons (Giuffrida 2017, 6–7), in some cases related to subsidiarity. The Netherlands and Malta joined in 2018.

The debate on the conformity of the EPPO with the subsidiarity principle shows that this principle is not only relevant to the decision of whether or not to regulate a particular issue at EU level, but also for the way in which the relationship of a new EU body with the relevant authorities at member states' level is shaped.

Secret service coordination beyond subsidiarity

Compared to police agencies, secret services are even more bound to nation states. While policing, since the Treaty of Lisbon, is one of the many policies for which the EU and its member states share competences, the starting point is different for secret service coordination (Aldrich 2012; Aden 2018). Their coordination is not part of the area of freedom, security and justice. Again, in the perspective of subsidiarity, the starting point seems clear: the EU does not have any authority, and therefore the subsidiarity principle does not apply. Decision-making should be left to the member states.

However, reality is somewhat more complicated. Secret services have already been cooperating bi- and multilaterally for a long time in order to fulfil their function of informing governments about developments in foreign countries which may be pertinent to foreign policy decisions. This cooperation is even more important for information that might be relevant to external or internal security. Since the 1970s, informal 'clubs' have been established in order to facilitate secret service coordination in Europe and beyond, mostly related to terrorism (Aldrich 2012). After the terrorist attacks of 11 September 2001, the boundaries between external and internal security lost importance, and secret services massively extended their cooperation in order to gather information about terrorist attacks that international networks might plan. This also made secret service work more similar to policing: preventing terrorists from committing attacks means that secret services either have to exert police tasks or that they have to cooperate more closely with police agencies (see Aldrich 2012).

What does this mean for the EU and subsidiarity? Over the past decades, it became clear that more coordination of secret service activities would be useful, even without formal EU legislative authority. The EU Intelligence

Analysis Centre (INTCEN) was first established in 1999 as Joint Situation Centre, (SitCen/JSC) in order to coordinate the sharing of secret information needed for governmental decision-making, e.g. in relation to terrorist threats. In 2012 it was integrated into the EU's External Action Service (Boehm 2012, 253–4; Cross 2013). The missing treaty base for this kind of coordination may be considered problematic. By contrast, in the perspective of subsidiarity, strong empirical evidence underlines the need for EU level coordination in activities combating cross-border terrorism. Officialising coordination in the EU framework would also facilitate accountability towards parliaments and the broader public.

Circumventing EU institutions?

Police agencies in the EU now widely accept and use standardised 'channels' of EU internal security cooperation such as the Schengen Information System. However, people working for police agencies and secret services sometimes tend to prefer informal coordination to cooperation through formally established institutions such as Europol. This overlaps with the interests of those who wish to keep the EU out of decision-making for internal security in order to protect the member states' national sovereignty.

EU institutions and especially the European Commission have made numerous attempts to convince the member states' security agencies to use the 'channels' established at EU level for their cooperation (Aden 2015; 2018). Nevertheless, informal networks and circles have been maintained. For policing, an 'inherent desire for autonomy in relation to the political-governance level' has been observed (van Buuren 2012, 3). The trust police leaders have in official channels established at EU level has often been limited, especially for sensitive information related to terrorism. Semi-institutionalised, but informal networks as the Police Working Group on Terrorism (PWGT), established in the 1970s, have been maintained and continue to be used. In relation to political decision-making and steering, security agencies enjoy considerable autonomy and discretion when they decide which 'channels' and institutional settings they use for cooperation (Aden 2018).

This demonstrates that, in administrative practice, the selection of an adequate institutional setting for police cooperation is not guided by the subsidiarity principle, rather it is reliant on other aspects, such as the personal and institutional trust in the 'channels' to be used for cooperation and in the officers involved. Trust in their reliability, especially for keeping information secret if necessary, plays an important role in practice (see Aden 2018).

Conclusion

This chapter has shown that for EU internal security policy the subsidiarity principle is often used as an argument to prevent formal power from being transferred to the EU, mostly by actors wishing to preserve a strong nation state and national sovereignty. By contrast, administrative coordination and cooperative practice is rather pragmatic, using the EU's institutional settings for standardised internal security cooperation, though still circumventing them for more sensitive issues such as terrorism.

Whether more or less internal security cooperation will take place at EU level in the future therefore depends upon two factors: firstly, on the development of old and new trans-border threats that may trigger intensified cooperation – and secondly, on the weight of euro-scepticism and the wish to maintain national sovereignty. Brexit might open a window of opportunity for more EU integration in the field of internal security among the remaining member states, as a powerful representative of internal security opt-outs will no longer influence EU decision-making.

References

Aden, H. (1998). *Polizeipolitik in Europa. Eine interdisziplinäre Studie über die Polizeiarbeit in Europa am Beispiel Deutschlands, Frankreichs und der Niederlande.* Wiesbaden: Westdeutscher Verlag.

Aden, H. (2015). Police Cooperation in the EU before and after the Treaty of Lisbon – Continuity and Innovation'. In Aden, H. (ed.) *Police Cooperation in the European Union under the Treaty of Lisbon – Opportunities and Limitations,* 15–22, Baden-Baden: Nomos.

Aden, H. (2018). 'Information Sharing, Secrecy and Trust among Law Enforcement and Secret Service Institutions in the European Union', *West European Politics* 41(4): 981–1002.

Aldrich, R.J. (2012). 'Intelligence and the European Union'. In Jones, E., Menon, A. and S. Weatherill (eds) *The Oxford Handbook of the European Union*, 627–42 Oxford: Oxford University Press.

Balzacq, T. and S. Léonard (2013). 'Information-sharing and the EU Counter-terrorism Policy: A "Securitisation Tool" Approach'. In Kaunert, C. and S. Léonard (eds) *European Security, Terrorism and Intelligence. Tackling New Security Challenges in Europe*, 127-42. Basingstoke: Palgrave Macmillan.

Bigo, D. (1996). *Polices en Réseaux: L'Expérience Européenne.* Paris: Presses de Sciences Po.

Boehm, F. (2012). *Information Sharing and Data Protection in the Area of Freedom, Security and Justice. Towards Harmonised Data Protection Principles for Information Exchange at EU-Level.* Heidelberg: Springer.

Buuren, J. van (2012). 'Runaway Bureaucracy? The European Police Chiefs Task Force', *Policing* 6(3): 281–90.

Craig, P. (2012). 'Subsidiarity: A Political and Legal Analysis', *Journal of Common Market Studies* 50(1): 72–87.

Cross, M.K.D. (2013). 'A European Transgovernmental Intelligence Network and the Role of IntCen', *Perspectives on European Politics and Society* 14(3): 388–402.

European Commission (2013). *Proposal for a Council Regulation on the Establishment of the European Public Prosecutor's Office.* Brussels: COM (2013) 534 final.

Giuffrida, F. (2017). *The European Public Prosecutor's Office: King without Kingdom?* Brussels: Centre for European Policy Studies (CEPS), Research Report No. 2017/03.

Goetz, K.H. and J.-H. Meyer-Sahling (2008). 'The Europeanisation of National Political Systems: Parliaments and Executives', *Living Reviews of European Governance* 3(2).

Gruszczak, A. (2016). 'Police and Customs Cooperation Centres and their Role in EU Internal Security'. In Bossong, R. and H. Carrapico (eds) *EU Borders and Shifting Internal Security*, 157–75. Heidelberg: Springer.

Kersbergen, K. van and B. Verbeek (2004). 'Subsidiarity of a Principle of Governance in the European Union', *Comparative European Politics* 2: 142–62.

Ligeti, K. and A. Weyembergh (2015). 'The European Public Prosecutor's Office. Certain Constitutional Issues'. In Erkelens, L.H., Meij, A. W. H. and M. Pawlik (eds) *The European Public Prosecutor's Office: An Extended Arm or a Two-Headed Dragon?*, 53–77. The Hague: Asser Press.

Lohse, K.M. (2015). 'The European Public Prosecutor: Issues of Conferral, Subsidiarity and Proportionality'. In Erkelens, L.H., Meij, A.W.H. and M. Pawlik (eds) *The European Public Prosecutor's Office: An Extended Arm or a Two-Headed Dragon?*, 165–82. The Hague: Asser Press.

Monar, J. (2014). 'EU Internal Security Governance: The Case of Counter-terrorism', *European Security* 23(2): 195–209.

Tekin, F. (ed.) (2012). *Differentiated Integration at Work. The Institutionalisation and Implementation of Opt-Outs from European Integration in the Area of Freedom, Security and Justice.* Baden-Baden: Nomos.

Weber, M. (1980 [1921]). *Wirtschaft und Gesellschaft.* Tübingen: Mohr Siebeck.

SECTION THREE

MIGRATION

8

Subsidiarity and Trafficking in Human Beings

MARCO BORRACCETTI

The European action against trafficking in human beings must be seen from a dual perspective. On the one hand, it is part of the action countering irregular migration as analysed throughout section three of this book; on the other hand, it is a serious form of crime included in EU cooperation concerning criminal matters in the area of freedom, security and justice (Title V of the Treaty on the Functioning of the European Union, TFEU) as explored in chapter seven. This dual perspective is also reflected in two different legal bases set out in Articles 79 and 83 TFEU. Both provisions are included in Title V, although they do not bind all EU member states as the UK, Ireland and Denmark have opted out of this set of regulations. However, the member states of EFTA are bound. In the area of freedom, security and justice the EU does not hold exclusive competence and, therefore, has to respect the principle of subsidiarity as mentioned in the treaties. More specifically Protocol no. 2 refers to the application of the principle of subsidiarity as well as that of proportionality. The aim of this chapter is to understand the role of the principle of subsidiarity in European actions as part of the fight against human trafficking. After an analysis of the principle in the EU legal framework and in the context of human trafficking, the focus will be on its contribution to adopting solutions against users of services that are provided by victims of trafficking.

The principle of subsidiarity in the area of freedom, security and justice

The principle of subsidiarity represents a filter between Union competences and their exercise. The EU may use its power to legislate in a given field, as conferred to it by the member states, only in a manner compatible with the subsidiarity principle. The Treaty of Lisbon retained this approach, even if the concrete guidelines for applying the subsidiarity test were not taken over in the new Protocol annexed to the Treaties (Lenaerts and Van Nuffel 2011).

The Treaty on European Union (TEU) specifies in Article 5 (1) that the use of EU competences 'is governed by the principles of subsidiarity and prop-ortionality'. More specifically, under the principle of subsidiarity, the EU can act if the objectives of the proposed action 'cannot be sufficiently achieved by the Member States, ... but can rather, by reason of the scale or effects of the proposed action, be better achieved at Union level'. Given its nature, it applies only in areas where the Union shares legislative competence with that of the member states (Article 5 (3) TFEU).

In practice, the subsidiarity principle tests Union action against a de-centralisation criterion as well as an efficiency criterion: the EU acts only if the proposed objectives cannot be sufficiently achieved by the member states, and if they can be better achieved by the Union (Lenaerts and Van Nuffel 2011). In other words, there is an assumption that EU action must have a better effect than the sum of single national actions in the specific policy area of concern.

Since the Treaty of Lisbon, the treaty formulation of the principle of sub-sidiarity explicitly refers to member state action 'either at central level or at regional and local level'. The philosophy is that decisions are taken 'as closely as possible to the citizen' (TEU preamble, last paragraph). The EU 'shall act only within the limits of the competences conferred upon it by the Member States in the Treaties' (Article 5 (1) TEU), and subsidiarity is one of the principles that governs the exercise of competences conferred to the EU. For this reason, EU action will conflict with the principle of subsidiarity only if the desired objective can be achieved just as much in all member states either by acting alone or by cooperation between the member states concerned (Article 5 (1) TEU).

The application of the principle of subsidiarity has to follow Protocol no. 2, adopted jointly with the Treaty of Lisbon. It implies that the actions of EU institutions are under the scrutiny of national parliaments in accordance with the specific procedures set out. This has the aim of contributing to the good functioning of the Union (Article 12 (b) TEU). In the case of the area of freedom, security and justice, Article 69 TFEU reaffirms the role of domestic representative bodies as controllers of EU institutional compliance with the subsidiarity principle. In particular, as suggested by Article 3 of Protocol no. 1, national parliaments can send to the presidents of the three political EU institutions a reasoned opinion whether a draft legislative act is in line with the principle. However, it is clear that subsidiarity concerns cannot be used to create new forms of crimes other than those already included in the part of the Treaty dealing with cooperation in criminal matters. In other words, subsidiarity cannot be exploited for creating different and new EU competences. Rather its specific use in the area of freedom security and justice serves to confirm the need for EU action. As it is not meant to restrain the use of centralised European measures, it stands in clear contrast to an interpretation that sees subsidiarity as a way of preserving the political function of national borders in EU-wide criminal law proceedings (Herlin-Karnell 2009, 352).

The preamble to Protocol no. 2 states clearly the aim of the principle of subsidiarity: to establish the 'condition for the application' and to establish a 'monitoring mechanism'. In fact, the main EU institutions have to guarantee its 'constant respect' (Article 1), justifying each version of a new piece of legislation through a detailed statement on compliance (Article 5). Indeed, any national parliament may – within eight weeks from the date of transmission of a draft legislative act – submit a reasoned opinion to the leadership of EU institutions stating that compliance was not ensured (Article 6). The lack of an explicit reference to such concerns may represent a violation of EU law as set out in the treaties.

The fight against human trafficking and its weakness

Trafficking in human beings is a serious form of crime and a grave violation of human dignity. Indeed, it is prohibited by Article 5 (3) of the Charter of Fundamental Rights of the European Union. It therefore has no legal or moral acceptance, and the exploitation of a person in coercive circumstances by another person must be seen as a reprehensible act in any system of criminal law and justice. As stated above, the European legal framework approaches the fight against human trafficking from a dual perspective: first, in connection with the fight against irregular migration and, second, as a crime with a European dimension that is subject to cooperation among the member states in criminal matters. As required by Article 79 TFEU, the EU:

> shall develop a common immigration policy aimed at ensuring,
> at all stages, ... the prevention of, and enhanced measures to
> combat, illegal immigration and trafficking in human beings.

For this purpose, EU institutions are requested to adopt specific combative measures in the area of trafficking in persons, in particular when the criminal practice concerns women and children. Yet, in this legal context the fight against trafficking in human beings is only one of the instruments meant to achieve the goal of counteracting irregular migration and thus forms part of

EU immigration policy. This follows from an emphasis on the external 'cross-border' dimension of trafficking as also reflected in the spirit of the UN Convention on Organised Crime (the Palermo Convention and its Protocol on Trafficking in Human Beings; United Nations, 2000) and the Convention of the Council of Europe against Trafficking in Human Beings (Council of Europe, 2005a).

Clearly, taking up the fight against trafficking in human beings exclusively in the context of migration policy would have severely limited EU action. All other constellations of trafficking, within or across member states, would not be followed up and could avoid further prosecution. For this reason, the explicit mentioning of trafficking in human beings in the list of crimes with a European dimension constitutes an added value. It covers all situations where EU citizens have become victims of traffickers without the need to establish a particular connection with migration issues. Therefore, Article 83 TFEU states that the

> European Parliament and the Council may, by means of directives adopted in accordance with the ordinary legislative procedure, establish minimum rules concerning the definition of criminal offences and sanctions in the areas of particularly serious crime with an internal 'cross-border' dimension resulting from the nature or impact of such offences or from a special need to combat them on a common basis.

Indeed, trafficking in human beings is one of these serious forms of crime with a cross-border dimension, albeit without a necessary linkage to a migration issue.

At the same time, the cross-country dimension set out in Article 83 refers to potential internal European constellations even though the area of freedom, security and justice is without internal borders. Nevertheless, such borders still exist for the prosecution of crimes in so far as the competence of law enforcement authorities is located within national jurisdictions and the legal measures in the hands of the member states are considered insufficient.

The EU's legal framework on trafficking in human beings includes the Anti-Trafficking Directive and the Residence Permit Directive (EU 2004; 2011). The former is the main source of the current framework and had a legal predecessor in the form of Framework Decision 2002/629 (see EU 2002; Krieg 2009). The latter was the first EU act that addressed trafficking in human beings from a criminal law perspective, and for this reason was adopted in the third pillar of the original treaty structure dealing with cooperation in the fields of justice and home affairs.

In the adoption process of the two directives, subsidiarity concerns came into play due to the added value deriving from EU actions in addition to the sum of national pieces of legislation. Arguably, the investigation and prosecution of respective crimes depends heavily on the cooperation of the member states concerned and is enhanced by harmonised criminal statutes. Yet, a satisfactory level of the required harmonisation 'cannot be achieved by national legislators on their own, even if they should choose to cooperate closely' (Satzger et al. 2013, 115–8).

Thus, the Anti-Trafficking Directive is aiming for a comprehensive approach in the fight against trafficking in human beings, also by including measures sanctioning traffickers regardless of the fact of whether they are natural or legal persons. Unfortunately, the piece of EU legislation does not contain similar provisions for the exploiters of victims who are not considered traffickers but are users of their services. In fact, according to the wording of Article 18 (4) of the Anti-Trafficking Directive, the member states should only 'consider taking measures' to punish 'the use of services which are the objects of exploitation'. Clearly, this must be considered the weakest part in the existing legal framework. Indeed, a system including sanctions for the users of services from victims of trafficking would be much completer and more effective by significantly reducing the possibilities for exploitation.

Although in line with the principle of subsidiarity, it might be worth noting that the choice of the European Parliament and the Council gives preference to the existing national approaches, leaving the consideration of criminal sanctions in the domain of domestic authorities. Therefore, a genuine European approach with potentially global reach is undermined as national governments maintain the last word in decisions on criminal law and policy. Not surprisingly, the envisaged solution has not worked so far, as it emerged from a recent Report on Criminalisation of the Use of Services issued by the Commission (EU 2016).

The report on the criminalisation of the use of services

In a nutshell, the report confirmed that national actions did not achieve the desired goals. For that reason, the Commission was requested to consider the possibility of issuing a specific proposal on the criminalisation of the users of services from victims of trafficking, while at the same time giving full respect to the principle of subsidiarity.

To develop its own position, the Commission made use of information received from the member states, although the latter did not elaborate in detail how 'they fulfilled the legal obligation to consider the criminalisation of users of victims stemming from Article 18 (4)' of Directive 2011/36/EU (EU 2016, 3). This formulation is telling and refers in substance to both parliamentary and governmental initiatives. Potentially, the obligation 'to consider the criminalisation of users of victims' could be satisfied by a simple discussion about the possibility of instituting different sanctions within the existing legal framework.

Due to limited cooperation by the member states, only a patchwork of data and information became available. Apparently, only ten EU countries (Bulgaria, Croatia, Cyprus, Greece, Lithuania, Malta, Portugal, Romania, Slovenia, and the United Kingdom) address all forms of exploitation and recognise the use of services in the context of trafficking of human beings as a criminal offence. Other EU countries have opted for a more limited and selective criminalisation of respective practices. More specifically, a second group of 14 member states (Austria, Belgium, Czech Republic, Estonia, France, Germany, Hungary, Italy, Latvia, Luxemburg, The Netherlands, Poland, Slovakia, and Spain) reported to have no explicit national legal provisions in place for establishing 'the use of services' as a criminal offence. Instead, in a smaller sub-group of member states, recourse could be made to provisions relating to sexual offences and child sexual exploitation (Belgium Italy, the Netherlands, Spain), or to the unlawful brokering and exploitation of labour more generally (Italy). Finally, in a third group, member states such as Finland, Ireland, and Sweden have introduced legislation targeting the use of victims of trafficking, but only as regards particular forms of exploitation: sexual exploitation in the case of Finland and Ireland, and the purchase of sexual services in the case of Sweden. In the meantime, the demand for services from victims fuels exploitative behaviour across Europe, while a comprehensive and coherent EU policy response is missing. As individual states appear to limit the required action against traffickers, the final result is increasingly fragmented EU action sporadically targeted at 'last consumers'.

As it stands, most legislative measures focus on sexual exploitation, bearing in mind that the biggest number of victims are women and girls (Eurostat 2015, 11). Yet, according to European and international definitions of trafficking, the exploitation for sexual reasons is just one category among many others. The latter, for example, also include 'forced labour or services, including begging, slavery, ... servitude, or the exploitation of criminal activities, or the removal of organs' (EU 2011, Article 2). Only the first country grouping has legislation in place covering diverse forms of exploitation. The second and third grouping may provide protection through rules not necessarily directed towards trafficking offences. By contrast, the EU legal framework applies, if the victims of trafficking are third country nationals who stay illegally in the territory of the Union. Then the member states have a legal instrument at their disposition in the form of the Employers' Sanctions

Directive (EU 2009). Under certain circumstances, this directive may justify the sanctioning of users of services, despite its prime intention to fight irregular migration.

Furthermore, a Communication by the European Commission clarifies that the member states have criminalised illegal employment in all the circumstances described in Article 9 of the Employers' Sanctions Directive, including those where the employer knows that the worker is a victim of human trafficking (EU 2014, 5). Yet again, the Commission points out that the member states are not necessarily sanctioning illegal employment when 'the employer was aware that the worker was a victim of human trafficking' (EU 2014, 5). Instead, the Employers' Sanctions Directive is applicable only in the rather specific case of victims residing illegally as third country nationals in a member state. It does not apply if potential victims are EU citizens or regular EU residents. Then none of the European acts is useful to counter the exploitative behaviour of users of services, and any other applicable legal instruments would have to be rooted in national legal orders.

Obviously, the current situation in the fight against human trafficking is influenced by different approaches and practices developed within the EU member states. Where national measures establishing a criminal offence exist, their individual scope is limited, for example, excluding recruiters. Moreover, all domestic legislation requires that the user had prior knowledge of the service provider being a victim of trafficking (EU 2016, 7). The need to find evidence for the intention or, indeed, knowledge of a wrongdoing by the users of services (*mens rea*) highlights the complexity of the issue. In most member states, the burden of proof rests with the prosecutor, while the suspect or defendant 'benefits from the presumption of innocence and has no obligation to prove his innocence' (EU 2016, 7). Similarly, an Explanatory Report of the Council of Europe pointed to this major obstacle, but still considered the evidence argument as inconclusive in terms of the criminal nature of a certain type of conduct (Council of Europe 2005b, 37).

What is more, the development of criminal law must go beyond a mere deterrent effect and protect people that are part of a larger community. This is particularly true for those most exposed to violence and who experience the use of force to exploit their individual vulnerabilities. Therefore, the focus must be on actors, legal persons, or groups of people engaged in exploiting victims of trafficking in the form of abuse or for the sake of profit. Investigations must also include promoters or facilitators of such behaviour who actively create an enabling environment for human exploitation. The potential linkage between exploitation and profit is not restricted to criminal organisations as it may involve a chain of legitimate businesses. These can include profit-takers such as relatives of victims, formal and informal recruitment agencies, labour market intermediaries, sub-contractors of global suppliers, travel agencies or transport enterprises as well as information technology companies (EU 2016, 9). The suggested criminalisation of the users of services from victims of trafficking would be a first step to protect vulnerable people and to incentivise law enforcement authorities to increase the reach of their activities.

The accountability of perpetrators as an anti-trafficking measure is a foundational aspect of EU action. However, the strength of this key element is undermined, if the users of services are not sanctioned in a complete and comprehensive way. In fact, this further impacts on the effective prevention of the crime of trafficking itself as it is 'less discouraged and even fostered ... through a culture of impunity'; and raising awareness of the demand side for different forms of trafficking may help to ensure that 'those who profit from the crime and exploit the victims are brought to justice' (EU 2016, 10). Again, in the words of the Commission (EU 2016, 10):

> The lack of criminalisation of the use of services of a trafficked person, especially with the knowledge that she or he is a victim of human trafficking, renders the overall fight against trafficking in human beings less effective.

While only a short time has passed since the Anti-Trafficking Directive came into force and the publication of a first evaluative report, its findings should ring an alarm bell. Successful implementation will not occur unless there is a more coherent and uniform EU approach towards the criminalisation of the users of exploitative services.

Application of the principle of subsidiarity

As mentioned above, the principle of subsidiarity supports European legislative action adding value to individual national efforts. In the described scenario, subsidiarity concerns must be examined from at least two perspectives: how, if at all, could a new EU act on the criminalisation of users of services of trafficked persons be considered a necessity; and does this follow from an inability of the member states to achieve the desired goal set out in the original directive?

As noted earlier, subsidiarity in EU legislation is not meant as an instrument to create new forms of criminalisation. In addition, trafficking in human beings has also been included in the list of serious 'euro-crimes'. What matters more here is the fact that the Union can exercise exclusive competences due to the 'nature' of the existing codification. In this context, it is worth noting the substance of Article 18 (4) of Directive 2011/36/EU:

> In order to make the preventing and combating of trafficking in human beings more effective by discouraging demand, Member States shall consider taking measures to establish as a criminal offence the use of services which are the objects of exploitation as referred to in Article 2, with the knowledge that the person is a victim of an offence referred to in Article 2.

According to the Report by the Commission, member states in their majority have not yet adopted comprehensive legislation sanctioning the use of services of victims of trafficking; and most legislation sanctions the use of services of trafficked persons for sexual reasons. On the one hand, this is justified due to the strong gender dimension of crime; on the other hand, it excludes all other forms of exploitation. It has also become clear that not all national measures target directly the users of services. Instead, domestic authorities are applying legal instruments already in place in their national legal framework to address this form of exploitative behaviour.

As a first result, therefore, taking into consideration the purpose of the Anti-Trafficking Directive, the demands of Article 18 (4) are respected and the actions of the member states are in congruence with the goal 'to consider taking measures' that establish a criminal offence. Arguably, though, the described provisions are only in partial fulfilment of the obligation on part of the member states. Again, the Commission Report is essential evidence as it demonstrates that only a minority of states has a comprehensive legal system in place, including rules on the criminalisation of the users of services. Moreover, the relevant national authorities are not able to prosecute all groups of users of exploitative services. Thus, national actions remain insufficient and inadequate, especially as the number of reported crimes is increasing at regional as well as global level. There can be little doubt that the demand side for the use of services of trafficked persons drives the criminal behaviour of traffickers further.

In sum, given the actual situation in the policy area under discussion further European legislative intervention can be justified, while simultaneously respecting fully the principle of subsidiarity. This is possible, as the member states so far have not been able to realise all the aims of Article 18 (4). Regardless of the complete implementation of Article 18 (4), its partial or entire lack of fulfilment, an argument in favour of a new legislative act on the criminalisation of users of exploitative services can be made in congruence with the principle of subsidiarity.

In this way, European objectives in the fight against the trafficking of human beings could be better achieved. Ideally, then, there would be no further discrimination or distinction among the users of services safeguarding potential victims from exploitation in various stages of the supply chain. Such genuine European action may also have a positive impact in the general fight against organised crime as a major source of specific types of exploitation.

Conclusion

The fight against trafficking in human beings demands a complete legal framework to target all its manifestations. This directs attention to the use of services of trafficked persons as a major aspect of the observed phenomenon. The Anti-Trafficking Directive created an obligation for EU member states to prosecute natural and legal persons as traffickers or as companies exploiting vulnerable people; it also enabled them to further consider the criminalisation of user behaviour. However, the Commission's own report showed the limits of the European system in addressing the identified problem. In short, national measures against the user population appear fragmented and piecemeal, while empirical data on the precise consequences of the implementation process of the directive is hard to come by. As reported crime rates of trafficking are not falling, the importance of an effective European legislative instrument in the hands of national prosecutors is reinforced. In this scenario, the principle of subsidiarity does justify EU action in the form of a new Commission proposal on the criminalisation of exploitative behaviour, thus adding value to the use of this policy instrument.

Nevertheless, the suggested legal interpretation of the principle of subsidiarity respects the limits set by the treaties as it does not serve to create a new form of crime. Instead, it attempts to develop the existing legal framework for a problem constellation with an already recognised European dimension. The latter has been repeatedly confirmed in official documents engaged with the subject matter, also stressing the social costs of human trafficking (see EU 2015). This chapter has argued that a revised Anti-Trafficking Directive must come to terms with the demand and supply side of a criminal transaction by 'changing the wider environment' that facilitates trafficking in human beings (EU 2011, Article 2; EU 2016, 9). Closing this existing legislative gap in the European legal order would give much needed support to national authorities in their mission to protect vulnerable persons from exploitation.

References

Council of Europe (2005a). Convention on Action against Trafficking in Human Beings of 3.5.2005. Council of Europe Treaty Series (CETS) no. 197. Available at: https://www.coe.int/en/web/conventions/full-list/-/conventions/treaty/197

Council of Europe (2005b). Explanatory Report to the Council of Europe Convention on Action against Trafficking in Human Beings, Council of Europe Treaty Series (CETS) no. 197. Available at: https://www.coe.int/en/web/conventions/full-list/-/conventions/treaty/197

European Union (2002). 'Council Framework Decision of 19 July 2002 on Combating Trafficking in Human Beings (2002/629/JHA)'. *Official Journal* L 203: 1, 1.8.2002 Available at: https://eur-lex.europa.eu/legal-content/EN/TXT/?uri=OJ:L:2002:203:TOC

European Union (2004). 'Council Directive 2004/81/EC of 29 April 2004 on the Residence Permit issued to Third-country Nationals who are Victims of Trafficking in Human Beings or who have been the Subject of an Action to facilitate Illegal Immigration, who cooperate with the Competent Authorities'. *Official Journal* L 261: 19, 6.8.2004 (Residence Permit Directive). Available at: https://eur-lex.europa.eu/legal-content/EN/TXT/?uri=OJ:L:2004:261:TOC

European Union (2009). 'Directive 2009/52/EC of the European Parliament and of the Council of 18 June 2009 providing for Minimum Standards on Sanctions and Measures against Employers of Illegally Staying Third-country Nationals'. *Official Journal* L 168: 24, 30.6.2009 (Employers' Sanction Directive). Available at: https://eur-lex.europa.eu/legal-content/EN/TXT/?uri=OJ:L:2009:168:TOC

European Union (2011). 'Directive 2011/36/EU of the European Parliament and of the Council of 5 April 2011 on Preventing and Combating Trafficking in Human Beings and Protecting its Victims, and Replacing Council Framework Decision 2002/629/JHA'. *Official Journal* L 101, 15.4.2011, p. 1 (Anti-Trafficking Directive). Available at: https://eur-lex.europa.eu/legal-content/EN/TXT/?uri=OJ:L:2011:101:TOC

European Union (2014). Communication from the Commission to the European Parliament and the Council on the Application of Directive 2009/52/EC Providing for Minimum Standards on Sanctions and Measures against Employers of Illegally Staying Third Country Nationals, COM (2014) 286 final. Available at: www.europarl.europa.eu/meetdocs/2014_2019/documents/com/com_com%282014%290286_/com_com%282014%290286_en.pdf

European Union (2015). Communication from the Commission to the European Parliament, the Council, the European Economic and Social Committee and the Committee of the Regions: The European Agenda on Security, COM (2015) 185 final of 28.4.2015. Available at: https://eur-lex.europa.eu/legal-content/EN/TXT/?uri=COM:2015:0185:FIN

European Union (2016). Report from the Commission to the European Parliament and the Council, assessing the Impact of existing National Law, establishing as a Criminal Offence the Use of Services which are the Objects of Exploitation of Trafficking in Human Beings, on the Prevention of Trafficking in Human Beings, in accordance with Article 23(2) of the Directive 2011/36/EU, COM (2016) 719 final of 2.12.2016 (Report on the Criminalisation of the Use of Services). Available at: https://ec.europa.eu/anti-trafficking/sites/antitrafficking/files/report_on_impact_of_national_legislation_related_to_thb_en.pdf

Eurostat (2015). Trafficking in Human Beings. Available at: https://ec.europa.eu/eurostat/de/web/products-statistical-working-papers/-/KS-TC-14-008-1

Herlin-Karnell, E. (2009). 'Subsidiarity in the Area of EU Justice and Home Affairs Law—A Lost Cause?'. *European Law Journal* 15(3): 351–61.

Krieg, S. (2009). 'Trafficking in Human Beings: The EU Approach between Border Control, Law Enforcement and Human Rights'. *European Law Journal* 15(6): 775–90.

Lenaerts, K. and P. Van Nuffel (eds) (2011). *European Union Law*, 3rd edition. London: Sweet & Maxwell.

Satzger, H., F. Zimmermann and G. Langheld. (2013). 'The Directive on Preventing and Combatting Trafficking in Human Beings and the Principles Governing European Criminal Policy – A Critical Evaluation'. *European Criminal Law Review* 3(1): 107–20.

United Nations (2000). 'Convention against Transnational Organized Crime of 15.11.2000 and its Protocol to Prevent, Suppress and Punish Trafficking in Persons, Especially Women and Children (Palermo Protocol)'. Available at: https://treaties.un.org/Pages/ViewDetails.aspx?src=TREATY&mtdsg_no=XVIII-12&chapter=18&clang=_en (Convention); https://treaties.un.org/Pages/ViewDetails.aspx?src=TREATY&mtdsg_no=XVIII-12-a&chapter=18&clang=_en (Protocol)

9

The Subsidiarity Principle and European Refugee Law

RALF ALLEWELDT

On 6 September 2017 the European Court of Justice handed down judgment on an action introduced two years earlier by Slovakia and Hungary against EU Council Decision 2915/1601 concerning the *ad hoc* relocation of 120 000 refugees. In connection with this action, the Hungarian parliament had adopted a reasoned opinion arguing that the suggested quota system would be in violation of the subsidiarity principle, as laid down in Article 5 of the Treaty on European Union (TEU) (Groenendijk and Nagy 2015; Varju and Czina 2017).

In a recent proposal aiming to establish, in the long term, a fairer and more sustainable asylum system in Europe, the European Commission, in the so-called draft Dublin IV Regulation, suggests, among other things, a 'corrective allocation mechanism'. Under this mechanism, whenever a member state is confronted with a number of asylum seekers exceeding a certain threshold, further applicants would be relocated to other EU countries (European Commission 2017, 15). In response to the proposed legislation, the parliaments of six member states (Czech Republic, Hungary, Italy, Poland, Romania, and Slovakia) raised objections against this particular component, and, subsequently, adopted reasoned opinions in line with Article 7 of the Subsidiarity Protocol. Reasoned opinions by national parliaments, as given in these two cases, must be taken into account by the EU legislative organs and may force them, depending on the number of opinions given, to review the draft (see Craig and de Búrca 2015, 97). Legally, the 'Protocol no. 2 on the application of the principles of subsidiarity and proportionality', forms an integral part of the Treaty on European Union (Article 51 TEU).

In an area as controversial as refugee policy, could the subsidiarity principle indeed lead the way to new solutions? If a common European approach in asylum matters is elusive, will it not make sense to look for national solutions instead? 'Are asylum and immigration really a European Union issue?' asks, for example, Joanne van Selm (2016, 60). These are legitimate questions which will be discussed in this chapter in the light of the motives leading to the creation of a common European asylum system.

The common European asylum system

In preparation for the single market, it was the intention of the EU to intensify freedom of movement for its citizens by removing all internal borders between the member states. This idea was put into legal terms in both Schengen Agreements, concluded in 1985 and 1990. At this point in time, not all actors may have been aware that such a decision would also entail the creation of a common asylum system. However, already the Convention implementing the Schengen Agreement of 1990 contained a chapter on the responsibility for processing asylum applications (Articles 28–38). Almost a decade later, in 1999, the European Council Tampere meeting established an 'area of freedom, security and justice'. On this occasion, the heads of state and government concluded:

> From its very beginning European integration has been firmly rooted in a shared commitment to freedom based on human rights, democratic institutions and the rule of law. ... This freedom should not, however, be regarded as the exclusive preserve of the Union's own citizens. ... It would be in contradiction with Europe's traditions to deny such freedom to those whose circumstances lead them justifiably to seek access to our territory. This in turn requires the Union to develop common policies on asylum and immigration.

It thus became obvious that the development of a common asylum policy will be necessary. In fact, given open internal borders, freedom of movement is available to everyone, including asylum seekers and refugees. Yet, without appropriate rules, asylum seekers might engage in 'asylum shopping': the practice by which applicants move to those countries where the procedures for granting asylum are softest and the conditions most generous; or where the highest amount of financial support is available. If, in the Schengen area, one member state opts for a strict asylum policy, while another maintains a 'soft touch', ultimately control powers will not rest in the hands of the former. Under an open border system, an applicant could always gain recognition in one country and move to the preferred destination later.

As a consequence, the member states conferred upon the EU certain legislative powers for a common asylum policy. These are laid down in Article 78 of the Treaty on the Functioning of the European Union (TFEU) which states:

1. The Union shall develop a common policy on asylum, subsidiary protection and temporary protection [...]. This policy must be in accordance with the Geneva Convention of 28 July 1951 and ... other relevant treaties.
2. For the purposes of paragraph 1, the European Parliament and the Council, acting in accordance with the ordinary legislative procedure, shall adopt measures for a common European asylum system comprising:

   a. a uniform status of asylum for nationals of third countries, valid throughout the Union;
   b. a uniform status of subsidiary protection for nationals of third countries who, without obtaining European asylum, are in need of international protection;
   c. a common system of temporary protection ... ;
   d. common procedures for the granting and withdrawing of uniform asylum or subsidiary protection status;
   e. criteria and mechanisms for determining which member state is responsible for considering an application for asylum or subsidiary protection;
   f. standards concerning the conditions for the reception of applicants for asylum or subsidiary protection; ... .

Accordingly, as foreseen in this Article, the Council and the European Parliament adopted the following directives and regulations:

- The revised Qualification Directive (2011/95/EU) lays down the grounds for granting international protection.
- The revised Asylum Procedures Directive (2013) describes minimum standards for the asylum procedure.
- The revised Dublin Regulation (Dublin III – 2013) regulates the process of establishing the State responsible for examining the asylum application. In most cases, under Article 13 the state is responsible where the asylum seeker first entered the European Union, i.e. very often Italy, Greece, or Spain.
- The revised EURODAC Regulation (2013) allows law enforcement access to the EU database of the fingerprints of asylum seekers.
- The revised Reception Conditions Directive (2013) aims to ensure that

there are humane reception conditions for asylum seekers across the EU and that their fundamental rights are respected.

Subsidiarity and the common asylum system

For assessing whether the existing EU asylum legislation is in line with the subsidiarity principle, the legal starting point must be Article 5 (3) TEU. It reads as follows:

> Under the principle of subsidiarity ... the Union shall act only if and in so far as the objectives of the proposed action cannot be sufficiently achieved by the member states, either at central level or at regional and local level, but can rather, by reason of the scale or effects of the proposed action, be better achieved at Union level.

Accordingly, under EU law, two criteria need to be fulfilled before Brussels can legislate in a certain field. First, a negative condition, in that the objectives of the proposed action cannot be sufficiently achieved by the member states on their own; and, secondly, a positive condition that these objectives can be better achieved at the level of the Union as a whole.

In this provision, the specific words 'the objectives of the proposed action' are obviously most important. Only once these objectives are clearly defined, it will be possible to assess whether the member states, or indeed the EU, are in a better position to achieve them. Thus, whatever political actor determines the 'objectives', largely controls the application of the subsidiarity principle in a particular policy area.

Who determines the objectives of proposed actions? The answer is fairly simple: it is the European Union. Typically, general objectives are stated in relevant provisions of the EU treaties; and, by definition, 'proposed actions' are those proposed by an EU institution. Moreover, the precise objectives of an action are usually given in the preamble of a legislative act, as proposed by the Commission, and, in line with the ordinary legislative procedure, amended and adopted by the Council and the European Parliament (see Articles 289, 294 TFEU). Therefore, the power to set the objectives of legislative action always remains with the EU institutions as central authorities in policy making. As can be seen from the clear wording of Article 5 (3) TEU, the subsidiarity rule refers only to the question as to who is best placed to achieve these objectives, as set by the EU. This finding is true for all policy fields where the treaties give the EU the power to legislate, including the field of immigration and asylum.

Who is best placed to achieve the desired objectives? To answer this second important question, the analysis proceeds by assessing, by way of example, three of the directives mentioned in the previous section. It will be necessary to set out the particular objectives of these legislative acts, before examining the relevance of the subsidiarity clause for each of them.

Revised Qualification Directive

The full title of the revised Qualification Directive reads as follows:

> Directive 2011/95/EU of the European Parliament and of the Council of 13 December 2011 on standards for the qualification of third-country nationals or stateless persons as beneficiaries of international protection, for a uniform status for refugees or for persons eligible for subsidiary protection, and for the content of the protection granted.

The preamble to the Qualification Directive proclaims, in its recital (paragraph) 49, that its objective is to

> establish standards for the granting of international protection to third-country nationals and stateless persons by member states, for a uniform status for refugees or for persons eligible for subsidiary protection, and for the content of the protection granted.

Revised Procedures Directive

The full title of the revised Procedures Directive reads as 'Directive 2013/32 EU of the European Parliament and of the Council on common procedures for granting and withdrawing international protection'. Again, the preamble to the directive states in recital 56 an objective 'to establish common procedures for granting and withdrawing international protection'.

In both cases, the objectives of legislative acts are already reflected in their titles; and are also largely identical with their content. It seems as if the legislating EU institutions consider these directives as objectives in themselves.

Reception Conditions Directive

In the Reception Conditions Directive, the legislator went a step further by claiming in recital 31 of its preamble that the subsidiarity principle has already been respected:

> The objective of this Directive, namely to establish standards for the reception of applicants in member states, cannot be sufficiently achieved by the member states and can therefore, by reason of the scale and effects of this Directive, be better achieved at the Union level.

Can these objectives of the three asylum directives be equally achieved by member states themselves? A negative answer to this question is a fundamental requirement for making use of the EU's legislative competence in the first place. If we accept, in accordance with Article 78 TFEU, that the European Union aims to have a common asylum system, it is hard to conceive how a single member state could create such a system. Indeed, it seems logically impossible. For example, the objective of the revised Qualification Directive concerning a uniform status of refugees cannot be achieved by one or several member states acting alone. The same would be true for the Procedures Directive. If again the objective is along the lines of Article 78 TFEU, common procedures cannot be created by a single member state. In other words, common procedures also presuppose some legislative acts coming from Europe.

For the Directive on Reception Conditions, the situation may seem slightly different as the objective is merely to establish 'standards for the reception of applicants'. Neither mentions the directive's explicitly 'common' standards, nor does Article 78 TFEU. Yet, the significance of this wording should not be overestimated. Under Article 288 TFEU, once certain binding standards are included in a directive, these have to be implemented by all member states; and become automatically 'common'. In addition, in a common asylum system, it appears sensible to establish minimal standards of reception. In the words of the 2009 Stockholm Programme of the European Council:

> It is crucial that individuals, regardless of the member state in which their application for international protection is made, are offered an equivalent level of treatment as regards reception conditions.

In this sense, the standards of reception conditions mentioned in Article 78 TFEU are exactly designed to secure an 'equivalent level of treatment'. Most certainly, the Reception Conditions Directive should be interpreted in the light of the Stockholm Programme. Therefore, as before, the desired objective is unlikely to be ever achieved by member states acting on their own. In short, all three directives confirm, as the result of a basic legal argument, that member states are not in a position to achieve the desired objective.

Furthermore, under Article 5 (3) TEU, the Union shall act only if the objectives of the proposed action can be 'better' achieved at EU level. This condition is closely connected to the previous legal reasoning. As long as the member states are not in a position to create a uniform status of protection, common asylum procedures, or equivalent standards of reception (at central, regional, or local level), the only option to achieve the objectives of the 'proposed action' is to turn to the Union. In sum, the intended common asylum system cannot be created by a member state, but it can be built – better and only – with the help of legislation coming from Brussels.

Individual provisions of the asylum directives

Do such considerations answer all questions regarding subsidiarity in the field of asylum? Probably not! While the mere fact that EU directives concerning qualification, procedures and reception conditions have been issued can be seen in line with Article 78 TFEU (and the subsidiarity principle), specific provisions within these pieces of legislation might not meet a stringent test. It cannot be excluded that certain objectives are achievable by individual member states. Hence, examining article by article of a directive may still reveal partial violations of the subsidiarity principle.

The Reception Conditions Directive, for example, contains the following provisions on:

- the obligations of member states to provide applicants with information relevant to their asylum claim, at least including information on any established benefits and on the obligations of applicants (Article 5),
- that member states shall ensure that applicants are provided with a document certifying their status (Article 6),
- the conditions of residence and freedom of movement (Article 7),
- conditions for the detention of an applicant (Article 8),
- the power of member states to require a medical screening of applicants (Article 13),
- the obligation of member states to ensure that victims of torture, rape or other serious acts of violence receive necessary medical and psychological treatment (Article 25).

As before, the guiding question remains whether particular issues can be regulated by member states themselves or whether this is better done at EU level. In each case, the stated objective cannot be achieved by governments acting on their own. Take, for example, the aim to provide psychological support and special treatment for victims of torture throughout the Union. If there were no such provision in a directive, then states may or may not decide to offer such support. If, on the other hand, there is a clear wish to issue documentation for all asylum seekers regardless of location, then only a European-wide rule makes sense. Likewise, limits on legitimate reasons for detention are best served when put into a legally binding EU norm. In short, common standards do not emerge by themselves, but require European actions in one form or another.

Obviously, these considerations are most relevant whenever EU law sets common minimum standards including state obligations. In fact, this is the case with most provisions of the asylum directives. There are, however, exceptions of individual provisions containing no genuine state obligations. As mentioned above, Article 13 of the Receptions Conditions Directive, states that member states 'may require medical screening for applicants on public health grounds.' Similarly, in Article 16, they may allow 'applicants access to vocational training irrespective of whether they have access to the labour market'. Provisions of this kind entitle member states to act in a certain way, but they do not establish a formal obligation. Indeed, one must doubt the contribution of these regulations either to specific objectives of the directive or to the common asylum system as a whole. It would be mere coincidence for common European standards in medical screening or vocational training to emerge. At the same time, the non-obligatory provisions do not harm national autonomy, highlighting instead that member states retain certain powers in a given area. As it appears reasonable for the EU to put these issues under the discretion of governments, the particular composition of the piece of legislation does not conflict with subsidiarity concerns.

Another case in point is the Qualification Directive, elaborating conditions under which refugee status, or a form of subsidiary protection, can be obtained. It is a complex exercise to interpret the concept of 'refugee' and to apply it to the facts of a specific case. For obtaining an equivalent level of refugee protection throughout the EU, member states need a common terminology and common definitions: to understand who can be an actor of persecution (Article 6); who can be an actor of protection (Article 7); what are the rules for internal protection; what are safe areas within the country of origin (Article 8); what are acts of persecution (Article 9); what are reasons for persecution (Article 10); and, what does it mean to be persecuted for reasons of 'political opinion', or 'religious conviction'? Eventually, a range of rules and regulations is applied to complex facts of real-world cases, frequently comprising long-term biographical data and general country profiles. Finally, decisions on asylum claims require notoriously difficult predictions of future events when applying the legal notions of 'danger' or 'well-founded fear of persecution' to individual cases.

In theory, it is possible to imagine individual provisions of the three asylum directives that are, strictly speaking, not relevant for achieving the objectives of a common asylum system. In reality, however, it is much harder to identify such a provision. What is more, even if within the existing body of law an example is found, it would not call into question the general assessment presented here: the objectives of the asylum legislation of the EU, as laid down in Article 78 TFEU and subsequent directives, cannot be achieved by member states acting alone; they can – better and only – be achieved by European Union action. In general, the examined legislation is in line with the subsidiarity principle set out in Article 5 (3) TEU.

Subsidiarity as a political principle

Up to this point the subsidiarity term has been used in the narrow, legal sense as established in Article 5 (3) TEU. This rule describes only how the EU should exercise certain powers that are conferred on it by international treaties. Essentially, its application requires that the EU has legislative competence. There can be no doubt that on the basis of Article 78 TFEU the power to regulate asylum matters rests with the Union. Once the EU has decided to make use of this power, it is, as discussed above, difficult to limit this power with the help of subsidiarity considerations as stated in Article 5 TEU.

Does this imply that the subsidiarity principle is irrelevant in European asylum law? Have member states, in other words, no option but to accept EU rules even if they are convinced that certain refugee issues are better regulated at national level? Clearly, there are some alternatives available. Firstly, recall that the common asylum system, as laid down in Article 78 TFEU, has not been forced upon the member states by some higher European power, but has indeed been introduced by the member states themselves who decided, unanimously, to amend the founding treaties of the EU. Secondly, and equally important, the EU legislative process contains an 'in-built' subsidiarity check. It should not be forgotten that national governments, sitting in the Council of the EU, play the strongest role in creating European law. They typically endorse power transfers to Brussels only to the extent absolutely necessary; and, in doing so, will try to avoid further legal obligations at home. Thus, the member states maintain a high degree of control over the entire legislative process, enabling them to reject European rules that would excessively tie their hands (Craig 2012, 81–3). Each and every new EU rule needs at least a qualified majority in the Council, and (since 2014) such a majority requires the votes of 55 per cent of the member states comprising 65 per cent of the EU population (Article 16 TEU). It is simply impossible for EU institutions to introduce legislative acts against the will of all (or a majority of) member states. National governments can always say 'no' in the Council, if they are not in favour of additional asylum legislation; and, potentially, can form a blocking minority with like-minded member states. In fact, many legislative proposals in the asylum sphere, and elsewhere, have failed because there was no qualified majority forthcoming in the main decision-making body.

Arguably, in terms of political deliberation and intergovernmental negotiation, subsidiarity does play a very important role in the EU's ordinary legislative procedure. If a representative of a member state defends national control powers against alleged EU intrusion, this behaviour is likely to find copycats in the Council, as the member states have a natural propensity to retain their power. As it stands, subsidiarity can be considered a highly relevant concept in the legislative procedure. It can help to build a strong case for national positions, lend credibility to general arguments and increase overall legitimacy of EU policy making.

In this sense, there is already a subsidiarity culture in the European Union. European institutions – in particular the Commission – are under pressure to justify why certain powers should be exercised by the EU. If they fail to convince governments about the need for EU action, the legislative act will not be adopted. By contrast, if an act is legally adopted, the member states confirm – at least by qualified majority – that the EU is in a comparatively better position to achieve the stated objectives of legislation. Of course, an increase in future legal challenges based on subsidiarity arguments is possible. In fact, it seems desirable that institutions offer stronger and more convincing justifications as to how subsidiarity is respected within a particular piece of legislation. Yet, the room for successful legal challenges is somehow limited due to the power of EU institutions to set their own objectives and the limited review process carried out by the European Court of Justice. The latter has never invalidated an existing EU law on grounds of subsidiarity (Craig and de Búrca 2015, 100). Once a government is outvoted in the Council, there is little chance to find redress in the court system on the basis of subsidiarity concerns. Potentially, this will also be the case for prospective acts of refugee law, including regulations on a quota system for asylum-seekers.

Although it is standard practice to accept majority decisions in the Council, there may be instances where member states find themselves in a minority position with fundamental national interests at stake. In refugee law, it is a question of general policy whether strong resistance by a member state should be overcome with the help of a majority vote. If several governments find the rules on relocating asylum-seekers (as envisaged by the draft Dublin IV Regulation) unacceptable, there might well be another escape route preventing deadlock in the Council, or a general political crisis in the EU. In this case, a majority of member states can consider devising a new distribution system only among themselves, using, as a last resort, the rules on enhanced cooperation as specified in Article 20 TEU (Kreilinger 2015). This solution, if feasible, might indeed reduce the area of conflict between European governments. In addition, it would leave resisting states an opportunity to join the proposed system at a later stage.

Occasionally, it can happen that subsidiarity considerations prevent the adoption of reasonable European solutions. However, the principle does not constitute a permanent stumbling block. If genuine European issues are not properly addressed at the member-state level, they will almost inevitably make a return to Brussels. Then, EU institutions enjoy an added degree of legitimacy to develop a common approach.

All said, law is not always the perfect problem-solver even with issues of a genuine European dimension at hand. In December 2016, for example, mayors from 80 European cities met in Rome and promoted their local entities as 'welcoming cities' (European Mayor's Summit 2016). In June 2017 an international conference in Gdansk, Poland, carried the title of 'Relaunching Europe Bottom-Up' and advanced the idea 'to transform the so-called refugee crisis into an inclusive European growth and development initiative'. The participants aimed to develop an explicit political strategy with solidarity and decentralised relocation of refugees at its heart. Their emphasis was very much on a multi-stakeholder approach that brings together political interests, the business community, and organized civil society at the regional level (Schwan and Höpfner 2017). These and other initiatives serve as a practical reminder that political solutions are also available at local rather than national or EU level.

Conclusion

Our analysis shows that EU asylum legislation is in line with the subsidiarity principle. The member states have agreed, by introducing Article 78 TFEU, to create a common asylum system. The objectives laid down in this provision – a uniform status of asylum, common asylum procedures, criteria and mechanisms which determine the member state responsible for considering an asylum application, or equivalent reception conditions – cannot be achieved by member states alone, but only by way of EU legislation.

Nevertheless, member states have many options to influence the contents of this legislation. Subsidiarity may be a strong argument in the political debate on draft legislative proposals. It is unlikely that new asylum legislation will contain any disproportionate or unreasonable demands, since such legislation always requires at least a qualified majority of member states' votes in the Council. Ultimately, as 'masters of the treaties', member states could even decide, by way of amending the founding treaties, to move legislative powers in asylum matters back to the level of national legislation. While such a step seems unlikely in the foreseeable future, in cases where individual governments hold very strong objections as regards specific legislative proposals, the majority of member states may consider using the enhanced cooperation procedure and introduce certain pieces of new legislation only for themselves.

References

Craig, P. (2012). 'Subsidiarity: A Political and Legal Analysis', *Journal of Common Market Studies* 50(1): 72–87.

Craig, P. and G. de Búrca (2015). *European Union Law.* Oxford: Oxford University Press.

Collett, E. (2014). 'Future EU Policy Development on Immigration and Asylum: Understanding the Challenge', *MPI Europe Policy Brief*, Brussels: Migration Policy Institute Europe.

European Court of Justice (2017). *Judgment of 6 September*, C-643/15 – Slovakia and Hungary v. Council. Available at: http://curia.europa.eu/juris/liste.jsf?num=C-643/15&language=EN

European Commission (2017). *Annual Report on Subsidiarity and Proportionality.* COM (2017) 600 final, 30 June. Available at: https://ec.europa.eu/transparency/regdoc/rep/1/2017/EN/COM-2017-600-F1-EN-MAIN-PART-1.PDF

European Mayors' Summit (2016). 'Final Statement of the European Mayors' Summit on Europe: Refugees are our Brothers and Sisters', 10 December. Available at: http://www.pas.va/content/accademia/en/events/2016/refugees/final_statement.html

Groenendijk, K. and B. Nagy (2015). 'Hungary's Appeal against Relocation to the CJEU: Upfront Attack or Rearguard Battle?', 16 December. Available at: http://eumigrationlawblog.eu/hungarys-appeal-against-relocation-to-the-cjeu-upfront-attack-or-rear-guard-battle/

Schwan, G. and C. Höpfner (2017). 'Relaunching Europe Bottom-Up –
Integration of Refugees as a Joint Municipal Development'. Conference
Report, Berlin: Humboldt-Viadrina Governance Platform. Available at: https://
www.governance-platform.org/wp-content/uploads/2017/09/HVGP_
RelaunchingEuropeBottomUp_WEB-1.pdf

Kreilinger, V. (2015). A Proposal to use Enhanced Cooperation in the Refugee
Crisis. Available at: http://www.delorsinstitut.de/en/publications/topics/
institutions-and-democracy/proposal-to-use-enhanced-cooperation-in-the-
refugee-crisis/

Van Selm, J. (2016). 'Are Asylum and Immigration really a European Union
Issue?', *Forced Migration Review* 51: 60–2. Available at: www.fmreview.org/
destination-europe

Varju, M. and V. Czina (2016). 'Hitting Where it Hurts the Most: Hungary's
Legal Challenge against the EU's Refugee Quota System', 17 February.
Available at: http://verfassungsblog.de/hitting-where-it-hurts-the-most-
hungarys-legal-challenge-against-the-eus-refugee-quota-system/

10

Subsidiarity Versus Solidarity? EU Asylum and Immigration Policy

MARCO BALBONI

This chapter investigates the relationship between the principle of subsidiarity and the principle of solidarity in the field of asylum and immigration policy of the European Union (EU). The question is whether or not these principles lead to the same results in the governance of the mentioned policy area. The basic assumption is that both principles move indeed in the same direction or imply similar solutions, even if these solutions seem difficult to adopt and encounter several obstacles. The following analysis explores first the principle of subsidiarity before considering the principle of solidarity.

The principle of subsidiarity was officially introduced in the legal order of the EU by the Treaty of Maastricht. The main rationale of the principle is to allocate the exercise of the power to the lowest level possible, provided that this level responds to satisfactory requirements of efficiency. As affirmed by Article 5 (3) of the Treaty on European Union (TEU), the principle operates only in areas not subject to exclusive EU competences in order to decide if legislative or operational powers can be exercised by the centralised level of the EU or the decentralised level of the member states. As a matter of principle, it requires a double scrutiny: at first establishing if the objectives of the proposed action cannot be sufficiently achieved by the member states; and establishing further, by reason of the scale or effects of the proposed action, if these objectives can be better achieved by the EU.

Although formally neutral, the principle has been adopted with a view to limit the exercise of competences by the centralised level of the EU. In fact, it implies that the European Commission, which has the power of legislative initiative, has to justify the adoption of an act or an action by virtue of the principle of subsidiarity. The Lisbon Treaty has provided national parliaments with a special mechanism of control, the so-called Early Warning System (EWS). Once national parliaments submit a certain number of reasoned opinions, the European Commission is compelled to review or justify its proposal. What is more, the European Parliament or the EU Council can abandon a proposal if they believe that the principle of subsidiarity is not satisfied. While the Court of Justice retains jurisdiction on the respect of the principle, it has been very reluctant to exercise its power due to the complex political implications this might have.

The principle of subsidiarity in comparative context

Strikingly, and contrary to what may be expected, in complex organisations with different levels of governance, the principle tends to imply that competences in the field of asylum and immigration are exercised at the most central level. The United States offers a significant example in this context. The United States and the EU as political systems differ in many respects. In fact, the principle of subsidiarity is not explicitly enunciated in the US legal framework. Yet, in so far as the consequences of the principle are concerned, a comparison can be justified given that both entities reflect organisational complexity (Delaney, 2013, p. 153).

In the early stages of American federalism, the competence in the field of asylum and immigration was shared between the federation and the member states, and it was unclear which level would ultimately prevail in cases of conflict. At the end of the 19th century, a number of cases reached the Supreme Court disputing restrictive legislative acts adopted by some members of the federation already burdened by high levels of immigration, most notably in the states of New York and California. Such local legislation was not welcomed by other states or the federation due to the consideration that immigration was necessary for economic growth at national level. The Supreme Court decided the matter in favour of the federation. Although the final decision was adopted on the basis of several grounds, one played a particularly important role. The majority view highlighted that the policy in the field of immigration concerns citizens of third countries. Therefore, immigration policy is intrinsically connected with foreign relations, and this implies an inherent policy competence of the federation. For example, unilateral action by a member state of the federation concerning citizens of a third country may entail consequences for the entire federation such as the risk of war. Hence, the exercise of competences in the field of the foreign relations suggests by its nature the exercise of competences in the field of immigration. While the respective debate continued for almost another century, nowadays nobody doubts that immigration policy essentially rests as a 'federal plenary power' in the hands of the US federation.

It is interesting to note that up to now similar justifications have been adopted in the EU context only to a limited extent, yet leading in practice to comparable results. As is well known, EU policy on asylum and immigration is based on a system of shared competence and, therefore, subject to the principle of subsidiarity. Some provisions reserve specific competence to the member states, but Article 67 (2) TFEU assigns a general competence to realise a common policy in the field of border control, immigration and asylum to Brussels, as specified by the subsequent provisions for each of these fields. Unfortunately, it is not entirely clear where the dividing line between the two is found. A relevant example refers to the recent process of adopting and enforcing the Directive on Seasonal Workers (European Parliament and Council 2014).

On the one hand, Article 79 (2) TFEU attributes to the EU the competence to adopt measures concerning the conditions of entry and residence of third-country nationals and the definition of their rights. On the other hand, Article 79 (5) TFEU reserves the competence to determine the volume of third country citizens admitted in their state to seek work to national governments. Based on Article 79 (2) TFEU, the proposed Directive on Seasonal Workers provided common criteria for the admission of third-country nationals within the EU and the definition of minimum rights to be granted to them as citizens legally residing in a member state. The European Commission, however, invoked different rationales to justify the exercise of the competence to adopt the directive under the principle of subsidiarity. Among these justifications, the following two stand out: the need to preserve open borders, while avoiding secondary movements in the flow of migrants within the Union; and the need to ensure effective cooperation with third countries on migration issues.

The proposed directive raised several questions in EU circles, precisely on the respect of the principle of subsidiarity. Although national parliaments have not been able to reach the required number of reasoned opinions, their opposition to the adoption of the directive has gathered an impressive consensus, rarely achieved on other occasions. The arguments invoked by national parliaments were based on two aspects: first, the directive was not necessary to preserve open borders within the EU as its purpose was only to ensure minimal rights to seasonal workers; and second, the directive was not necessary for ensuring efficient EU cooperation in migration matters with third countries. The first reasoning was difficult to reject by the European Commission, whereas national parliaments were not able to provide valid arguments in support of the second.

In fact, given that member states are free to provide for better living conditions or workers' rights, it is not easy to argue on part of the Commission that the directive is strictly necessary to prevent secondary movements of third-country nationals. By contrast, it is far more difficult to deny the existence of a strong connection between the adoption of the directive and the need to ensure effective cooperation with third countries on migration issues. As further specified by the Commission, the treaties also confer competences in development policy to the EU level, which in line with Article 208 (1) TFEU, has the duty to take into account respective objectives in the implementation of all policies 'which are likely to affect developing countries', including asylum and migration policy. Clearly, actions from member states alone are not sufficient to attain the objectives of development policy, especially in cases of extensive and widespread migration. This necessarily requires a common EU approach. As the Commission (1995, 2) explained, immigrants often,

> retain strong links with their countries of origin, and the economies of the latter benefit from welcome contributions in the form of salary remittances. If planned cooperation with the countries in question fails to produce a methodical way of tackling migration pressure, friction could easily result, hurting not just international relations but also the groups of immigrants themselves.

Frequently more concerned with national sovereignty, member states have only occasionally shared a joint vision, for example, when acting in the framework of common responsibilities. Accordingly, the French EU Presidency stated in 2008 with reference to migration policy: 'decisions taken by a Member State will have repercussions for all other Member States'.

The principle of solidarity

To a large degree, the principle of solidarity suggests similar consequences. In legal terms, the principle has its roots in the international regime for refugees. After World War II, on 3 December 1949, the UN General Assembly adopted, with Resolution 319 (IV) on Refugees and Stateless Persons, one of the first codified texts in the field. Its preamble explicitly recognised that 'the problem of refugees is international in scope and nature'. Moreover, the fourth sentence of the preamble of the Geneva Convention relating to the Status of Refugees (1951) affirms that,

> the grant of asylum may place unduly heavy burdens on certain countries, and that a satisfactory solution of a problem

of which the United Nations has recognized the international scope and nature cannot therefore be achieved without international co-operation.

Although the lack of a direct mentioning leaves practical consequences unclear, there is little doubt that the preceding statements are motivated by the principle of solidarity (**Karageorgiou 2016, 3**). Any solution to the refugee problem would demand consultation and cooperation between states due to its international dimension. Indeed, countries on their own are not able to deal properly with all its causes and consequences. Yet, depending on perspective, it may be questioned whether the principle of solidarity as a guidance for European asylum and immigration policy does originate in international law rather that in a notion meant to govern the relations between EU member states.

As a guiding principle for asylum and immigration policy, solidarity is recalled in Article 67 TFEU and then further developed in Article 80 TFEU, forming the last provision of the Treaty chapter devoted to policies on border checks, asylum and immigration. Article 80 TFEU states that,

> policies of the Union set out in this Chapter and their implementation shall be governed by the principle of solidarity and fair sharing of responsibility, including its financial implications, between the Member States. Whenever necessary, the Union acts adopted pursuant to this Chapter shall contain appropriate measures to give effect to this principle.

Despite the reference to solidarity and fair sharing between member states, it should be stressed that the first addressee of both elements is the EU legislator, who is called upon to transform abstract ideas into operational policies. Furthermore, given its direct enunciation, it appears that the principle of solidarity within the European legal order goes a step further than what it is implied by its recognition in the international context. As **Karageorgiou (2016, 4)** points out,

> the provision explicitly couples solidarity with fair sharing of responsibilities. The fact that two distinct terms are deployed to describe the drafters' intentions is rather telling; the concept of solidarity is chiefly concerned with approaching an issue collectively, in support of each other, whereas fair sharing of responsibilities is related to a concrete division of labour.

The principle of solidarity goes beyond the mere adoption of measures at a centralised or common level in order to ensure a better cooperation between states. Thus, it implies more than the same principle proclaimed at international level. As solidarity fundamentally requires the sharing of responsibilities on the basis of a criterion of fairness, it comes with institutional *as well as* substantive policy implications.

Regardless of its standing in the EU Treaty, the solidarity principle has experienced serious implementation gaps, either in the legislation adopted by the EU or in the concrete behavior of national governments. Arguably, this is the causal factor to understand the apparent deficiencies in the EU's common policy on asylum and immigration. The example of the EU's Dublin system, established by an EU regulation of the same name, explains some of the practical consequences stemming from the principle's inadequate implementation (European Parliament and Council 2013).

The relevant piece of legislation states that the member state competent for the examination of an application by any asylum seeker is the country of first entry. In this way, the main burden shifts to the member states directly located at the borders of the Union. In fact, the European Commission specified in its own reform proposal the Dublin system not as a burden-sharing mechanism, but as one of straight burden-shifting (European Commission 2016, 13). In the words of Advocate General Sharpston (2012, 83): 'the whole system of providing protection for asylum seekers and refugees is predicated on the burden lying where it falls', and on the basis of a simple 'situation of fact'. As a consequence, there is an almost natural tendency of the most burdened countries to evade the proper application of core rules of the Dublin system and to make their asylum system as unattractive as possible in order to reduce the practical demands placed on them.

Similarly, a lack of attention to the principle of solidarity is evident in other types of measures which were supposed to help the most burdened countries. The German initiative of 2015 is a case in point as it applied unilaterally the discretionary clause provided by Article 17 (1) of the Dublin Regulation. The latter states that,

> by way of derogation from Article 3 (1), each Member State may decide to examine an application for international protection lodged with it by a third-country national or a stateless person, even if such examination is not its responsibility under the criteria laid down in this Regulation.

The adoption of this unilateral measure outside a concerted framework had the effect of passing on negative repercussions to other member states. Thus, the initiative became a pull factor for the arrival of new migrants in countries other than Germany and further increased the pressure on member states already exposed to the phenomenon (Shisheva 2016, 4). Not surprisingly, the European Commission has restricted the remit of the relevant clause in its proposals for reform of the Dublin arrangements.

In light of the above, it is fair to say that, within the EU legal order, both the principle of subsidiarity and the principle of solidarity move in the same direction and imply similar consequences, despite some remaining differences. The impact of the principle of subsidiarity is more institutional or procedural in character, in the sense that it essentially asks for the adoption of collective measures at a coordinated, if not central, level. The impact of the principle of solidarity, by contrast, has either an institutional or a substantive dimension. In other words, it implies not only coordinated or central measures, but also real burden-sharing to make more sustainable policies possible for all member states.

All said, it is necessary to clarify how deep the intervention at central EU level should be. How can the central intervention by Brussels be balanced and preserve national competences? Even if the principle of subsidiarity and the principle of solidarity would require a more resolute centralised intervention and more joint measures, it should not be forgotten that the EU model does not aspire to be identical with US style federalism.

To answer the question, the treaties give only a few partial indications. The second sentence of Article 80 TFEU, for example, states: 'whenever nec- essary, the Union acts adopted pursuant to this Chapter shall contain appropriate measures' to give effect to the principle of solidarity. Yet, this particular provision assumes an already resolved problem as regards the subject exercising the competence. In fact, finding a proper balance for the application of the subsidiarity and solidarity principles in their institutional as well as substantive dimension depends more on non-legal factors than on provisions inscribed in the treaties.

A number of such factors can be enumerated: first, there is a lack of consensus on the values which should have priority at European level. In contrast to other European crises, the migration problem is more profound as it challenges directly principles and values held by individual member states and depends 'on solutions to address life and death of human beings fleeing war zones and persecutions' (Pascouau 2016, 17). Second, there is a lack of trust among EU states in their mutual capacity to adequately meet the duties of common burden-sharing. It is no coincidence that Northern member states typically defend their strict approach by demanding from the Southern countries calling for more solidarity to ensure their national asylum systems are up to scratch with European standards. Third, and probably at the heart of the matter, there is a fundamental misunderstanding of this policy area since the very beginning of European cooperation and reflected in the narrative that settled in the collective memory. Indeed, the core of EU asylum and migration policy has always been driven by the emphasis on the positive effects of the elimination of internal borders, while disregarding the necessity to set up a common regime for the Union's external borders. Abolishing borders between France and Germany might be a good idea, but this does not mean that France and Germany will not have any external border. Instead, it means that the external border of France and Germany is now placed somewhere else, for instance, in Italy or in Greece (with significant consequences in terms of available resources and commitments to a larger set of responsibilities) (Shisheva 2016, 5). Taking care of the EU's Mediterranean borders cannot just be a problem for Italy and Greece since their borders have to be considered the borders of all European member states. No one can expect two countries alone to do the job for everybody else in the common European space.

In combination, the factors listed above produced a rather inconvenient situation for the European project. Not only does it negatively affect the possibility to address current challenges, but it also precludes a clear strategy for the future. The measures adopted in EU asylum and immigration policy appear to respond more to contingent circumstances than to reflect long-term aims and objectives. A confirmation of this claim can be found in the documents adopted by the European Commission, admitting that only limited policy actions are feasible and that more long-standing measures are unlikely to be scheduled in the absence of more favourable political conditions. Furthermore, the lack of systematically collected, objective data frequently prevents the conduct of a more thorough analysis as a potential starting point for new policy initiatives at European level.

Conclusion

In EU policy on asylum and immigration, the principle of subsidiarity and the principle of solidarity point in the same direction. Both ask simultaneously for the adoption of measures at a more centralised or coordinated level and for more balanced commitments by the member states. Despite the persistence of serious obstacles to achieve this result, success stories can be found within narrow limits. The adoption of the Directive on Seasonal Workers is a case in point. In terms of the EU's institutional profile, however, the risk of a rather ambiguous framework cannot be excluded. The frequent incapacity of the EU to adopt adequate measures may coexist with occasional peaks showing centralised efforts. Certainly, from the perspective of a neutral observer, this does make little sense in terms of policy coherence and consistency.

For this reason, an effort should be made to find a sound balance between measures which have to be adopted at central or coordinated level and measures which need to remain in the hands of national governments. Obvious examples for the latter are issues of migrant integration where actual needs change from country to country, or external migration flows that ultimately affect individual member states to different degrees. In the final analysis, what creates most concern is the apparent lack of a long-term strategy. Of course, the general political climate is not conducive, but processes of public deliberation must be initiated and sustained by European institutions to develop a more solid policy approach better aligned with existing needs.

References

Commission of the European Communities (1995). 'Communication from the Commission to the Council and the European Parliament, Strengthening the Mediterranean Policy of the European Union: Proposals for Implementing a Euro-Mediterranean Partnership'. COM (95) 72 final. Brussels.

Delaney E. F. (2013). 'Justifying Power: Federalism, Immigration, and "Foreign Affairs"'. *Duke Journal of Constitutional Law & Public Policy* 8(1): 153–95.

European Commission (2016). 'Proposal for a Regulation of the European Parliament and of the Council establishing the Criteria and Mechanisms for Determining the Member State Responsible for Examining an Application for International Protection Lodged in One of the Member States by a Third-country National or a Stateless Person (Recast)'. COM (2016) 270 final/2. Brussels.

European Parliament and Council (2013). 'Establishing the Criteria and Mechanisms for Determining the Member State Responsible for Examining an Application for International Protection lodged in one of the Member States by a Third-country National or a Stateless Person (Recast)'. Regulation 604/2013. Available at: http://eur-lex.europa.eu/legal-content/EN/TXT/HTML/?uri=CELEX:32013R0604&from=en

European Parliament and Council (2014). 'Conditions of Entry and Stay of Third-country Nationals for the Purpose of Employment as Seasonal Workers'. Directive 2014/36/EU. Available at: http://eur-lex.europa.eu/legal-content/EN/TXT/HTML/?uri=CELEX:32014L0036&from=en

French Presidency (2008). 'The European Pact on Immigration and Asylum'. Available at: http://www.immigration.interieur.gouv.fr/content/download/34482/258636/file/19_Plaquette_EN.edf

Karageorgiou, E. (2016). 'The Law and Practice of Solidarity in the Common European Asylum System: Article 80 TFEU and its Added Value'. Available at: http://www.sieps.se

Pascouau, Y. (2016). 'From Conflict to Equilibrium: The Construction of a Common Ground for Social and Political Consensus on Migration'. In *Improving the Responses to the Migration and Refugee Crisis in Europe*, 14–29. Lisbon: Calouste Gulbenkian Foundation. Available at: https://www.researchgate.net/publication/313036740_Improving_the_Responses_to_the_Migration_and_Refugee_Crisis_in_Europe

Sharpston, E. (2012). 'Opinion on Case CIMADE, Groupe D'Information et de Soutien des Immigrés (GISTI) v. Ministre de L'Intérieur, de L'Outre-mer, des Collectivités Territoriales et de L'Immigration, C179/11'. Available at: http://curia.europa.eu/juris/liste.jsf?num=C-179/11

Shisheva, M. (2016). 'Schengen, Security and Solidarity: Sending the Right Message to EU Citizens, Research Project Migration, Borders Control and Solidarity: Schengen at Stake?'. Available at: https://www.iedonline.eu/publications/2016/schengen-reseach-papers.php

United Nations (1951). 'Convention Relating to the Status of Refugees'. Available at: http://www.unhcr.org/3b66c2aa10.pdf

United Nations, General Assembly (1949). 'Refugees and Stateless Persons', Resolution 319 (IV), 3 December. Available at: https://documents-dds-ny.un.org/doc/RESOLUTION/GEN/NR0/051/38/IMG/NR005138.pdf?OpenElement

11

Global Migration and Local Integration: The European Refugee Crisis

JÖRG DÜRRSCHMIDT

There was a sense of looming crisis when the EU heads of state and government met in Bratislava in September 2016. It was the first summit after the Brexit vote. Finally, the EU leadership had to face up to the organisation's limited ability to develop an effective and sustainable response to the refugee crisis. In the wake of the crisis, cleavages had appeared between member states in the East and the West as well as the North and the South of the Union, discursively focussed around lacking principles of responsibility and burden-sharing. Some member states castigated others about their inability to implement agreed responsibilities within the common European immigration and asylum policy. Yet, at the same time, these others complained about the lack of previously agreed material solidarity to help them to do so. A third group suggested to renegotiate the actual type of solidarity requested. As a consequence, the EU summit during this existential crisis conveyed a certain sense of desperation articulated in appeals to 'co-operate or bust!', but without a guiding principle to put general commitments into a working policy. Instead, the term of flexible solidarity made the round. Accordingly, the Bratislava Declaration only vaguely refers to principles of responsibility and solidarity as a recipe to avoid future uncontrolled flows of migrants. Nevertheless, its principles were meant to ensure the safety of EU external borders and to offer a basis for a long-term European migration policy.

Against this background, this chapter draws on general implications of the subsidiarity concept. Due to the paradoxical nature of migration policy, subsidiarity aspects of European asylum and migration policy can be examined along two dimensions: first, by looking at the EU's integrated border management as an illustration of external (or internationalised) subsidiarity between the member states; and second, by highlighting its internal dimension in the case of the Lampedusa refugee disaster in terms of local integration policy. Both examples show that the practice of subsidiarity pushes an otherwise narrow political-institutional construct towards a wider sociological usage.

Locating the concept

In the migration debate, several commentators recalled subsidiarity as a forgotten concept and a potential key to solve Europe's refugee problem. Following this principle, power and responsibility should be located at those levels of government, where the required resources, political accountability and interest representation can be best established. Thus, distributive justice and economic efficiency desired by ordinary citizens would be observed most effectively. While the subsidiarity principle was deeply enshrined in the Maastricht Treaty of 1992, from today's perspective it might look as 'a road not taken'. On the one hand, leading experts involved in the initial discussions still praise their *Making Sense of Subsidiarity* (Begg et al. 1993) as a useful guiding principle and political tool to address the EU's current governance dilemma. If only EU legislation is properly implemented, i.e. in accordance with the institutional matrix provided by the subsidiarity principle, everything will be fine. Seen from this angle, the key towards a solution of the European refugee crisis rests with finding the right trade-off between centralised and decentralised decision-making creating adequate implementation capacities for the common migration and asylum policy.

On the other hand, there are observers who doubt that a satisfactory solution to the refugee crisis can be found through a more stringent implementation of subsidiarity alone. In their view, various challenges faced by the EU's immigration and asylum system cannot be addressed by adding a few policy instruments or by providing better organisational and financial support. For them, the refugee crisis is not the cause of EU governance problems but rather their consequence. The disputes about shared border management and common standards in asylum procedures has anything but revealed the structural limitations of EU migration policy and the tools at its disposal. What is needed to regain policy coherence is not an institutional quick fix to a temporary crisis, but a serious change in the dominant policy rationale. Part of a solution must come from the recognition that refugee policies have gotten tangled up with the dynamics of globalisation and international migration. Critical voices refer to an irrevocably broken refugee system that sys-tematically produces the 'survival migrant', while trying to disentangle the human right to take refuge from the right to migrate (Betts and Collier 2017).

Therefore, the flaws in the EU asylum and immigration regime have to be seen as a deficit in global governance. Its driving force is the 'liberal paradox' inherent to any modern, not just European, migration regime (Hollifield 1992). Although domestic stability and welfare protection demand control of state borders with a premium on national sovereignty, the globalised economy together with humanitarian obligations drives the imperative for mobility and the right to migrate. Both the Schengen (free movement within the EU borders) and Dublin (regulating access to the EU) agreements attempt to juggle this paradox in line with the EU's self-image as an area of freedom, security and justice. Indeed, in the context of subsidiarity, they underline the need for a guiding principle as regards intergovernmental burden-sharing, responsibility and solidarity; yet, as part of a genuinely new global architecture built around transnational migration, asylum and welfare.

Therefore, it makes sense to differentiate a rather restricted version of the subsidiarity principle from a much broader use of the concept. In the narrow version, it refers to the distribution of responsibilities between institutions and levels of governance. In the wider version, it provides a hierarchical matrix for mobilising and organising the potential of human society. The former alludes to the ongoing search for a compromise between federalists and confederalists, i.e. between those who prefer more centralisation and integration and those who argue for a more decentralised and inter-governmental approach to the European polity. The latter, by contrast, takes a look beyond state institutions to the internally available social capital that can be mobilised by civil society.

Historically, this wider version of subsidiarity is embedded in the social thought of the Roman Catholic Church. There the concept comprises a key formula for the legitimate provision of aid and welfare. Essentially, it proposes that social support should be organised in a way that sustains – but does not absorb – smaller forms of collective organisations. In general, action by smaller social units is preferred, unless larger social units provide a positive benefit that cannot be obtained by the smaller ones (Spicker 1991, 4). Accordingly, there is a fine line separating welcome support from unwanted intervention. In fact, subsidiarity works with two main guiding principles for social obligation: solidarity as well as constraint; both exercised to maintain agency for the smaller social unit. It follows that the basic idea of subsidiarity structures responsibility and obligation in a way that prefers individual action over action by the community, local policy over national policy, national deliberation over supranational regulation, and so on. Thus, in a sociological definition, it denotes a stratification of the lifeworld in zones of familiarity, trust, and motivation that are built around everyday needs. In this 'organic view of society' (Spicker 1991, 3), subsidiarity champions the decentralised capacity of the lifeworld to organise social intelligence spontaneously and to mobilise social capital within existing social networks and beyond the confines of formal institutions.

This contrasts with the narrow definition as a political principle by which complex states organise the architecture of their governance institutions. Formally, subsidiarity still advocates levels of governance at the smallest possible level of political organisation (guaranteeing self-determination, transparency and loyalty), but in practice it serves to control the level of discreteness granted to supranational bodies. In the EU context, the principle emphasises the relative autonomy of national and sub-national bodies to curb the centralising and strategic ambitions of the European Commission. Arguably, the strengthened role of national parliaments through the 1997 Lisbon Treaty as monitors of compliance and early warning systems even brought the principle into an unhappy alliance with the principle of sovereignty (see Spicker 1991, 9).

Initially, the subsidiarity principle was situated in the evolving relationship between nation states and the Union. Gradually, this has been extended to include the local and regional level in a single model for the procedures of interlinked decision-making and divided sovereignty typical for federal political systems (Friesen 2005). Therefore, subsidiarity must be regarded as an intrinsic aspect of multi-level governance (MLG) that has established itself as a dominant analytical framework for networked governance across local, regional, national and European institutions. Accordingly, recent debates on the rescaling of the state (the transformation of socio-spatial relationships in the context of neoliberal globalisation) have further highlighted an increased significance of sub-national units through subsidiarity concerns ensuring political efficiency in multi-level arrangements. As global migration is also part of this rescaling process, respective policy and management issues feature most prominently in this area (Zapata-Barrero and Barker 2014). Moreover, the 'local turn' in the MLG approach as applied to migration and immigration policy has revived the wider understanding of subsidiarity by drawing specifically on the role of non-state actors and civil society (Zapata-Barrero et al. 2017).

A common migration and asylum policy?

In 2015, the EU Commission's *European Agenda on Migration* stated that 'no member state can effectively address migration alone' and that 'we need a European approach'. In retrospect, this sounds like a repetitive mantra endorsing European integration as an empowerment of traditional state actors. Of course, national governments might gain rather than lose sovereignty (and thus maintain their capacity to rule) by sharing administrative competence and ceding territorial autonomy in the face of complex political issues such as migration. This general capacity of an organisation to transform its own structure and guiding principles to better adapt to a changing environment is referred to as 'governability' (Paquet 2001, 188).

Since its first outline at the Tampere Summit of 1999, the European policy on migration and asylum has embraced a 'paradigm of multi-level governance' (Hampshire 2015a, 541). In a minimalist understanding, the EU's architecture consists of three dimensions shaping the governance of this policy area: relations between the European Commission, the European Parliament and the European Council; relations between these institutions and national governments; and finally, relations that link both national governments and supranational institutions with sub-national authorities. Within this set-up, the relations between national governments and supranational EU institutions form the most contested core. While the latter have steadily acquired strategic influence over migration policies, nation states sought to retain decision-making power on crucial aspects of migration policy, such as the right to decide on the actual number of migrants admitted into their territory from outside the Union.

Due to the contested nature of the policy field, the EU Commission has gradually implemented a *Common European Asylum System* (CEAS). The Dublin regulations are the cornerstone of the CEAS stipulating that asylum seekers have their claim assessed in the member state of first entry. This mechanism aims to foreclose 'asylum hopping' in a Union with diverse regional welfare standards, but simultaneously creates a classic 'weakest-link' problem. In recognition of this issue, the EU introduced three asylum directives (the Qualification Directive, the Procedures Directive, and the Reception Condition Directive) which address key questions, such as who is a refugee, how is the quest for asylum properly processed, and what rights should asylum seekers and refugees receive?

Moreover, to enhance harmonisation on asylum policy and to foster practical cooperation as well as interoperability between the national and EU level of governance, a set of EU-based organisations and institutions has emerged. Since 2003, EURODAC has provided a computerised fingerprint database for identifying illegal border crossings and asylum seekers, while EUROSUR, established in 2013, has provided an integrated border surveillance system equipped with smart border technologies, such as video observation, satellite tracking and miniature drones. Two further EU agencies are crucial for providing operational support in border management: In 2011, EASO became active to provide staff training and quality assessment for the implementation of common asylum standards in the member states; and already since 2005, FRONTEX has been operating with steadily increasing budgets as the co-ordinating agency for the EU's external borders. Its central task is 'integrated border management', best understood as multi-level governance in action. As a strategy, it implies an accumulation of modalities of coercion, although without centralising the authority over these modalities. In other words, it softly *Europeanises* border management by installing technology-based cooperation and by trying to induce at the same time a shared organisational culture and common doctrine (Jeandesboz 2015).

At first sight, the multi-level architecture of asylum and migration policy might look like an exemplary manifestation of subsidiarity. Political authority is pooled at the supranational level because it is deemed necessary by the member states which have recognised the limits of unilateral action. However, asylum and migration policy remains an area of shared competence, meaning that national governments retain a final say over issues of access and integration. In its strategic ambition, the EU as the aggregate political unit remains dependent on the parts of which it is constituted. This is most notable when it comes to 'integrated border management'. The governance arrangement does not fundamentally challenge national sovereignty over borders, but reworks the conditions under which the exercise of this sovereignty is practically possible.

Therefore, EU asylum and migration policy illustrates that subsidiarity does not simply amount to governance at the smallest possible level. Instead, and next to divided sovereignty, it also implies solidarity and support between different territorial units and layers of governance. The member states, for example, carry out their specific responsibilities within CEAS as an obligation towards the functioning of the shared European asylum and migration policy. Similarly, prospective member states have to demonstrate their capacity to adapt to and eventually implement the requirements of an integrated border management. In turn, the EU offers financial and operational support to member states carrying the burden of a sudden influx of migrants and asylum-seekers. An EU programme labelled 'solidarity and management of migration flows', running between 2007 and 2013, serves as an illustration how financial aid has been distributed to immigration hot-spots in Greece. Likewise, the creation of rapid intervention teams (RABITs) and asylum support teams by FRONTEX and EASO have offered operational support to particularly challenged member states such as Italy and Bulgaria.

Certainly, this understanding of the common migration and asylum policy held together by the principle of subsidiarity is exceptional for the EU's institutional architecture. Yet, increasingly sober voices can be heard when reviewing the results of almost twenty years of policy making. The assessment ranges from an implementation fatigue and practical 'hibernation' to a growing discrepancy between rhetoric and practice or a looming policy failure. Despite considerable efforts to create a common asylum policy, 'asylum legislation and practices across European states are anything but common' (Hampshire 2015a, 539). There are, for example, considerable differences in recognition rates across member states and the standards for decision-making and reception tend to vary. In fact, already before the climax of the refugee crisis in 2015, one could conclude that EU migration policy 'looked to be running out of steam' (Hampshire 2015a, 543).

From this perspective, subsidiarity appears rather distorted without unfolding its full potential. A weak version of subsidiarity dominates, safeguarding the sovereignty of nation states from strategically minded EU institutions. As a consequence, levels of governance are not taken seriously to transform into graduated relations of mutual responsibility and obligation. Despite formal competence, EU institutions were unable to identify and articulate a general European interest beyond the national interests of the member states. Thus, EU policy is neither complete nor visionary. It is instead one-sided towards elements of control and interested in externalising migration movements. The enabling aspect of immigration remains rudimentary, factually perpetuating an unhappy mix of 'survival migration' towards Europe. Serious enforcement problems undermine sustainable commitments and encourage opportunistic behaviour by individual member states. The latter is reflected in familiar practices by national authorities simply 'waving through' potential applicants, encouraging secondary movements to neighbouring countries or allowing for lucrative citizenship sales. The operational support given by FRONTEX and EASO is well-meant and sometimes well-staged, but both agencies remain underfunded and understaffed. Most importantly, they do not have direct operational authority over national border services. Finally, the financial assistance offered to overstretched member states was seen by them as little more than token money.

Overall, these developments have undermined the emergence of a sustainable subsidiarity culture long before the peak of the latest refugee crisis. At best, it brought to the fore previously latent asymmetries of national interests. Positive notions of subsidiarity working with coordinated actions at various levels of governance based on principles of solidarity and shared responsibility, transformed more or less openly into burden-shifting. Frontline member states, in particular Greece and Italy, felt that the initial responsibility with regard to new entries in line with the Dublin agreement quickly turned into an exclusive responsibility to deal with the refugee crisis on behalf of the EU. As the asylum system of these frontline states showed signs of fragility and sub-standard application of existing European legislation, other member states such as Germany and Sweden stepped in on humanitarian grounds. Ironically, through their intervention, Brussels was saved from violating the Geneva Convention on Human Rights, albeit at the price of circumventing its own Dublin convention. Conceptually, this is best captured as an *ad hoc* or make-shift mode of subsidiarity.

The unprecedented numbers of refugees coming to European shores in 2015 have exposed the deficiencies of the EU asylum system. For a technical explanation, one could point to a gap between legislation and implementation that needs closing; or, one could refer to a broader crisis scenario where economic downturn, financial constraints and rising populism have made it difficult for frontline states to keep their asylum system functioning along European standards. Perhaps, one could also mention the rising number of actors involved in complex governance arrangements for this particular policy area. The EU's Eastern enlargement of 2004 and 2007 as well as the growing influence of international organisations such as the International Organisation for Migration (IOM) come to mind. However, the fundamental underlying issue remains the inequity of the European asylum system (Hampshire 2015a, 547). As it stands, it tries to impose responsibility and solidarity on a historically grown asymmetric landscape of national power and interests. All this without seriously acknowledging European country profiles in terms of geographic location, (post)colonial histories, migration legacies or competing welfare systems and labour markets. In addition, it pushes economically weak member states to the frontline of a controversial policy problem while effectively shielding the more affluent member states. Current showings of financial and operational solidarity cannot hide the fact that the EU has failed to establish an effective regime of mutual obligation. The particular constellation risks undermining subsidiarity concerns in other policy areas as well. Thus, the official discourse around solidarity and responsibility that periodically flares up in official documents seems emblematic for a broken subsidiarity debate.

Europe's reception culture: subsidiarity meets hospitality

The Italian island of Lampedusa has become a symbol of a flawed migration and asylum system, unable to rebalance the asymmetric burden it imposes on member states due to the contingencies of geography. On 3 October 2013 more than 360 migrants from Libya died drowning off its coast. The disaster brought the ambivalence of EU policy making to public attention. The moral outrage following the Lampedusa shipwreck led the Italian government to authorise the 'Operation Mare Nostrum' to patrol and safeguard the Mediterranean Sea. It failed, however, to convince its European partners to share the costs of this search and rescue mission estimated at 9.0 million euros per month. Eventually, the national effort was replaced by the Frontex-led operation 'Triton', working with a significantly smaller budget (2.9 million euros per month) based on voluntary contributions and tasked with the gathering of intelligence rather than humanitarian rescue efforts. This shift in emphasis towards surveillance mechanisms in the control of European sea borders has been seen as another indicator of the organised irresponsibility with which the Union approaches its migration crisis.

In this context, it is worth noting that before the disaster Lampedusa was one of the most popular entry points to Europe, and as a consequence, a pioneer in developing a welcoming reception culture. This, also, long before the march of Syrian refugees along the Balkan route brought other countries and their behavioural responses to the fore. Before the switch of media attention, the first boatpeople arriving on the Italian island were met by a local culture of spontaneous hospitality. Yet, this long-established ethos similar to un-questioned help between fishermen became increasingly challenged and 'professionalised' with increasing numbers of arrivals, attempts of political intervention and economic profiteering. Within a few years, locals required special permits to visit reception centres, and refugees felt the need to protest against the impact of political clientelism on their day-to-day lives. A declining fishing industry and dependence on tourism had contributed further to the fragmentation of the local community and rising resentment towards refugees and asylum-seekers (see Friese 2010).

The case of Lampedusa thus moves the analysis to another dimension of subsidiarity, replacing the linkage between national and supranational governance with an individual-societal or citizen-state nexus. The question here is not how authority is organised and exercised at different levels, but how the primary responsibilities of care and solidarity are organised by the social body. In this sense, subsidiarity refers to the conditions of individual subsistence and community support. This widened understanding of the principle could be described as the 'unbinding' of subsidiarity towards everyday capacities of self-organisation and empowerment.

One such crucial capacity of the everyday is to welcome strangers and to accommodate those in need without immediately enquiring their identity. This anthropological moral imperative of granting temporary asylum could be observed in the voluntary reception culture (*Willkommenskultur*) once prevalent on Lampedusa and evident in cities such as Passau or Malmö more recently. Its cultural roots can be traced back to the widely shared belief that God reveals himself in the beggar or stranger knocking at your door (Friese 2010, 326). Arguably, without being able to draw on this eternal sense of hospitality in the everyday integration of refugees, state actors would have faced an immediate humanitarian catastrophe.

Seen from this angle, state intervention in the realm of self-organised hospitality culture seems undesirable. Yet, next to ethical reasoning, there is also a clear judicial-political argument when it comes to the hosting of refugees and migrants. The latter addresses questions of human rights, citizenship and institutionalised welfare. In practice, it will tend to curtail access to and formalise content of traditional hospitality. While unconditional hospitality is offered instantly by the lifeworld, it has an uneasy relationship with notions of sovereignty, the real-world borders of existing political communities, and institutionalised forms of welfare. Hence, the anthro-pological view of hospitality would need government legislation that limits state involvement for pre-existing hospitality to be effective. Moreover, if state-centric asylum procedures 'deface individuals' in a cold and technical manner, the spontaneous hospitality of everyday life could offer warmth and compassion instead (Wilson 2010). Understood in this way, subsidiarity would imply a mutually supportive relationship between state institutions and civil society actors for the purpose of an effective protection of refugees.

It is important to note that this link between the state and civil society cannot be confined to a partial inclusion of hospitality ethics into technocratic asylum procedures. Insofar as these procedures offer an entry point towards political citizenship as well as social membership, any respective policy will be tied up with key principles of societal openness and closure. In fact, EU member states have fought hard to retain their position as fundamental structures for individual lives; essentially by tying biographies to their national institutional clusters of education and welfare. In doing so, they organise individual claims and duties via carefully graded modes of social and political citizenship. Not surprisingly, therefore, migrant recognition and integration has crystallised as the one of the most contested policy issues within the Union.

At the same time, it is a truism that the integration of migrants needs to take place within a societal microcosm of localities. It is at this particular territorial level that 'migrants seek full participation in the social, economic, and cultural life of the host community' (Hepburn and Zapata-Barrero 2014, 5). Here, civil society actors yield a considerable amount of power as gatekeepers to everyday participation and belonging. In addition, they are able to shift the emphasis of subsidiarity from notions of efficient service delivery to notions of social coherence and local identity. Then, subsidiarity carries meaning much more in relation to processes of sustainable migrant integration beyond an initial reception culture (*Willkommenskultur*), and would also imply greater sensibility towards the orderly structure of lasting solidarities. The latter follow rules of social closeness and relative distance embedded in the customised everyday practices of sub-national spaces. Accordingly, these cannot be ordained or prescribed from above, but need to emerge from ongoing public deliberation. If robust solidarity for migrant integration is merely administered by higher levels of governance, it is likely to breed resentment within the disadvantaged fragments of the European population. EU citizens living in the region's poorer periphery, for example, might feel tempted to 'fast track' into one of the affluent core economies and follow a pattern first observed among 'survival migrants' (Hann 2015).

Conclusion

From a sociological perspective, subsidiarity refers to the allocation of responsibility and solidarity at various levels of governance. However, as a consequence of societal globalisation there is an ongoing process similar to the 'unbinding of politics' in the context of migration and asylum policy. Firstly, the 'unbinding of subsidiarity' matters in the EU's external dimension as a negative policy that passes on migration challenges by striking ambivalent deals with regional neighbours. Undoubtedly, EU institutions still have some way to go to develop a genuine global approach in line with their ambition to speak with one voice in the governance of 'survival migration'. Secondly, the 'unbinding of subsidiarity' matters more positively in the EU's internal dimension when recognising the autonomous problem-solving capacity of everyday life. This, for example, has been manifested in the spontaneous hospitality offered to migrants as part of a local reception culture. The neglect of such bottom-up practices in the exercise of mutual responsibility and solidarity would run the serious risk to accept further social fragmentation and individual isolation.

Both cases discussed in this chapter show that subsidiarity is more than just the effective management of several levels of governance. More comprehensively, the concept includes the moral resources a society may or may not mobilise. Therefore, discussing the local as well as global aspects of subsidiarity in a highly contested setting transforms traditional questions of formal decision-making and implementation. As it stands, the European policy on asylum and migration leaves us wondering how we want to live together in the 21st century.

References

Begg, D. (1993) *Making Sense of Subsidiarity. How much Centralisation for Europe?* London: CEPR.

Betts, A. and P. Collier (2017) *Refuge: Transforming a Broken Refugee System.* London: Penguin.

Hepburn, E. and R. Zapata-Barrero (2014) 'Introduction: Immigration Policies in Multilevel States'. In Hepburn, E. and R. Zapata-Barrero (eds) *The Politics of Immigration in Multilevel States: Governance and Parties*, 3–18. Basingstoke: Palgrave.

Friese, H. (2010) 'The Limits of Hospitality: Political Philosophy, Undocumented Migration and the Local Arena', *European Journal of Social Theory* 13(3): 323–41.

Friesen, M. (2005) 'Subsidiarity and Federalism: An Old Concept with Contemporary Relevance for Political Society', *Federal Governance* 2(1): 1–22.

Hampshire, J. (2015a) 'European Migration Governance since the Lisbon Treaty: Introduction to the Special Issue', *Journal of Ethnic and Migration Studies* 42(4): 537–53.

Hampshire, J. (2015b): 'Speaking with One Voice? The European Union's Approach to Migration and Mobility and the Limits of International Migration Cooperation', *Journal of Ethnic and Migration Studies* 42(4): 571–86.

Hann, C. (2015) 'The Fragility of Europe's Willkommenskultur', *Anthropology Today* 31(6): 1–2.

Hollifield, J. F. (1992). *Immigrants, Markets and States: The Political Economy of Postwar Europe*. Cambridge, MA: Harvard University Press.

Jeandesboz, J. (2015). 'EU Border Control: Violence, Capture and Apparatus'. In Jansen, Y., Celikates, R. and J. de Bloosis (eds): *The Irregularisation of Migration in Contemporary Europe: Detention, Deportation, Drowning*, 87–102. London: Rowman & Littlefield.

Paquet, G. (2001). 'The New Governance, Subsidiarity, and the Strategic State'. In: *Governance in the 21st Century*, 183–214. Paris: OECD.

Spicker, P. (1991). 'The Principle of Subsidiarity and the Social Policy of the European Community', *Journal of European Social Policy* 1(1): 3-14.

Wilson, E. K. (2010): 'Protecting the Unprotected: Reconceptualising Refugee Protection through the Notion of Hospitality', *Local-Global* 8: 100–22.

Zapata-Barrero, R. and F. Barker (2014). 'Multilevel Governance of Immigration in Multinational Sates: Who Governs? Reconsidered'. In Hepburn, E. and R. Zapata-Barrero (eds) *The Politics of Immigration in Multilevel States: Governance and Parties*, 19–40. Basingstoke: Palgrave.

Zapata-Barrero, R., Caponio, T. and P. Scholten (2017). 'Theorizing the "Local Turn" in a Multi-Level Governance Framework of Analysis: A Case Study in Immigrant Policies', *International Review of Administrative Sciences* 83(2): 1–6.

SECTION FOUR

INTERNATIONAL DIMENSION

12

European Foreign Policy and the Realities of Subsidiarity

JÖRG MICHAEL DOSTAL

This chapter discusses subsidiarity considerations in the broader theoretical and empirical context of European foreign policy. The argument advanced here integrates the policy conduct of key member states as well as that of the Brussels-based institutions. It is guided by the assessment of Gammelin and Löw (2014, 266–7; author's translation) appropriate for the best part of the post-Cold War period: 'the last word in foreign policy still rests with the nation states' and 'what exactly one should understand by joint foreign policy is only vaguely defined'. A proper understanding of the concept of subsidiarity, therefore, requires some foundation in the European history of international relations (IR) and an awareness of the major administrative changes in the European Union (EU), implementing programmes such as the Common Foreign and Security Policy (CFSP), the European Security and Defence Policy (ESDP), the Common Security and Defence Policy (CSDP) and, most recently, the policy of Permanent Structured Cooperation (PESCO).

Each of these practical steps follow on from the consolidated version of the Treaty on European Union (TEU) establishing 'general provisions of the Union's external action' (Articles 21 and 22 TEU) and 'specific provisions of the Common Foreign and Security Policy' (Articles 23 to 46 TEU). The limits of the subsidiarity concept are apparent in this empirical dimension, despite the further analytical specification suggested in chapter one. To explain convincingly the track record of EU member states in international affairs, the standard realist and liberal approaches to IR must be included. So far, the integration process – and one of its more sophisticated mechanisms – has not been able to overcome the self-interested behaviour of EU member states in an international system showing clear signs of increasing multipolarity.

Europe in international relations

The international order of the 19th century was dominated by European powers. After the defeat of Napoleonic France in 1815 and before the start of World War I in 1914, the British Empire had become the dominant global actor. Yet, already in the second half of that century this hegemony declined and, gradually, the United States (US) and imperial Germany overtook the lead country in terms of industrial strength. In fact, by the turn of the century, the global order had turned increasingly multipolar with Great Britain now facing serious challenges from other powers such as France, Germany, Italy, Russia and the US, as well as the Austro-Hungarian and Ottoman Empires.

The shift towards multipolarity became even more pronounced as a result of World War I. Britain and France reorganised large sections of Central and South East Europe by creating new nation states. The respective territories were mostly carved out from the geographic space of the dissolved Austro-Hungarian Empire, but included large minority communities later subjected to assimilationist policies in order to 'strengthen' the dominant nationality. This policy intervention was vindicated with reference to US President Woodrow Wilson's concept of national self-determination, even if, in practice, this served as a fig leaf to reorganise the central European state system according to the geostrategic interests of the victorious powers (in particular, France and Great Britain). This helped, more specifically, to separate the two major defeated states of World War I and to form a *cordon sanitaire* made up of smaller European states around Weimar Germany and Soviet Russia. Similar foreign policies were implemented in the Middle East, redrawing borders in the Arab world after the dissolution of the Ottoman Empire. Not surprisingly, these divisions gave rise to new territorial disputes, some of which are still relevant today.

The international system as it emerged after the 1919 Treaty of Versailles was very much based on conflict between victorious allied powers and defeated revisionist states. Once this constellation had led to another major conflict between Hitler's Germany and Stalin's Soviet Union (resulting in the military capitulation of fascist Germany and imperial Japan), the international order turned bipolar. Eventually, the US and the Soviet Union emerged as the undisputed leaders of two ideological 'camps', each covering large parts of the European continent.

In Western Europe, the post-World War II order produced unprecedented efforts to establish a system of closer cooperation among key government actors in economic affairs and security matters. While initially triggered by US economic assistance (in the form of the European Recovery Programme

(ERP) or 'Marshall Plan'), European integration in its early phase took the form of legal documents negotiated as the 1951 Treaty of Paris, establishing the Coal and Steel Community (ECSC), and the 1957 Treaty of Rome, creating the European Economic Community (EEC). Yet, at the time, not all major integration projects were successful. Most importantly, from the angle of subsidiarity, the drive towards the European Political Community and the European Defence Community (EDC) was stopped by respective votes in the French national assembly. An unusual coalition of right-leaning Gaullists concerned about national sovereignty and left-leaning Communists with pro-Russian sentiment presented an insurmountable hurdle in the domestic ratification process.

With the United Kingdom (UK) joining the EEC in 1973 and the end of the Cold War in 1989, the scene was set for further integration steps and a real power transfer to EU institutions. The signing of the Treaty on European Union (the 1992 Maastricht Treaty) marked a new window of opportunity for accelerated integration, kept open by the subsidiarity principle, now explicitly stated in the legal text. Through successive treaty reforms, EU enlargement to Central and East European states could go hand in hand with the deepening of political integration. The latter necessarily included provisions for the future development of the CFSP. Nevertheless, more than two decades later, the results of the efforts to develop a genuine European foreign policy must be considered disappointing.

European foreign policy after the Cold War

Formal subsidiarity mechanisms do not matter in the CFSP. This is a direct legacy of the failed EDC which instead gave rise to the North Atlantic Treaty Organisation (NATO) as the major instrument of transatlantic military cooperation. Moreover, the Hague Summit in 1969 could only agree on an intergovernmental version of European Political Cooperation (EPC). The coordination of foreign policy measures among individual member states was preferred to any real transfer of competence, and, thus, sovereignty.

This situation did not change with the Single European Act (SEA) of 1986, despite linking up supranational EC elements with the intergovernmental EPC in one unified document (Allen 2012, 643). Later, the Maastricht Treaty introduced a three-pillar structure. The first Community pillar covered mainly economic, social and environmental policies and limited aspects of foreign policy, such as development cooperation and humanitarian aid, while the entire second pillar was dedicated to the CFSP. Most importantly (as was the case with a third pillar on Justice and Home Affairs), the latter had to follow intergovernmental decision-making procedures based on the principle of unanimity.

At best, with the CFSP informal subsidiarity concerns did enter through the backdoor. The 1997 Amsterdam Treaty created the post of a 'High Representative' (HR) and facilitated two years later the appointment of Javier Solana, a former NATO Secretary General. Over the next decade he managed to refocus CFSP in the new format of the ESDP. His suggested policy reforms did also touch on the emerging EU-NATO relationship, even if most member states (except the five neutral states of Austria, Finland, Ireland, Malta and Sweden) still saw the Atlantic alliance as the primary source of military security.

In 2009, with the entry into force of the Lisbon Treaty, ESDP was changed to CSDP, replacing the general term 'European' with the more specific 'common'. Thus, alluding to the fact that security and defense matters might, as other policy areas discussed in this volume, justify a centralised EU competence. What is more, the CSDP entailed a strengthening of the role of the HR, who now acted simultaneously for the EU Foreign Affairs Council and the European Commission as one of its Vice-Presidents. More recently, joint EU-NATO summits also reconfirmed the desire for a better task division between the executive arms of the two organisations. There is no questioning of the fact that this type of structured cooperation 'constitutes an integral pillar of the EU's work aimed at strengthening European security and defence' and that 'a stronger EU and a stronger NATO are mutually reinforcing' (EEAS 2017).

To detect subsidiarity concerns in the EU efforts towards a common foreign policy, one needs to distinguish smoke and mirrors from what is substantially important. The frequent renaming of policy initiatives and the creation of new narratives is not helpful, as indicated by the current shift from CSDP to PESCO. As it stands, the HR continues to represent the original CFSP with action capacity very much dependent on a unanimous vote in the Council. Article 18 (2) TEU notes that the 'High Representative shall conduct the Union's common foreign and security policy', while Articles 21 to 46 TEU outline the institutions and practices of the CSDP (but only Article 42 (6) and Article 46 TEU mention PESCO explicitly). Therefore, the CFSP continues to be an overarching paradigm, whereas the CSDP constitutes the actual effort that puts forward EU policy instruments. Accordingly, in the formulation of Article 42 (1) TEU, CSDP is 'an integral part of the CFSP' (EEAS 2016).

From the subsidiarity angle, PESCO can be interpreted as a specific format of CSDP in which member states make contractual commitments to participate in a set of narrowly defined, joint projects. Indeed, PESCO is a subsidiary activity compared to the more general member state engagement through NATO membership or CFSP participation. In this context, it is noteworthy that

Denmark and Malta have opted out of PESCO, while the remaining 26 EU member states have joined at least one of the ongoing 47 projects. By allowing for a high degree of flexibility, the intention is to 'reinforce the EU's strategic autonomy to act alone when necessary and with partners whenever possible' (EEAS 2018, 5).

It is too early to tell whether subsidiarity thinking together with bureaucratic organisational change will gradually narrow the expectations-capability gap in European foreign affairs. The experiences made with the European External Action Service (EEAS) give no reason for optimism. Among other things, the idea of an EU Minister for Foreign Affairs had been rejected by the Dutch and French referenda on the Constitutional Treaty, but in 2011 still paved the way for the EU diplomatic service with around 5000 employees. While the limited reforms of the Lisbon Treaty fell back on the term 'High Representative', they could not prevent ongoing turf battles between national foreign offices and the emerging EEAS. Crucially, the institutional ambiguity of the EU's top foreign policy role has not been resolved. In the words of Fabbrini (2015, 42):

> The Lisbon Treaty left unanswered the question of whether the HR should be a policy entrepreneur promoting a common foreign policy position, thus reframing the interests of the member states in a more integrated perspective, or a mere policy coordinator of the Ministers of Foreign Affairs who make up the Council. The institutional solution has not resolved the puzzle of who speaks on behalf of the Union in international relations, given also the important role that the President of the European Council, the President of the Commission and the Trade Commissioner are allowed or expected to play in the external relations of the Union.

In fact, if one opts for more personalised versions of subsidiarity, a further complication arises from subsequent HR appointments (Catherine Ashton, Federica Mogherini, Josep Borrell) and their relative political standing in comparison to Javier Solana. More importantly, intergovernmentalism, defined as the autonomy of the more powerful member states to frame their own policies, remains in place. National foreign policy actions can go ahead despite a lack of agreement at EU level. Therefore, the conceptual problems of consistency and coherence, addressed by formal subsidiarity in other policy areas, continue in the context of European foreign policy (Edwards 2011, 47–8). Strictly speaking, member states have maintained their responsibility to formulate and conduct a national foreign policy excluding any far-reaching EU ambition to accommodate 28 different geopolitical positions for the sake of global governance (Allen 2012, 650–4).

Subsidiarity and theories of international relations

As has been highlighted in chapter one, subsidiarity refers to the positive interaction between two institutions with one being able to support the other in cases of need. The roots of the concept in Catholic thought suggest an appropriate division of labour between individual households and state agencies. More specifically, higher level authorities should recognise the autonomy of lower-level entities and only take on tasks that cannot be delivered at the subsidiary level. As has been pointed out before, the idea of subsidiarity has been recognised in formal EU treaties and features prominently in the analysis of multi-level governance as well as that of federal political systems. Such densely institutionalised frameworks show a tendency to favour *downward subsidiarity* whereby political power is exercised at the lowest possible level that is able to fulfil a certain political purpose. Yet, if lower units of political authority cannot deliver desirable outcomes, there is a need for *upward subsidiarity.* In other words, there is no categorical rejection of centralisation, and the relocation of power can be a legitimate act depending on circumstances. Consequently, subsidiarity remains a contested concept when exploring the normative and functional reasons to justify the allocation of political authority.

In the internal dimension of the CFSP and the external EU-NATO relationship, the subsidiarity concept can be applied in various downward and upward directions. Yet, the intergovernmental nature of European foreign policy remains firmly in place. The Lisbon Treaty in Article 24 (1) TFEU demands unanimity in the field of the CFSP, 'except where the Treaties provide otherwise'. The potential use of qualified majority voting on foreign policy issues is further constrained by Article 31 (2) TFEU, in so far as it gives member states a veto 'for vital and stated reasons of national policy'.

Firstly, in terms of upwards subsidiarity, European defence could be deferred to NATO, accepting the primacy of the latter, while certain NATO tasks might still be devolved to individual member states voluntarily offering a set of supplementary activities. The European Parliament, for example, claims that CSDP concerns the ability to 'handle crisis outside the Union where the US does not want to intervene', further suggesting a task division between CSDP's 'soft defence outside European territory' and NATO's 'hard defence within European territory' (DG for External Policies 2017, 10-6). If pushed to the extreme, this could imply 'to merge CSDP into NATO, to take over, step by step, command of the major agencies in NATO, and to allow the US to focus on the areas of the world that are of the most strategic importance to Washington' (DG for External Policies 2017, 32).

Secondly, in terms of downward subsidiarity, PESCO includes EU member states voluntarily agreeing to participate in several of its 47 shared defence projects. It is seen as a new way to achieve 'strategic autonomy' on part of the Union by filling its capability gaps with the help of quantitative spending targets. Yet, only a few of the projects appear of political significance and are viable without participation of the 'four frontrunners' France, Germany, Italy and Spain (Blockmans and Macchiarini Crosson 2019, 23). In the first PESCO wave, cooperative efforts concentrated on 'military mobility', 'logistics hubs' and 'training mission competence centres' attracting 24, 13 and 13 countries, respectively (Council of the EU 2018). Against this background, strategic autonomy might be a misnomer for what has been described as a form of differentiated integration. Moreover, critics may interpret these activities as an effort to drive EU militarisation further. The frequent complaints about Germany's lack of readiness 'to commit to tough military operations' supports this line of reasoning (DG for External Policies 2017, 24).

Beyond these two examples, subsidiarity has also been invoked with reference to global governance arrangements. The United Nations (UN), as the international organisation tasked with conflict resolution, can delegate responsibility for peace-keeping missions to regional organisations drawing on their capabilities to add to its own effectiveness (Peou 1998, 440). Accordingly, Article 42 (1) TFEU mentions the 'principles of the United Nations Charter' and outlines in Article 43 potential EU tasks within this framework.

Setting formal preconditions aside, the question remains how the EU should organise its own foreign policy activities to achieve institutional coordination across multiple levels of governance. In the post-Lisbon constellation, the terminology of 'subsidiarity' and 'coherence' has often been used with similar intentions – to counteract the fragmented and divided setup of EU external relations. This broadly defined policy area is full of challenges as it includes exclusive (common commercial policy) and shared competences (area of freedom, security and justice) as well as *sui generis* powers (CFSP) and parallel responsibilities (development cooperation and humanitarian aid). One of the resulting ambiguities has been captured by Hertog and Stroß (2013, 383–4):

> In the areas of development cooperation and humanitarian aid, the Union shall have competence to carry out activities and conduct a *common policy*; however, the exercise of that competency *shall not result in Member States being prevented* from exercising theirs.

Arguably, a rather unspecified notion of upward and downward subsidiarity serves the interests of the most powerful EU member states well, keeping different CFSP manifestations outside the scope of the community method. The uncoordinated and spontaneous nature of subsidiarity in European foreign policy is a deliberate choice. It follows on from the principles of intergovernmentalism that avoids the jurisdiction of the European Court of Justice and side-lines other supranational institutions.

Liberalism

Setting the version of subsidiarity identified above into the context of IR theory helps to understand the limitations of the general concept. The liberal approach suggests that inter-state tensions under conditions of anarchy can be managed in a peaceful and mutually beneficial manner. Its proponents believe that a more cooperative international system can be built in a step-by-step process based on the construction of international organisations. Relevant actors in this process include states and their governments as well as members of civil society working below and above the state level. Once institutionalised, this process is expected to produce shared norms and values such as subsidiarity that can strengthen cooperation and mutual trust in a virtuous cycle.

However, early liberal efforts to produce a cooperative international system between the two World Wars, especially the League of Nations, failed to live up to proclaimed expectations. This was due to the existence of double standards on the part of supporters of international cooperation. For example, the concept of 'national self-determination' – closely related to the idea of subsidiarity – was advocated by Anglo-American liberals when it suited their own political interests but rejected in all other cases. Thus, US President Woodrow Wilson supported national self-determination in Central and Eastern Europe, yet ignored similar demands by Arab, Indian and Korean nationalists in their part of the world. In short, there was no tendency toward increased cooperation at state or civil society level during the interwar period and in the League of Nations system. In fact, its very foundation in the idea of collective security broke down prior to World War II.

After World War II, liberalism became less influential in international affairs. For example, the UN, as the successor organisation of the League of Nations, was based on a mixed approach. The hierarchy of power – a realist element – was represented by granting the status of permanent membership in its Security Council to victorious powers (China, France, Great Britain, the US, and the Soviet Union). Other states were given representation in the UN General Assembly according to the 'one state-one vote' principle. Crucially, the Security Council is more powerful, since its ten non-permanent members (with short-term access to the five permanent members on a rotating basis) do not enjoy any veto power. It can adopt binding resolutions if at least 9 of 15 votes are provided and no permanent member issues a veto. By contrast, the UN Assembly can only adapt non-binding resolutions and, therefore, is limited to a consultative role.

Since the mid-1980s, neo-liberal theorists have reformed their analysis of international relations. While they maintain the original liberal thesis about the ability of international cooperation to trigger value change in security relations, there is a new starting point. Not too different from realist thinkers, the self-interest of states in cooperative behaviour has the purpose to realise absolute gains as opposed to relative (individual state) gains. The liberal approach stresses that absolute gains are unattainable for individual states, if they focus exclusively on their own short-term interests. However, cooperative behaviour might improve the position of all participating states, especially if cooperation takes place across different issue areas, allowing states to engage in bargaining that compensates losses in one field by gains in others. Indeed, such inter-state bargaining might result in the formation of 'international regimes' through formal international organisations that include formal or informal norms of behaviour (such as subsidiarity) to collectively improve the security and prosperity of member states.

Liberal and neo-liberal approaches aim to explain the upward and downward processes as previously identified in the specific case of the EU. More generally, they expect these to occur in the interaction between the state and civil society. The upward move is the consequence of foreign policy preferences formed via competitive domestic politics, and then used as the decisive terms of reference for a country's foreign policy at the international level (Brummer and Oppermann 2014, 39). At the same time, domestic interest aggregation in favour or against certain foreign policy decisions is only half of the story. There is also the downward move, explained in neo-liberalism by 'asymmetric interdependencies' between states. As in realist accounts, there is a recognition of the fact that states might be influenced in their foreign policy choices by other powerful states.

Realism

In comparison to liberal approaches, realism has a more serious problem with subsidiarity. For its protagonists, states are the main actors in an anarchical international system. There exists no higher authority, such as a world government, or a global governance mechanism in the form of subsidiarity to control the conduct of individual states. Each state must turn to self-help to guarantee its security *vis-à-vis* other states. For example, individual states can strengthen their capabilities by growing the economy and having more money for military expenditure. As state executives conduct their business independent from each other, and sometimes in secrecy, neighbouring states might feel obliged to 'retaliate' by strengthening their own armed forces.

While there is an element of balancing – as in global governance accounts of subsidiarity presented in chapter 13 – here it is a reactive, horizontal effort to perceived threats from competing states. Attempts to address a 'security dilemma', therefore, often lead to local, regional and global arms races (Jervis 1978). The efforts of states to increase their own security result in perceptions of a related loss elsewhere. The relative gains in the security of state A result in the relative loss of security for state B.

An alternative option for states to strengthen their security is to engage in inter-state bargaining to form alliances against perceived threats. The international system might be characterised by unilateralism (an individual hegemonic state), bilateralism (competition between two main powers), or multilateralism (three or more powerful states). With weaker states entering formal alliances with a strong state, or quietly following the demands of a hegemon, their behaviour might resemble subsidiary arrangements in the international system. For realists, however, 'bandwagoning' would be a much more appropriate strategic term.

Again, if weaker states aim to build counter-alliances against a hegemonic power, they might engage in 'external balancing' by forming new alliances to strengthen their relative position in the international system. In practice, then, weaker states might advance a combination of internal balancing (the mobilisation of a larger share of domestic resources for security purposes) and external balancing (the forming of inter-state alliances against a hegemon). Even if such arrangements are codified in international law, the dominant anarchy of the international system implies that no state can have absolute confidence in the long-term stability of formal commitments.

Under conditions of bi- or multipolarity, some realists also identify balancing efforts. Any unilateral aggressive action will trigger countermoves on behalf of other great powers. The recovery of Russia as a major power, the rise of China, and the formation of alliances without the US – the Shanghai Cooperation Organisation (SCO) – indeed point to the re-emergence of multipolarity. Conversely, if US unilateralism prevails, the superpower 'will be tempted to impose its will on the world through ambitious wars and interventions' (Adams 2013, 42-3). Most importantly, all versions of realism remain highly sceptical of the role of international and regional organisations as well as that of non-state actors. Soft mechanisms such as subsidiarity are unlikely to constrain the behaviour of states and to impose limits on the role of anarchy in IR.

IR theories and the EU

Most EU scholars have advanced theories that combine liberal and realist arguments. At the liberal end, neo-functionalism suggests that increasing complexity and interdependence of advanced industrial societies enforces delegation of regulatory authority to supranational institutions. International organisations are empowered to exercise authority beyond the nation state. This argument, initially advanced in the early post-war period for the case of the European Coal and Steel Community (ECSC), suggested that the logic of delegation to supranational bodies would gradually 'spill over' from one field of policy making to another. Thus, the upward move of authority over a sector of the economy vital for the ability of states to fight war would not be an endpoint. Instead, it sets in motion a logic of shifting loyalty towards neutral policy experts, holding superior knowledge on specific issues, and less exposed to the constraints of bargaining at the domestic level (Haas 1958).

At the realist end, liberal intergovernmentalism argues that nation states will pursue their own interests and delegate authority to supranational bodies only after extensive inter-state bargaining. Major states and their most powerful domestic constituencies are the principal actors, ultimately driving state behaviour. Rather than small states and weak constituencies, they determine the content and substance of history-making decisions and, subsequently, the outcomes of integration policy (Moravcsik 1998). The member states continue to be the ultimate power holders. The delegation of EU authority, for example via subsidiarity mechanisms, is not seen as a factual one-way street as in neo-functionalist accounts. If powerful domestic actors located in strong member states desire to do so, respective competences could be withdrawn through treaty reform.

Finally, a variation of this argument can be advanced by arguing that inter-state bargaining at the level of the EU was facilitated by the persistence of external threats. The Soviet Union during the Cold War or the US as the global hegemon strongly encouraged the internal re-balancing efforts in Western Europe. Accordingly, once these external constraints are gone, realists might expect a crumbling of EU institutional structures. Liberals, by contrast, trust in the resilience and persistence of norms given their central role in the integration process over time. Liberals, for example, might interpret codified subsidiarity mechanisms as evidence for mutual learning, allowing EU institutions to survive under new circumstances of multipolarity.

The realities of EU foreign policy

In sum, the IR-inspired debate of subsidiarity highlights certain features of the EU's track record in foreign policy. Its underlying assumptions fit many aspects of the CFSP, CSDP and PESCO; especially, when different levels of EU policy making interact with the external institutional environment of NATO or the UN. There is also a clear potential of extension to other regional organisations, such as the Organisation for Security and Cooperation in Europe (OSCE) and the African Union (AU). In all these cases, the required international sharing of capabilities raises immediate questions about the internal organisation of cooperation and the distribution of competences among EU member states.

At the same time, the UN suffers from a lack of authority in various dimensions of international security too. Formally, the EU has accepted UN jurisdiction, but still cannot prevent member states from acting alone or taking advantage of unclear UN resolutions (as in the case of Libya) (Ganser 2017). There are, therefore, instances where regional actors are a stumbling block to an emerging global security system. While the subsidiarity perspective allows useful case-by-case observations on the EU's foreign policy role, it must accept the limitations imposed by the nature of the international system and the behavioural constraints of states elaborated in the two standard IR theories.

The realist approach, for example, explains the sporadic and fragmented use of subsidiarity mechanisms in European foreign affairs after the Cold War. Historically, the most powerful member states – France, Germany, and the UK (as well as the aspiring powers of Italy, Poland, and Spain) – have made quite different geopolitical investments, and their individual interest calculations stand firmly in the way of common EU agency. Arguably, EU countries share wider security concerns for the European continent, but abstract joint interests have not translated into consistent and coherent foreign policies. Rather, member states continue to compete in fields such as intelligence, military procurement and external relations and, frequently, choose to work against each other. From a realist point of view, the balancing idea explains the persistence of intergovernmentalism and inter-state bargaining in the long run. Similarly, further steps towards institutionalisation – the office of the HR and the EEAS – are met with deep scepticism. Their action capacity can always be traced back to the policy positions taken by the most powerful member states.

The liberal approach, by contrast, appreciates EU joint efforts in the area of foreign policy. At the European level, common institutions and their policy deliberations help to socialise foreign policy actors to accept formal or informal subsidiarity norms, ultimately paving the way for better policy making. In fact, smaller member states might favour procedural solutions to gain some input into EU foreign policy, thus addressing their specific dilemma in international politics. In addition, the creation of a common regime allows – on the output side – the sharing of absolute gains among all participants rather than mere relative gains that derive from inter-state competition.

Take, in this context, the classic liberal promise to achieve a more effective (or *better*) use of national resources through joint military spending. All member states would benefit from the sharing of military technology, instead of focussing exclusively on national capabilities and inter-state competition. Unfortunately, this argument ignores the theoretical ambiguity of subsidiarity and the factual persistence of networks of mutual obligation between arms producers and national policy makers. Weapons procurement and expenditure is notoriously difficult to control and moving such a system upwards to the EU level could potentially make things worse (or *less effective*). Indeed, such a result will be just as likely, if the mere duplication of traditional network structures occurs. Most certainly, member states with an already developed military-industrial complex are hesitant to share freely their knowledge and expertise, acutely aware of their domestic tax expenditures. Eventually, the aura of common policies and the appeal of subsidiarity mechanisms might overcome the resistance of national publics, vindicate higher military spending, and facilitate military sales to non-EU states. Then, however, liberal good intentions would have resulted in rather 'realist' outcomes.

Conclusion

This chapter identified a significant disconnect between the EU's proclaimed foreign policy aspiration as manifested in diverse institutional arrangements and the actual behaviour of key member states. The cases of Libya, Iraq and Syria show the consequences of traditional power politics in Europe closely aligned with US foreign policy and embedded in transatlantic networks rather than joint EU efforts. As security and stability within EU borders and surrounding regions has also declined, the detrimental external roles of France and the UK have been widely criticised. In fact, in an act of practical subsidiarity, the UK House of Commons was able to refuse a direct military intervention in Syria due to high levels of domestic civil society mobilisation. Yet, further self-criticism in this matter from Brussels has been noted only by its absence. This episode fits the general assessment of subsidiarity advanced here as a sporadic and fragmented mechanism severely constrained by the workings of the international system.

The latter constitutes a worrying challenge to the EU's geopolitical future afflicted by the contested nature of US relations with rising powers such as Russia and China. Under conditions of increasing multipolarity, the various guises of EU foreign policy revert to another format of state power. The subsidiarity mechanisms identified in this chapter are neither consistently applied nor widespread enough to fulfil the liberal hope of Europe speaking with one voice. If member states continue to pursue different aims in ever more complex institutional arrangements, the EU's promise to offer protection in a world of rising insecurity might be misleading. Thus, given the realities of subsidiarity in European foreign affairs, low expectations are least likely to generate disappointment.

References

Adams, K. R. (2013). 'Structural Realism: The Imperialism of Great Power'. In Sterling-Folker, J. (ed.) *Making Sense of International Relations Theory*, 2nd edition, 21–46. Boulder, CO: Lynne Rienner.

Allen, D. (2012). 'The Common Foreign and Security Policy'. In Jones, E., Menon, A. and S. Weatherhill (eds) *The Oxford Handbook of the European Union*, 643–58. Oxford: Oxford University Press.

Blockmans, S. and D. Macchiarini Crosson (2019). 'Differentiated Integration within PESCO – Clusters and Convergence in EU Defence'. *CEPS Research Report* 2019/04, December.

Brummer, K. and K. Oppermann (2014). *Außenpolitikanalyse*. Munich: Oldenbourg Verlag.

Council of the European Union (2018). 'Council Decision of 6 March 2018 establishing the List of Projects to be developed under PESCO'. Available at: http://www.consilium.europa.eu/media/33065/st06393-en18-council-decision-pesco_press.pdf

Directorate General (DG) for External Policies (2017). 'Permanent Structured Cooperation: National Perspectives and State of Play'. Available at: http://www.europarl.europa.eu/RegData/etudes/STUD/2017/603842/EXPO_STU(2017)603842_EN.pdf

Edwards, G. (2011). 'The Pattern of the EU's Global Activity'. In Hill, C. and M. Smith (eds) *International Relations and the European Union*, 2nd edition, 44-72. Oxford: Oxford University Press.

European External Action Service (EEAS) (2016). 'Military and Civilian Missions and Operations', 3 May. Available at: https://eeas.europa.eu/ headquarters/headquarters-homepage_en/430/Military%20and%20 civilian%20missions%20and%20operations

European External Action Service (EEAS)(2017). 'EU-NATO Cooperation Factsheet', 18 October. Available at: https://eeas.europa.eu/sites/eeas/files/ eu-nato_cooperation_factsheet_18-10-2017_0.pdf

European External Action Service (EEAS)(2018). 'Permanent Structured Cooperation (PESCO) – Factsheet', 28 June. Available at: https://eeas. europa.eu/sites/eeas/files/pesco_factsheet_2018-09-29.pdf

Fabbrini, S. (2015). *Which European Union? Europe After the Euro-Crisis.* Cambridge: Cambridge University Press.

Gammelin, C. and R. Löw (2014). *Europas Drahtzieher: Wer in Brüssel wirklich regiert.* Berlin: Econ.

Ganser, D. (2017). *Illegale Kriege. Wie die NATO-Länder die UNO sabotieren. Eine Chronik von Kuba bis Syrien.* Zürich: Orell Füssli.

Haas, E. B. (1958). *The Uniting of Europe: Political, Social and Economic Forces, 1950–1957.* Stanford, CA: Stanford University Press.

Hertog, L. den and S. Stroß (2013). 'Coherence in EU External Relations: Concepts and Legal Rooting of an Ambiguous Term'. *European Foreign Affairs Review* 18(3): 373–88.

Jervis, R.A. (1978). 'Cooperation under the Security Dilemma', *World Politics* 30(2): 167–214.

Moravcsik, A. (1998). *The Choice for Europe: Social Purpose and State Power from Messina to Maastricht.* Ithaca, NY: Cornell University Press.

Peou, S. (1998). 'The Subsidiarity Model of Global Governance in the UN-ASEAN Context'. *Global Governance* 4(4): 439–59.

13

Subsidiarity: A Principle for Global Trade Governance?

GÜNTER WALZENBACH

One day, evolution in governance might lead to a world state with the ability to develop globally binding norms and rules. Then a world government would stand above individual countries and make the most of an irrevocable transfer of sovereignty. Yet, this power transfer would be partial, if this world republic is organised along federal lines with considerable autonomy remaining in the hands of constituent units of formerly independent nation states. In fact, global governance as a vertical system operating at multiple levels entices large groups of political actors to demand subsidiarity as a tool that effectively constrains the exercise of global authority. In the case of the World Trade Organisation (WTO) and its economic liberalisation policy, for example, this process is already under way and has progressed further than in some other issue areas discussed in this volume. What started out as gradual tariff reduction and the phasing out of import quotas, now targets differences in national health and safety standards as well as social and environmental regulation. As a result, a general preference for domestic or regional decision-making in trade policy is much harder to construct, and the subsidiarity principle has become more than a convenient default rule for global governance or a synonym for decentralisation.

The increasing recognition of subsidiarity in global affairs exercises an important balancing function that acts as a stepping-stone towards further codification. Traditionally, the benefits of trade liberalisation as measured in economic growth rates have consistently offered the 'good reasons' for shifting decision-making upwards, but the neglect of social costs and societal contestation asks for a more considered evaluation (Jachtenfuchs and Krisch 2016, 6). In other words, the same rules, norms and regulations have considerably different costs, benefits and social implications across countries due to diverse conditions and preferences, and this provides some stimulus for non-standardisation. It is in this light that this chapter depicts subsidiarity as a medium- to long-term policy mechanism that serves as a balancing tool in an emerging global system of multi-level governance. In short, it is more than a mere decision-making criterion with prime impact for a scaling down of governance arrangements. International economic organisations and institutions of global economic governance are the prime location for an assessment of this hypothesis. More specifically, highly technical, at times log-jammed and circular arrangements of global trade governance form an ideal testing ground for some of its more far-reaching promises in terms of political legitimacy. The mechanisms analysed in three case studies of EU-WTO interaction below may appear sporadic and overly selective, but in the current stage of global economic governance they put subsidiarity into practice as the only viable option to settle conflicts between the preferences of domestic political communities and the wider demands of the global market system.

Subsidiarity and global governance

At the global level, subsidiarity is a principle that gives guidance to reform processes across governance arrangements (Lamy 2012). Quasi-federal mechanisms achieve policy effectiveness by allocating competences to the lowest possible level of authority and by recognising relevant costs and benefits. This ordering activity is applicable to a range of international forms of authority, including international institutions, international organisations, and international courts. Regardless of their specific remit, they recognise and respect degrees of self-governance at various levels and do so in diverse issue areas.

Within such a global system of multi-level governance, the European Union (EU) takes on a special position as it is a federal system in the making with fragmented constitutional foundations. In contrast to global ambitions, here the high degree of institutionalisation documented in this volume appears 'ripe for the kind of federal legislative self-discipline that subsidiarity implies' (Berman 1994, 455). Yet, the practical implementation of subsidiarity remains challenging and contested at all levels. This follows, for example, from the need to accommodate diverse preferences and interest constellations in the multi-actor setting of international negotiations; or, the constant interplay of subsidiarity concerns with other issue areas of international relations asking for sustainable compromises to resolve trade-offs of an essentially political character.

As the contributions to this volume show, subsidiarity can be a very useful tool to structure the political process across several levels of EU decision-making. While it promises to keep government power and action as closely as possible to citizens, it also takes questions of resource limitations and practicality seriously. For this reason, there is no single answer where to find the 'lowest possible level – closest to the individuals and groups affected by the rules and decisions adopted and enforced' (Slaughter 2004, 30). For subsidiarity to become a more established part of global governance, its dynamic character must be recognised. Gradually, as with other principles of international law, a growing number of international organisations become the hub for the implementation of governance mechanisms as a result of extended cooperation among diverse state and non-state actors.

Most of the time, the burden of proof for whether a scaling-up of power to the global level makes sense rests with representatives of national governments, their ministers and top civil servants. It is up to their judgement when and how specific policy functions require additional institutionalisation, also beyond the EU. Once successful, though, international and supranational organisations themselves need to provide evidence that new governance arrangements and power allocations produce complementary or superior results to traditional forms of inter-state cooperation. In no small measure, therefore, implementation of subsidiarity depends on its skilful application by highly qualified people at adequate levels of governance following fair procedures and general rules of appropriateness (Howse and Nicholaidis 2016).

The management of the global trading system involves a complex set of actors: technocratic insiders of bureaucratic networks with high levels of expertise in economic liberalisation; lawyers and judges with the task of adjudicating and implementing transnational rules; and elected politicians ensuring the accountability of international bargains. Civil society actors enter the equation too, especially when respective reform agendas imply fundamental changes in the allocation of authority. In this constellation, subsidiarity acquires an important discursive, consensus-building quality that helps to moderate 'the balance of authority and legitimacy between different levels of governance' (Broude 2016, 56).

Trade facilitation

The first case study refers to a WTO working group originally set up during the organisation's 1996 ministerial conference in Singapore. It was the joint EU effort that ultimately opened the way for a recognition of subsidiarity considerations in international trade policy as regards customs arrangements. Despite longstanding disagreements between developed and developing countries, and in contrast to other technical 'Singapore issues' – such as investment, government procurement and competition policy – the EU succeeded to keep trade facilitation in an elevated position on the Doha development agenda. Then, step-by-step, the important reform item of customs and border procedures was addressed with the constant support of the international business community and an unusual alliance among developing countries. In addition to the transaction cost argument in trade relations, the EU position specifically emphasised the need for global regulations to be compatible with the norms of the single market (Woolcock 2012, 79).

Once organised properly, the co-ordination of national, regional, and global trade facilitation initiatives can create welfare gains for all participants. The subsidiarity principle here suggests to formally identify the extent of cross-border spill-overs of trade measures by individual countries and to adjust the administrative management of the exchange of goods to the same level at which most of the trade volume occurs. Complex transit arrangements and border checks for the exchange of goods and products between world regions are a case in point. These involve significant transnational effects whenever a trade relationship is built around international shipping routes or long-distance follow-on transport. Then region-wide arrangements become vital to realise the benefits of free trade as a national regulatory approach would strongly disadvantage and discriminate landlocked countries (Maur and Shepherd 2017). In this scenario, trade facilitation measures work best when upscaled and managed at macro-regional level.

In fact, the WTO trade facilitation agreement concluded at its ninth ministerial conference in 2013, and coming into force four years later, marked an important step in the practical implementation of the subsidiarity principle. It indicates a breakthrough for multilateral negotiations that in many other issue areas of the global trading system has not been forthcoming. In procedural terms, preference was given to a decentralised, bottom-up approach explicitly recognising the resource and capacity limitations of many developing countries. In term of substance the new agreement entailed an element of refocusing on the 'hardware issues' of international trade where a lack of adequate infrastructure is regularly causing frictions and delays in economic exchanges across borders (Neufeld 2014, 3).

Negotiators faced the dilemma to find a common framework, while at the same time giving special and preferential treatment to developing and least-developed countries noting a potential North-South stand-off. Previous WTO deals had merely granted transition periods for certain groups of countries and created long delays before actual policy change was put into practice. The trade facilitation agreement, however, broke new ground. Although country-specific reforms and time-lags are an aspect of the regime, it contains a new, comprehensive 'flexibilities package' that establishes a crucial link between the commitment to trade facilitation and the actual implementation capacity on the ground. More precisely, if the necessary financial and logistical support for anticipated infrastructure projects at national border crossings is not made available, the involved developing country is under no formal obligation to honour relevant parts of WTO agreements on trade liberalisation.

In this way, subsidiarity concerns establish a workable mechanism that ensures consultation and transparency between two different sets of regime actors operating at domestic and international level. The available implementation capacity, and therefore the practical feasibility of the principle, is assessed on a country-by-country and measure-by-measure basis. In other words, the traditional one-size-fits-all approach of global trade agreements is given up. The trade facilitation model terminates an increasing number of general exceptions for developing countries and favours a tailor-made approach paying tribute to the development needs of individual countries.

Importantly, the deliberations around this governance arrangement were embedded in a subsidiarity discourse reflecting long-standing demands from least developed countries. Previously, their ambition to have more policy space through the ownership of economic reform efforts failed by signing up to international commitments they were unable to fulfil. Paragraph two of the trade facilitation agreement now explicitly states that its members 'would not be obliged to undertake investments in infrastructure projects beyond their means'. It continues by clarifying the remit for least developed countries in so far as these 'will only be required to undertake commitments to the extent consistent with their individual development, financial and trade needs or their administrative and institutional capabilities'.

This wording is indicative of the changing narrative surrounding the subsidiarity-inspired components of the WTO trade facilitation agreement. Initially, its conceptual bearings were formulated by country groupings of the developing world in the negative sense of policy exemptions from general obligations. Yet, learning from past experiences, multilateral negotiations over the last decade finally succeeded in search for positive mechanisms that simultaneously strengthen implementation capacity, make room for issue-specific trade facilitation and respect for individual country needs.

Inter-regional trade agreements

For many, given the institutional gridlock in the WTO, major inter-regional deals appeared as a more promising alternative to generate global economic growth. In this second case of the analysis of applied subsidiarity, trade negotiations between the EU and the United States entailed stronger engagement with members of parliament, non-governmental organisations, trade unions, and business groups. However, apparent shortcomings, such as selective access of civil society actors and numerous veto points at different stages of the negotiation cycle, undermined the search for a workable solution. Ultimately, changes in trade-offs during the bargaining process and the changing position of a variety of domestic actors led to the failure of the intended mega-deal between two major players in the global trading system.

Thus, subsidiarity raises specific questions about overlapping jurisdictions and the appropriate level of civil society activism in inter-regional negotiations. On the one hand, consultation processes add value through the maintenance of escape clauses and clarification of exceptions in controversial areas of international trade. On the other hand, legitimacy and efficiency gains through public debate and improved compliance also require a clear focus and location of parliamentary and public deliberation within a multi-level system. Despite an intended compatibility of inter-regional with global arrangements, the WTO only reluctantly accepted legal mechanisms negotiated among sub-groupings of its membership to enhance its own legitimacy base.

Indeed, legitimacy considerations ranked high in the negotiation phase of inter-regional trade regimes. In the prominent example of the Transatlantic Trade and Investment Partnership (TTIP), the envisaged liberalisation drive generated unprecedented levels of mobilisation by civil society organisations operating either locally, nationally or regionally in the extended EU setting. Yet, a consensus on the substance of regulatory convergence across the Atlantic was mainly found in the business community and less so among other civil society actors. The latter could not rally under a unifying banner comparable to the structural imperatives of global value chains and capital investments.

In the EU, setting the TTIP agenda inspired domestic politics as it invigorated societal activism in sectors such as public health and local government; previously untouched by free trade agreements and related negotiations. Consumer organisations and trade unions with a long-term interest in agenda-shaping intensified their engagement and provided critical assessments during the negotiation process. In short, 'the breadth and depth of TTIP's ambition has raised the stakes for civic interest groups beyond those narrowly opposed to globalization' (Young 2016, 364). Two features of the proposed transatlantic regime explain best unprecedented levels of mobilisation and lasting tensions due to subsidiarity concerns: enhanced regulatory cooperation and global lock-in of investment arbitration.

Subsidiarity in trade relations has appeal because it comes with procedural safeguards to protect societal preferences, but the de- and re-regulatory content of TTIP sparked worries about a further dis-embedding of European market economies. In the health care sector, for example, cost escalation would offer opportunities for US American service providers to crowd out traditional public sector agencies (Inman 2016, 36). More generally, a finalised TTIP deal would challenge the European policy mix between the state and the market, upsetting a careful balance in vital areas of social security. Similarly, opponents doubted the alleged benefits from regulatory cooperation at the transatlantic level: how, if at all, could the equivalence of EU and US standards be ensured without further guarantees for shared authority to deliver high levels of consumer protection? Neither party to the negotiations found previous experiences with scandals in the processed food market or the handling of genetically modified organisms particularly reassuring.

Furthermore, TTIP's investment arbitration system would shift authority away from the state by giving foreign investors the right to initiate proceedings against government actors if public policy measures harm their revenue expectation. As respective court tribunals and arbitration panels depend on a small circle of highly trained lawyers, the risk of organisational capture is particularly high. Due to resource limitations, the same type of expertise would simply move between public and corporate clients.

With the failure of TTIP negotiations, many grey areas in operational aspects of the proposed partnership remain. Whenever substantive issues suggest a formal deference to national decision-makers, subsidiarity considerations rank high. Comparative analysis, for example, can show that existing investment treaties at bilateral level have already in place a more elaborate investor-state dispute settlement mechanism than proposed in TTIP (Von Staden 2012, 1047). Interestingly, in times of economic crisis, these reserve the right to initiate rescue efforts to national governments regardless of any detrimental effects for international business. After all, it appears reasonable to prioritise the restoration of public order (or peace and security) over the profit motive, and to do so by relying on democratic procedure and public accountability.

Ironically, the ultimate failure of viable subsidiarity mechanisms in TTIP had more to do with the influence of representative bodies controlling government than irreconcilable differences in specific issue areas. In the US, a final deal requires a congressional-executive agreement and as such could only come into effect after approval by both houses of Congress. In the EU, the Commission decision to designate TTIP as a mixed agreement triggered the need for ratification by national legislatures, in addition to endorsement by the EU Council and the European Parliament. Eventually, the large number of policy objectives set by government against numerous veto-players determined an overall negative outcome. The task to assess correctly the overlap between parliamentary and governmental majorities at different levels of decision-making proved to be an insurmountable obstacle (Jančić 2017, 216). Ultimately, it was not possible to replicate the relative success of the EU-Canada Economic and Trade Agreement (CETA) originally meant as a blueprint for more advanced forms of global trade governance. In the case of the latter, competing subsidiarity claims on both sides of the Atlantic were settled by accepting significant compromises in international regulatory cooperation.

WTO dispute resolution

Despite its mixed record, much of the subsidiarity debate in the WTO has focused on the Dispute Settlement Mechanism (DSM). Sophisticated pro-cedural arrangements, including arbitration panels and an appellate body, protect extensive jurisdiction to assess national and European trade policies. The third case study of a subsidiarity mechanism underlines the legitimacy of government discretion for the sake of human health, food safety, environ-mental protection and animal welfare.

Traditionally, critics of the DSM have challenged its judgements highlighting structural deficiencies due to the disproportionate influence of a small group of powerful Western states. With new and emerging trading states in the global system, WTO members still rely on a community of private trade lawyers to manage their conflicts. Accordingly, internal reform attempts have focused on procedural modifications while maintaining stability and predictability as a major organisational goal. Therefore, the high level of transparency achieved through the DSM allows to shed some further light on the balancing effect of subsidiarity. Three prominent examples of EU encounters with the WTO mechanism confirm the important, yet time-consuming, aspect of arbitration in trade policy. The evidence presented below clearly rejects any quick fix assumption in the application of the subsidiarity principle.

As early as 1998, it became obvious that time is a crucial factor in decision-making. Controversially, a WTO panel concluded that an EU import ban on hormone treated beef was based on inadequate risk assessments (WTO 2009). And although the EU Commission sought to provide better justifi-cations, it was unable to do so within a reasonable period, allowing the US and Canada to impose retaliatory sanctions. Until 2003, a Brussels Directive still upheld trade restrictions for specific growth hormones stressing that more comprehensive scientific evidence on their health risks was not available. The US and Canada remained unconvinced while DSM proceedings continued without conclusive decisions. Only in 2009, the US (and two years later Canada) finally arrived at a bilateral compromise with EU authorities dropping the sanctions regime in return for enhanced market access of hormone-free meat.

In a similar way, it took France three years to defend an import ban on asbestos and other products containing the harmful substance. Eventually, a WTO panel agreed that the decision of the French government aimed to protect human life and health, and that 'no reasonable available alternative measure' did exist (WTO 2001). It was within its power to do so as the ban neither led to arbitrary or unjustifiable discrimination of importers, nor constituted a disguised restriction on international trade.

More recently, the EU justified an import ban on seal products with moral concerns confronting animal cruelty. It explicitly disapproved of the complicity by consumers who inflict suffering by purchasing products derived from seal hunts. In fact, referring to Article XX (a) of the General Agreement on Tariffs and Trade (GATT), the supranational organisation considered restrictive measures 'necessary to protect public morals' (WTO 2014). Subsequently, only specific aspects of the EU ban were challenged as it allowed for two exceptions to the general prohibition: seal products derived from hunts conducted by indigenous communities and for the purpose of marine resource management could still enter legally the internal market. This market access, however, was only granted in an immediate, unconditional way to exporters from Greenland and withheld from Canadian and Norwegian producers. Accordingly, the WTO found inconsistencies with two of its key working principles on 'most-favoured nation status' and 'national treatment' as laid out in Article I (1) GATT and Article III (4) GATT.

Only in 2015, four years after the initial WTO proceedings, the EU revised internal legislation to comply with the rules of the global trade regime. A modified regulation removed all exceptions that would have accepted seal hunts for resource management purposes. It also amended the exceptions given to the Inuit, an indigenous community inhabiting the Arctic regions of Greenland, Canada and Alaska. The reworked document now ensured that a meaningful exception remains despite the adding of animal welfare considerations. It leaves EU authorities with the power to act in cases of circumvention which may include further prohibitions or limits to the quantity of seal products placed on the market; for example, if hunts are conducted primarily for commercial reasons.

What is more, a follow-up regulation by the EU Commission did add detail to the implementation of the Inuit exception. It required the setting up of an attestation body that ensures compliance with the conditions of the EU seal regime and introduces a certification scheme specifying the type of products that are permitted to enter the EU market. At the time of the WTO ruling, only Greenlandic Inuit (citizens of Denmark, but not the EU) were effectively using the exception for indigenous communities. Subsequently, the Commission continued to engage with third countries and formally recognised the sub-national government of Nunavut (in the northern territories of Canada) as an attestation body for the certification scheme thereby taking subsidiarity in trade matters seriously and spreading the benefits of the seal regime further.

No doubt, for many proponents of global subsidiarity these three examples of compromise in the day-to-day running of the DSM will not go far enough. From a system perspective, other principles than pure subsidiarity concerns frequently rank higher in global trade governance. A complaint system, as operated through the DSM, will always struggle to address macro-considerations of power distribution, economic inequality and sustainability head on. Indeed, the presence of power politics in the form of an EU-US compromise to establish this WTO mechanism in the first place was able to trigger positive policy change in the medium- to long-term.

Re-balancing the global trading system

The three case studies presented above do not provide an exhaustive list of mechanisms helping to avoid gridlock in global trade governance. From the subsidiarity angle, the widely respected consensus requirement of the WTO should not be forgotten. It necessitates an approach to negotiation by which 'nothing is agreed until everything is agreed'. The so-called 'single under-taking' allows the participants to engage in detailed cost-benefit calculations before making any new commitments in terms of issue-linkages or demanding package deals (Hoekman 2014, 557). Yet, not only is this practice slow and time-consuming, it might also lead to stalemate when it is impossible for negotiators to strike a balance between global regulations and national exceptions. The WTO decision-making process in this respect leaves important power resources with national delegates of trade ministries. They form relevant access points at the national level to facilitate policy formation and to address information deficits on part of the general public as regards the intricacies of the global trade agenda.

The EU as a supranational organisation with formal compliance arrangements holds clear advantages when it comes to the operation of global subsidiarity mechanisms. The pattern derived from the case studies shows how the anticipated EU compliance itself became part of a deliberative process within the WTO acting as a significant constraint on the implementation of global trade regulations (Young and Peterson 2014, 146). Internally, of course, WTO compatibility is but one element in a complex and cumbersome policy making process in Brussels; and a crisis-ridden global environment does not make it easier to follow through with the Union's liberal trade policy orientation. Nevertheless, with exclusive competences in place, an open mind towards mixed agreements and the ability to take, if need be, unilateral defensive measures, EU actorness in trade policy was never in question. In the issue areas discussed here, only post-Brexit policy options of the United Kingdom stand in the way of a largely untarnished success story.

For the time being, and closer to the WTO's internal policy cycle, the use of waiver power granted to the Ministerial Conference and the General Council constitutes one of the strongest organisational statements on global subsidiarity. In principle, at least, the suspension from any obligation under its legal framework is possible, if requested by one of its 164 member states. While ultimate approval depends on 'strong collective preferences' and adherence to detailed political procedures, it enables key executive actors to carve out international policy space and to delineate more precisely the division of competences between a global authority and its constituting members (Feichtner 2016, 97).

Will a combination of some – or all – subsidiarity-inspired mechanisms be enough to outweigh opportunity and transaction costs in the reform of the global trading system? Rodrik (2011, 253), for one, demands a more fundamental re-balancing of global governance by advocating a radical overhaul of WTO rules on safeguards. Currently, these allow higher import tariffs whenever domestic firms experience severe competitive pressures from foreign firms. In his view, turning them into a catch-all category for general country opt-outs from liberalisation would be a promising way forward. Thus, an element of choice would be handed back to national governments allowing for a more thorough review of distributional issues, social regulations, labour and environmental standards, or development priorities. Most importantly, an extended safeguard system would have to satisfy the highest standards in line with the democratic credentials of domestic institutionalisation and decision-making.

In sum, the political interpretation of a global subsidiarity principle suggests a stringent conduct of good governance tests – with assessment criteria ranging from evidence-based deliberation to heightened transparency levels, and from executive accountability to civil society inclusiveness – preceding actual implementation. In fact, a prerequisite for successful balancing is to reset trade liberalisation on a more equal footing with social goals at the global level. This is much easier said than done, as key policy actors in different world regions do not always share the political preferences of their constituencies. Trade ministers, civil servants and legal experts among the diverse WTO leadership would need to see social ambitions to reduce inequality and economic growth strategies as much more interconnected, if they were to instigate true system reform.

Conclusion

This chapter has explored the subsidiarity principle in the context of case studies on global trade governance with strong EU involvement. The emerging WTO agenda shows several challenging trajectories away from the earlier focus on tariff reductions facing new challenges and thus requiring new balancing mechanisms. With more attention now paid to beyond the border issues, such as health and safety requirements or social and environmental standards, to non-tariff barriers as well as regulatory divergence among countries, multilateral negotiations risk severe and lasting gridlock. Politically, there appears to be less appetite to introduce regulatory change that would even out diverse social preferences and historically grown economic structures. Consequently, the WTO is under pressure to find a better balance between common disciplines and country specific com-petences under the control of governments. Therefore, the time is right to think about a more systematic recognition of subsidiarity in the global rulebook in order to strike a new balance between achieving globally universal rules while permitting, at the same time, greater diversity to meet specific local conditions.

A more explicit acknowledgement promises to resolve the recurrent tensions between diverging societal preferences and the continuing drive towards international market integration. As has been realised at the national and regional levels, global economic governance cannot neatly separate political deliberation from market decision-making, and neo-liberalism is not the model around which a global consensus can be constructed, let alone with ease. Instead, more research is needed to map the global reach of subsidiarity – or subsidiarity like mechanisms – and to verify its impact as a decentralising or centralising, vertical or horizontal force. Arguably, many trade policy actors drawing on individual country experiences and familiarity with federalised political cultures now consider a more nuanced approach towards the interplay of national, regional, and multilateral levels as most appropriate. From the perspective of the subsidiarity debate elaborated in this volume, global economic governance needs a specific type of reform to prevent ultimately destructive unilateralism while at the same time leaving a dynamic policy space for states to accommodate changing societal preferences. In this balancing exercise the precise nature of implementation mechanisms matter, as does the time that is needed to make them work efficiently. Yet, if global governance is to be more than a proxy for a bargain between powerful states, the calibration and fine-tuning associated with further codification seems inevitable.

References

Berman, G. A. (1994). 'Taking Subsidiarity Seriously'. *Columbia Law Review* 94: 331–456.

Broude, T. (2016). 'Selective Subsidiarity and Dialectic Deference in the World Trade Organization'. *Law and Contemporary Problems* 79(2): 53–74.

Feichtner, I. (2016). 'Subsidiarity in the World Trade Organization: The Promise of Waivers'. *Law and Contemporary Problems* 79(2): 75–97.

Hoekman, B. (2014). 'Global Trade Governance'. In T.G. Weiss and R. Wilkinson (eds) *International Organization and Global Governance*, 552–63. London and New York: Routledge.

Howse, R. and K. Nicholaidis (2016). 'Toward a Global Ethics of Trade Governance: Subsidiarity Writ Large'. *Law and Contemporary Problems*, *79*(2): 259–83.

Inman, P. (2016). 'A Deal for Freer Trade or Corporate Greed? Here's the Truth about TTIP'. *The Observer*, 3 January, 36–7.

Jachtenfuchs, M. and N. Krisch (2016). 'Subsidiarity in Global Governance'. *Law and Contemporary Problems* 79(1): 1–26.

Jančić, D. (2017). 'TTIP and Legislative-Executive Relations in EU Trade Policy'. *West European Politics* 40(1): 202–21.

Lamy, P. (2012). 'Governance of a Multipolar World Order'. Speech at the Rajaratnam School of International Studies, Singapore, 21 September. Available at: https://www.wto.org/english/news_e/sppl_e/sppl248_e.htm

Maur, J.-C. and B. Shepherd (2017). 'Regional Integration and Trade Facilitation'. Available at: https://www.wto.org/english/res_e/publications_e/wtr11_forum_e/wtr11_7jun11_e.htm

Neufeld, N. (2014). 'The Long and Winding Road: How WTO Members Finally Reached a Trade Facilitation Agreement'. *Staff Working Paper* ERSD-2014-06. Geneva: WTO Economic Research and Statistics Division.

Rodrik, D. (2011). *The Globalization Paradox*. Oxford: Oxford University Press.

Slaughter, A.-M. (2004). *A New World Order*. Princeton and Oxford: Oxford University Press.

Von Staden, A. (2012). 'The Democratic Legitimacy of Judicial Review Beyond the State: Normative Subsidiarity and Judicial Standards of Review'. *International Journal of Constitutional Law* 10(4): 1023–49.

Woolcock, S. (2012). *European Union Economic Diplomacy*. Farnham: Ashgate.

WTO (2001). 'European Communities — Measures Affecting Asbestos and Products Containing Asbestos', DS135. Available at: https://www.wto.org/english/tratop_e/dispu_e/cases_e/ds135_e.htm

WTO (2009). 'European Communities — Measures Concerning Meat and Meat Products (Hormones)', DS26. Available at: https://www.wto.org/english/tratop_e/dispu_e/cases_e/ds26_e.htm

WTO (2014). 'European Communities — Measures Prohibiting the Importation and Marketing of Seal Products', DS401. Available at: https://www.wto.org/english/tratop_e/dispu_e/cases_e/ds401_e.htm

Young, A. R. (2016). "Not Your Parents' Trade Politics: The Transatlantic Trade and Investment Partnership Negotiations'. *Review of International Political Economy* 23(3): 345–78.

Young, A. R. and J. Peterson (2014). *Parochial Global Europe*. Oxford: Oxford University Press.

14

Subsidiarity and European Governance: Export and Investment Promotion Agencies

MAXIMILIAN BOSSDORF

The concept of subsidiarity has gained prominence as an organising principle for systems of multi-level governance (MLG). It captures the process by which political authority is allocated to the lowest practical level. In the European context, supranational institutions shall only take measures, if a 'proposed action cannot be sufficiently achieved by the Member States, either at central level or at regional and local level' (European Union 2012). Given the lack of a formal EU constitution or a centralised EU government, subsidiarity appears as an ideal method of mediating between the concerns of various actors at different levels of the European polity. As Davies (2006, 64) points out, 'what could be more liberal than allowing the Member States to do anything that is not forbidden?'. In addition, Article 5 (3) of the Treaty on European Union (TEU) places the burden of proof regarding the advantages of a centralised approach firmly on the EU (Craig 2012). Indeed, 'the Union shall act only if and in so far as the objectives of the proposed action cannot be sufficiently achieved by the Member States' (European Union 2012, 18).

However, there are inherent flaws within the legal capacity of subsidiarity to govern effectively. Impartiality, for example, in respecting the interests of higher and lower tiers of the EU system could only be assured if there were 'no conflict between the objectives of the various levels' (Davies 2006, 78). As the principle impacts on core responsibilities of the state as well as of EU institutions, it will not suffice to achieve a compromise between diverging interests at different decision-making levels. To this end, it would also require the implementation of closely related legal concepts such as proportionality; or acceptance of the top-tiered, ultimate authority of the European Court of

Justice. As Scharpf (2010, 230) points out: 'European law has no language to describe and no scales to compare the normative weights of the national and European concerns at stake'. Therefore, the mediation effects and organisational merits of the legal subsidiarity concept are strongly contested. From the angle of political theory, subsidiarity is better understood as a general guiding principle to examine and design complex systems of MLG. Accordingly, this chapter does not interpret subsidiarity as a strict legal doctrine, but as an organising principle which underpins key aspects of the MLG approach. To make this point, this chapter explores the case of Export and Investment Promotion Agencies (EIPAs) and, thus, offers new insights into a key component of German and European trade policy. More specifically, it focuses on how normative subsidiarity mechanisms shape MLG in practice without following the legal prescriptions of Article 5 (3) TEU.

The complexity of governance arrangements

EIPAs are a new and understudied phenomenon from the perspective of European governance. Given the diversity of such agencies within as well as across states, the multitude of actors involved does challenge standard comparisons. Traditionally, investment promotion activities have been associated with embassies, consulates, and national delegations to trade fairs. More generally, the design and implementation of foreign economic policy was considered the responsibility of sovereign institutions. For national governments, trying to attract foreign direct investment (FDI), this meant the creation of a favourable domestic regulatory environment and direct negotiations with foreign counterparts. In turn, export promotion policy was driven by producer initiatives through chambers of commerce, trade associations and guilds, including services such as export advice, export credit insurance and marketing support. Yet, due to economic globalisation, the dividing line between state services and private sector provision has been blurred. Most states now experience the pressure to increase their global competitiveness if they want to attract foreign capital. In addition, sub-state regions seek new ways of accessing international markets and try to develop their local economies apart from national or supranational policy measures.

Within the EU, for example, each member state has – under the direction of foreign or economic ministries – created a dedicated investment promotion agency, usually in the form of a state-owned enterprise or service provider. More specifically, respective agencies can take the form of limited public liability companies, crown corporations, contracted consultancies, government departments or industry-run initiatives and associations. Frequently, this organisational set-up and the division of governance competences is the result of distinct country experiences.

To complicate things further, there has been a notable EU impact on the operation of the mixed economy. Germany, with one of the oldest and most complex systems for export and investment promotion in Europe, is a case in point. While the Federal Republic recognises subsidiarity as a key principle (Article 72 Basic Law), it differs from similar arrangements in Westminster democracies. The federal competence is subject to subsidiarity requirements as outlined in Article 72 (2) Basic Law as well as a requirement for legislative power in the specific subject matter (Taylor 2006). In fact, the 16 German state entities (*Länder*) insisted on the inclusion of the principle of subsidiarity in the EU treaties (Scharpf 2010). As a result of a strong domestic subsidiarity tradition, the Federal Republic operates EIPAs through a two-tiered system: one at the federal level, and one at the regional 'Länder' level.

Accordingly, this chapter identifies multiple levels of governance in the German and European EIPA system. Due to overlapping spheres of responsibility, the principle of subsidiarity can be observed at the core of respective EU efforts, even if it is unable to account for all EIPA activities. Instead, there is a system of shared authority across an institutionalised set of actors which works with varying degrees of unity and policy coherence as well as 'commitment to EU norms, and power resources' (Smith 2004, 743). In other words, the EIPA system is characterised by a loose MLG approach – or MLG type II – in the terminology advanced by Marks and Hooghe (2004). This emphasises voluntary cooperation among actors at multiple levels, sharing their authority without clear vertical hierarchies. It suggests a bottom-up approach to authority that comes with a natural delegation of authority to various working levels. However, as this chapter concludes, the recent creation of the European External Action Service (EEAS) resembles a traditional federalist top-down approach affecting EIPAs in line with Marks and Hooghe's MLG type I approach. Regardless of MLG type, though, both system characteristics remain compatible with a general, underlying conception of subsidiarity. This recognises overlapping spheres of authority at several levels, enabling key actors to engage in vertically fluid exchanges for the sake of purposeful policy making.

EIPAS at regional and federal state level

Before assessing the impact of the supranational MLG component, it is important to understand the governance relationship between EIPAs at regional and national level. Prior to the Lisbon Treaty, most European EIPAs were found in two different policy sectors (government/non-government) and at two levels of governance (local/regional – national/federal). Therefore, respective agencies could fall into one of the four categories outlined in Figure 1 for the case of Germany. The coordination system indicates a further sectoral differentiation as well as the possibility of overlapping governance arrangements.

Figure 1

Traditional EIPA Tiers/Levels

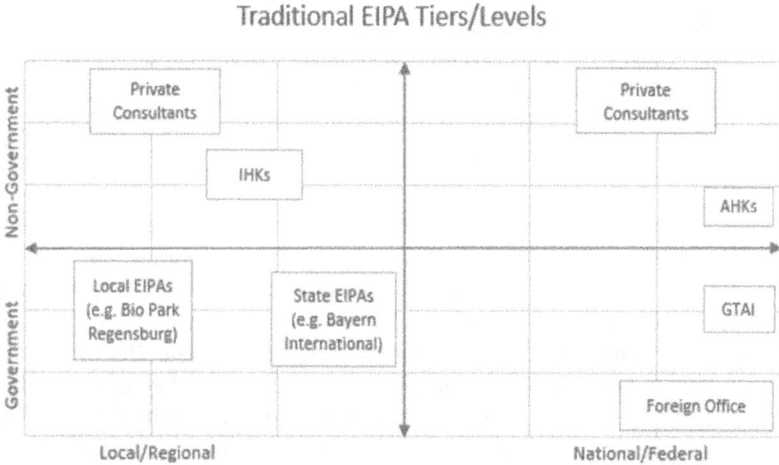

Along the right quadrants of the vertical axis, there is the economic development agency of the Federal Republic (*Germany Trade and Invest*, GTAI), as well as the German system of Chambers of Commerce Abroad (*Auslandshandelskammern*, AHKs). Both organisational forms promote investment flows into the country, while simultaneously representing German export interests abroad. At the local or regional level, EIPAs follow more closely the principle of subsidiarity through an exclusive focus on sub-state promotion efforts. This includes EIPAs of the German Länder such as Bayern International, Baden-Württemberg International, and Berlin Partner, or region-specific Chambers of Commerce (*Industrie- und Handelskammern*, IHKs). Frequently, these too operate with a dual task division of inward FDI promotion and external trade support. In the case of Bavaria, for instance, the relevant state ministry operates two separate companies, one dealing with FDI (*Invest in Bavaria*), and one dealing with export promotion and foreign market development (*Bayern International*). In the case of neighbouring Baden Württemberg, by contrast, the task division is achieved through two different departments within a single official agency (*Baden-Württemberg International*, BW-I).

Along the horizontal axis, the traditional relationship between local and national EIPAs does not follow a centralised or hierarchical pattern. The actors at national or federal level have no legal authority over their counterparts at local or regional level. Given the federal political system, the local and regional EIPAs interact with their respective state governments (*Landesregierungen*), and do not maintain institutional ties with the federal government (*Bundesregierung*) or centralised private business initiatives. In fact, the local and regional EIPAs are owned and operated by state governments, whereas local Chambers of Commerce (IHKs) are private non-profit associations, joined up in a federal network with the Association of German Industry and Trade Chambers (*Deutscher Industrie und Handelskammertag*, DIHK) as their umbrella organisation. Again, the latter has no control over the activities of individual IHKs but represents their views for lobbying purposes at national level.

Some regional EIPAs follow a hybrid commercial model with several shareholders coming from the public and semi-public arena. BW-I, for example, is financed by the *Land*, its state bank, and the industry association of Baden-Württemberg, as well as an umbrella organisation of local chambers of trade and commerce. It is also worth noting that neither of the two identified levels has a centralised planning or coordinating committee to streamline activities within different segments of the system. Thus, subsidiarity is not an official component of German foreign economic policy and, instead, finds its recognition in the informal practices of organisational actors adhering to the related principle of federal comity.

The German system in practice

At federal level, GTAI and AHKs work closely with local EIPA actors and involve them in their own initiatives. Local EIPAs are feeder organisations providing federal agencies with export-ready contracts, new clients and emerging opportunities through direct access to valuable information from the local business community. Moreover, for the externally operating AHKs, local agencies in Germany are potential customers and a source of income, providing funding for trade delegations, marketing events or contracts of representation. Usually, this collaboration is based on personal relationships that are fostered and maintained informally on behalf of federal agencies. Therefore, EIPAs in the German system are free to cooperate with each other across different levels as this is perceived to be in their own economic interest.

In practice, local promotion agencies have become tenants in the foreign offices of their federal counterparts, outsourcing the planning of trade delegations, making budgetary contributions or co-financing members of staff to represent their specific interests internationally. For example, already since the 1990s the state of Bavaria has operated its own network of 20 global business representations with major support coming from the staff of German Chambers of Commerce Abroad (AHKs) (Bayerisches Staatsministerium 2017). In this set-up, subsidiarity arrangements allow local regions to run international promotion networks independently of federal interference. The MLG approach is a useful tool in analysing the related cooperation and coordination efforts between different groups of actors.

The federal government endorses this system despite rare cases where centrally funded EIPAs have concentrated excessively on the collaborative relationship with a single local provider. Under such circumstances, it will issue a reminder to the federal agency about the obligation to serve the economic development of the whole country rather than handing competitive advantages to individual regions. Due to the lack of an overarching organisational structure, the system relies on shared economic concerns as part of Germany's national interest. Thus, the country-specific governance structure follows neo-functionalist understandings as embedded in the MLG type II concept. Here, authority is not exercised around pre-existing vertical hierarchies but evolves with specific problem constellations (Hooghe and Marks 2003). This has the advantage to allow for competitive processes among different sets of actors in overlapping areas of jurisdiction. True to the spirit of subsidiarity, individual levels of governance must prove their ability to outperform others in their capacity to realise new business opportunities. Potentially, this competition can also be used as a deliberate policy instrument to increase the quality or efficiency of service delivery (Benz 2007). Overall, the relative autonomy of EIPAs in the German system has led to a high degree of specialisation and resource maximisation in external promotion efforts. Similarly, in terms of inward investment acquisition, the GTAI as the key federal actor with worldwide presence is well-positioned to identify local and regional partner organisations for foreign customers. While the EIPAs at higher and lower levels can operate independently in this market segment, they are likely to cooperate with each other for the sake of cost effectiveness.

Consequently, the effectiveness of the co-ordination process across several levels depends largely on communication flows in interpersonal networks and the readiness of key actors to engage in voluntary exchanges. If personal relationships break down, or individual representatives have not sufficiently internalised subsidiarity norms, significant financial burdens can follow in terms of duplicate institutional structures or identical service provision. Together with inefficient resource allocation, this may add to a degree of confusion among domestic exporters and external investors in the day-to-day running of the system. What is more, the complexity of the coordination system makes EIPAs particularly sensitive to changes in the external environment. The absence of clear delineations of competences between levels of governance complicates public-private interactions and requires political decision-making to respond adequately to new funding streams and business opportunities.

Take, in this context, the rapid organisational change that occurred in the regional promotion system of the state of Lower Saxony (*Niedersachsen*). In 2009, the *Land* brought its dedicated investment promotion agency into public-private ownership, now constituted as a limited liability company (*NGlobal GmbH*) and equipped with an international network for export promotion. The shares of the reformed entity were held by the state of Lower Saxony, a regional trade fair organiser (*Deutsche Messe*), a local state bank (*NordLB*), local chambers of commerce, as well as a semi-public academy for management training (*Deutsche Management Akademie*). Already two years later, the official state component dealing with investment acquisition was relocated to another semi-private company, supposedly to serve the specific purpose of business innovation (*Innovationszentrum Niedersachsen GmbH*) (Niedersächsisches Ministerium 2013a). Finally, in 2013, NGlobal was dismantled to give way for a new government department in the Ministry for Economic Affairs, Labour and Transport, re-uniting investment acquisition, export promotion as well as the related delegation and networking activities in a single public entity. In the words of the responsible Minister, Olaf Lies (Niedersächsisches Ministerium 2013b; author's translation):

> After analysing the existing export promotion system, the criticism of the business community, and the requests of the ministerial bureaucracy, I have decided to re-integrate foreign trade development into the Ministry for Economic Affairs, Labour and Transport.

The observed tension between public and private provision of promotion activities has a historical legacy. Not only was the creation of Chambers of Commerce Abroad perceived as an unnecessary duplication of services, it also challenged the sovereign monopoly of the state to conduct international trade policy. Parliamentary debates going back as far as *Reichstag* sessions in the period from 1899 to 1901 indicate the critical attitude held by the Foreign Office (*Auswärtiges Amt*) in response to the opening of the first German Chamber of Commerce in Brussels (Reichstagsprotokolle 1903). More than a century later, the non-governmental sector represented by the domestic IHK system and the externally located AHKs is considered an important element of official governmental policy and formally recognised as the third pillar of external trade promotion. Currently, the respective network spans 139 international offices (with more than 1500 members of staff) and with up to 20 per cent of their budgets covered by direct federal grants. By contrast, the private non-associational sector populated with consultancies such as Price Waterhouse Coopers (PwC) or Ernst and Young (EY) plays a much smaller role. In recent years, their activities have concentrated on the winning of government contracts to conduct advertising campaigns, to organise trade delegations and to attract inward FDI.

The impact of the EEAS

From the German perspective, the practical EU attempts to implement the principle of subsidiarity are anything but clear cut, especially if responsibilities are supposed to be allocated to the lowest possible level. Comparable to other policy areas addressed in this book, the empowerment of actors at the EU member state level has not been a prime target. Recurrent EU efforts in the field of export and investment promotion have clashed with organically grown national promotion systems, while attempting to supersede their mandate by the formation of genuine European actor capacity. Hence, it would be misleading to connect subsidiarity with a bottom-up approach. Instead, the insertion of an additional top- layer serves to by-pass national governments while directly engaging with local or regional agencies. With the ratification of the Lisbon Treaty, the ambition of a pan-European approach has become much more obvious.

In particular, the creation of the EEAS has impacted external trade promotion and the EIPAs of the member states. Following Council Decision 2010/427/ EU, the diplomatic service has seen a dramatic expansion to 139 inter-nationally operating offices. With a budget exceeding 600 million euros, a workforce of 4237 people, and more than half of those active in EU delegations abroad, actor capacity in European foreign policy cannot be denied (EEAS 2017). In analogy to the turf battles between the EEAS and national foreign services, similar skirmishes are expected with the actors of domestic promotion systems (Adler-Nissen 2014). The EU already holds exclusive competences in external trade relations and negotiates on behalf of the member states through the Directorate General for Trade of the Commission (DG Trade). In addition, the EEAS (2019) interprets the portfolio of its delegations rather broadly in so far as they are

> responsible for all policy areas of the relationship between the EU and the host country – be they political, economic, trade or on human rights and in building relationships with partners in civil society.

Unfortunately, the 2013 reform review of the EEAS neither mentioned subsidiarity concerns nor suggested alternative forms of sharing authority in a strengthened system of European governance. This, by the way, is in stark contrast to the vision originally outlined for lower-level actors in the 2009 White Paper on Multilevel Governance (Committee of the Regions 2009). In fact, the EEAS (2013, 18) seems to harbour even more far-reaching ambitions by addressing

> residual competence issues to ensure that EEAS and EU delegations are the single channel for EU external relations issues, including in areas of mixed competence and in multilateral fora.

Therefore, *de facto*, the EU has already established a third level of authority, which ultimately acts within the same sphere as traditional trading states. This poses a long-term challenge to the policy instruments in the hands of national export promotion agencies as well as the lobbying activities of embassies and consulates.

Towards a European EIPA system?

Of course, an additional sphere of EU responsibility does not automatically undermine all subsidiarity concerns as expressed in Article 5 (3) TEU. It is an empirical question how the practical interaction with the member states impinges on domestic action capacity in trade matters. In this respect, a major point of contestation has been the role of EEAS delegations in initiating and co-funding European Chambers of Commerce (ECC) in third countries. In contrast to German AHKs, these reveal no standardised structure in their formal set-up or exhibit regulatory constraints in their external promotion activities. Accordingly, they are recognised as an emerging challenge to the dominant business model of national EIPAs. If their numbers increase – while offering comparable services within a larger network – private companies at local, regional and national levels could be easily persuaded to switch providers.

On the one hand, representatives of the German EIPA system appreciate the positive advocacy role of EEAS delegations in multilateral trade relations. From this angle, it makes sense for larger member states to actively cooperate and shape new pan-European initiatives. On the other hand, this entails the risk that over time the EEAS and ECC services will be in direct competition with national provisions once these have gained access to EU-wide funding opportunities. Indeed, the recent EU efforts point in the direction of a federalist type I approach to MLG. Although the actors at lower levels are not centrally controlled within a strictly hierarchical relationship, the top-layer tries to delegate authority downwards without allowing for a more fluid, interactive exchange. The first step towards a European EIPA system challenges the *raison d'être* of established national organisations, even if it is welcomed by some of the smaller member states hoping for a better resource flow to their export and investment projects.

Paradoxically, the traditional EU policy strategy in this sector, originating in the pre-Lisbon period, was closer to MLG type II. Due to an emphasis on common problem-solving and resource maximisation rather than hierarchical ordering, it better incorporated the subsidiarity considerations of Article 5 (3) TEU. In fact, the EU continues to support national export promotion efforts through the European Regional Development Fund (ERDF), which leaves actual implementation in the hands of downstream actors.

Take, for example, the ongoing Bavarian 'Go International' project for small and medium-sized enterprises (SMEs). The participating businesses are entitled for reimbursements of up to half of their export promotion expenses within an individual limit of 20,000 euros over a three-year period. The overall organisation rests with regional chambers of commerce and trade, who administer the joint funding from the ERDF and the *Bavarian Ministry for Economic Affairs,* Media, Energy and Technology. Importantly, the precise co-funding arrangements depend on the geographic location and industrial sector of the participating SMEs. For this purpose, as Figure 2 shows, the ERDF identifies priority areas and funding opportunities targeted at specific government districts and city regions in Bavaria (BIHK Service 2017). Despite their complexity, such funding streams are more suitable for the classic MLG type II environment of the German case. The established EIPAs can still tap into EU resources, yet without sacrificing their operational independence.

Similarly, the role of the European Commission in providing grants or co-funding arrangements for EU external promotion projects aligns more closely with subsidiarity demands. Consider, in this context, the joint EU-Gulf Cooperation Council (GCC) Invest project, running for three years from 2012 to 2015. It did join up traditional AHK actors in the form of the German Emirati Joint Council for Industry and Commerce and the German-Saudi Liaison Office for Economic Affairs with relatively new arrangements such as the GCC Federation of Chambers and *Eurochambres,* an ECC umbrella organisation. The partnership, furthermore, intended to engage all European EIPAs in the Gulf region through the conduct of conferences, workshops and study programmes.

Figure 2: ERDF priority areas in Bavaria, 2014–2020. Source: BIHK Service (2017, 4).

Essentially, the Commission does not implement policy measures on the ground but calls for proposals from the EIPAs of the member states. The project offer came with an EU co-funding promise of 60 per cent, if other partners contributed through their workforce to the remaining costs. Different to the Bavarian ERDF project, the Brussels institution insisted here on an inclusive approach. For EU-GCC Invest, the explicit aim was to involve as many member state EIPAs as possible in programme activities, also to disseminate widely the available information on European investment promotion systems. Moreover, the participation of national providers from Europe was entirely voluntary; the UK's former Trade and Invest department (UKTI), for example, preferred to chart its own path in the Gulf region. In fact, even the participating German AHK offices remained autonomous and, ultimately, in charge of the implementation process through their own members of staff. In short, the EU programme did not attempt to establish competing governance structures and, instead, had the objective to foster those already in place. In sum, the examples presented in this section show that MLG type I and II coexist in the complex space of European export and investment promotion. However, if subsidiarity is taken seriously, it champions a traditional bottom-up use of policy tools in support of local, regional and national agencies.

Conclusion

The MLG approach is particularly useful to understand the sharing of authority across different levels of the European polity. In the case of German export and investment promotion policy, bottom-up and top-down processes coexist. For the actors in the observed EIPA systems, informal conceptions of subsidiarity matter when setting out the general direction of their organisational relationships. Rather than suggesting mere decentralisation to the lowest working level, the policy area analysed here suggests sharing arrangements by autonomous actors operating at different organisational levels and with various sectoral divisions. Instead of centrally enforced governance, EIPA efforts are dominated by voluntary, market-driven cooperation. Under such conditions, the concept of subsidiarity works as a compass steering the fluid transfer of authority in promotion systems with strong vertical dynamics.

Traditionally, a similar relationship existed in the EU dimension when using Commission and ERDF funding. At first sight, therefore, the expansion of EEAS delegations and creation of ECCs constitutes a significant challenge to the EIPA structures of the member states, and especially to those of the Federal Republic. Yet, given the fact that the new 'top' EU tier neither bans nor supersedes the promotion activities of national EIPAs, the relevance of the subsidiarity principle remains intact in the European dimension of foreign economic policy. Regardless of whether the adaptation to changing trade relations occurs at home or abroad, the distinction between two MLG types, advanced in this chapter, is vital to understand the normative implications of subsidiarity.

References

Adler-Nissen, R. (2014). 'Symbolic Power in European Diplomacy: The Struggle between National Foreign Services and the EU's External Action Service'. *Review of International Studies* 40(4): 657–81.

Bayerisches Staatsministerium für Wirtschaft und Medien, Energie und Technologie (2017). *Bayerische Repräsentanzen im Ausland - Bavarian Representative Offices Worldwide.* Available at: https://www.stmwi.bayern.de/fileadmin/user_upload/stmwi/Publikationen/2017/20170117-Bay_Repraesentanzen_im_Ausland_TB_Januar_2017.pdf

Benz, A. (2007). 'Inter-Regional Competition in Co-operative Federalism: New Modes of Multi-level Governance in Germany'. *Regional and Federal Studies* 17(4): 421–36.

BIHK Service (2017). *Förderbestimmungen über das Förderprojekt 'Export Bavaria 3.0 - Go International'.* Available at: http://www.auwi-bayern.de/awp/foren/go-international/anhaenge/foerderbestimmungen-go-international.pdf

Committee of the Regions of the EU (2009). *The Committee of the Regions' White Paper on Multilevel Governance*, CdR 89/2009 fin. Available at: http://www.europarl.europa.eu/meetdocs/2009_2014/documents/afco/dv/livre-blanc_/livre-blanc_en.pdf

Craig, P. (2012). 'Subsidiarity : A Political and Legal Analysis'. *Journal of Common Market Studies* 50(1): 72–87.

Davies, G. (2006). 'Subsidiarity: The Wrong Idea, in the Wrong Place, at the Wrong Time'. *Common Market Law Review* 43: 63–84.

European External Action Service (2013). *EEAS Review.* Available at: http://collections.internetmemory.org/haeu/20160313172652/http://eeas.europa.eu/library/publications/2013/3/2013_eeas_review_en.pdf

European External Action Service (2017). *Annual Activity Report 2016.* Available at: https://eeas.europa.eu/sites/eeas/files/aar2016_final_final.pdf

European External Action Service (2019). About the European External Action Service (EEAS). Available at: https://eeas.europa.eu/headquarters/headquarters-homepage/82/about-european-external-action-service-eeas_en

European Union (2012). 'Consolidated Version of the Treaty on European Union'. *Official Journal of the European Union* C 326/13, 26 October. 13–46. Available at: https://eur-lex.europa.eu/resource.html?uri=cellar:2bf140bf-a3f8-4ab2-b506-fd71826e6da6.0023.02/DOC_1&format=PDF

Hooghe, L. and Marks, G. (2003). 'Unraveling the Central State , but How ? Types of Multi-Level Governance'. *American Political Science Review* 97(2): 233–43.

Marks, G. and Hooghe, L. (2004). 'Contrasting Visions of Multi-level Governance'. In Bache, I. and M. Flinders (eds) *Multi-level Governance,* 15–30. Oxford: Oxford University Press.

Niedersächsisches Ministerium für Wirtschaft, Arbeit und Verkehr (2013a). Antwort vom Minister für Wirtschaft, Arbeit und Verkehr Olaf Lies auf die mündliche Anfrage der Abgeordneten Jörg Bode, Gabriela König und Christian Dürr (FDP). Sitzung des Niedersächsischen Landtages am 01.11.2013 – Top 26. Available at: http://www.mw.niedersachsen.de/aktuelles/ presseinformationen/unternehmensansiedlung-119422.html

Niedersächsisches Ministerium für Wirtschaft, Arbeit und Verkehr (2013b). Außenwirtschaftsförderung wird neu aufgestellt und Chefsache. Available at: http://www.mw.niedersachsen.de/aktuelles/presseinformationen/ auenwirtschaftsfoerderung-wird-neu-aufgestellt-und-chefsache-118175.html

Reichstagsprotokolle (1903). *Stenographische Berichte über die Verhandlungen des Reichstags.* Berlin: Norddeutsche Buchdruckerei.

Scharpf, F.W. (2010). 'The Double Asymmetry of European Integration Or : Why the EU Cannot Be a Social Market Economy'. *Socio-Economic Review* 8: 211–50.

Smith, M.E. (2004). 'Toward a Theory of EU Foreign Policy Making: Multi-level Governance, Domestic Politics, and National Adaptation to Europe's Common Foreign and Security Policy'. *Journal of European Public Policy* 11(4): 740–58.

Taylor, G. (2006). 'Germany: The Subsidiarity Principle'. *Institutional Journal of Constitutional Law* 4(1): 115–30.

15

Subsidiarity and Fiscal Federalism in Canada

BARRIE B. F. HEBB

While Canada's historical evolution from a centralised nation state in 1867 to a decentralised one can be viewed as unique, the country shares a common dilemma with other nation states, and federations, in particular. Decisions need to be made over how decision-making authority will be divided between multiple levels of government. There is no single global solution for the division and jurisdiction of powers within a nation state or multi-level government structure (Friesen 2003). Some have opted for a more centralised structure while others favour greater decentralisation. In this context, the principle of subsidiarity can provide guidance. This principle holds generally that decision-making authority should be held as close to the constituents affected by the decision as possible while higher levels of authority should hold a subsidiarity role; delegation of authority essentially moves from the lower level upwards when a case can be made that the issue to be decided upon is of a common character, affecting more than one of the members, or could not be dealt with adequately at the lower level. Examples of each, respectively, could be common defence, trans-boundary water rights for a river across members' territories, or a response to a natural disaster.

While in Canada's case, subsidiarity is not formally declared in the Constitution of 1982 or the British North America Act (BNA) of 1867, it has arisen directly and indirectly through Supreme Court of Canada (SCC) decisions through modern cases involving disputes over the division of powers (Kong 2015). This is in contrast to the EU case, where the principle has been more formally adopted in treaties (Broullet 2011). It has, however, also arisen specifically over fiscal issues, namely different governance level's ability to tax and spend. The argument here is that subsidiarity alone would not be enough to genuinely provide meaning and substance over the distribution of powers without the fiscal dimension being addressed. The principle of subsidiarity, in other words, is less meaningful, if a level of government does not have adequate revenue sources to act in its area of jurisdiction. The fiscal division of powers plays a vital role for this principal since it would essentially be violated if taxation and revenue raising powers did not match the remaining division of powers, in scope and intent.

This chapter has two core objectives. The first is to provide for the reader that is more familiar with the EU than with Canada some general characteristics that may be useful in understanding why Canada is likely to function more effectively and efficiently as a decentralised federation as opposed to a highly centralised nation state (Follesdal and Muñiz Fraticelli 2015, 90-1). On the one hand, considerable scope for autonomy exists at the provincial and territorial level, while on the other there is reason and interest for the thirteen members to see value in being together in a federation as opposed to separate nation states; despite the wide diversity in the population sizes of the Canadian provinces and territories, economic interests, and tensions over other areas such as language. The second objective is to examine the fiscal division of powers, notably over the powers to tax and spend.

Subsidiarity and fiscal decentralisation

The choice a multi-level government has over its structure can essentially be reduced to two sets of related questions. The first is the decision over which levels of government within the nation state should have jurisdiction over which areas. Should schools, healthcare, defence, infrastructure, education and language be held at the national, provincial/territorial, or municipal level of government? The second set of questions has to do with which level of government has ultimate power or authority over this set of decisions. Which level gets to decide in the end whether the jurisdiction is supposed to be at the local, provincial or national level? The nation-state may be viewed as being comprised of lower-level units which hold authority, for example, and delegate power upwards on a case-by-case basis. The reverse may also be true where the national level of government is deemed to hold the power to decide to delegate powers and jurisdiction downwards.

The principle of subsidiarity provides guidance not only over this division of powers, but also over how the decision over the division should take place. In its simplest form, this principle holds generally that decision-making authority should be held as close as possible to the people in whose interest the decision is going to be made. This means that the starting point is the local level with authority or jurisdiction being delegated upwards when a case can be made that the decision affects a wider group of people, or there are efficient and effective reasons to do so, such as responses to natural disasters. In these extreme situations the local level may not be able to respond. It follows from this principle further that the national level would essentially receive its reason for existing based on consent from below and it would play a subsidiary role, acting in those areas of common interest across the lower levels of government (Halberstam 2009).

The principle of subsidiarity can also be interpreted as providing guidance over the division of powers in a multi-level government structure in other essential ways. For instance, it also follows from this principle that the nation state is essentially the sum of its parts because it has derived its authority from the lower levels and not the reverse (Friesen 2003). This means that the nation-state itself is only legitimate so long as it is held as legitimate by the lower levels of government. In the case of a federation, it would be legitimate only in so far as the members of the federation viewed it as legitimate. The national level exists to serve the common interests of the members and cannot pursue policy, legislation or other activities that hinder or harm the lower levels.

Further, with powers and jurisdiction divided according to this principle, there are positive and negative aspects of subsidiarity (Cyr 2014). In particular, the principle outlines and protects the lower levels from infringement into areas specified as within their jurisdiction. This is the negative dimension in that it prevents the national level from undue interference. However, there is also a positive dimension in that the national level is expected to act, potentially interfering, in some situations for the benefit of citizens residing there, such as through providing assistance. This can be justified in cases where the lower level is unable to act effectively or efficiently. This could take place during an invasion, natural disaster, or perhaps even poor economic times where insufficient revenues may mean that citizens suffer. The idea that the higher level can step in provides substance and reason for being a member, after all, of the nation. Other cases may include when a decision by a lower level of government affects another region, such as regulating river flows or dams.

Modern interpretations of the principle of subsidiarity, beyond this element of strict division of conditions when one level could act in another, also stress the cooperative nature of the principle (Hueglin 2013). The different levels of government, therefore, according to subsidiarity are not meant to compete so much as complement each other. Citizens of a region of the country are both local and national citizens. It would not make sense for the federal level of government to pursue a policy that hinders lower levels of government from serving their own constituents. This is due to the fact that citizens in that polity are both local and national, and it would follow that the national level of government would be harming, not serving, some of its citizens. Further, a local level of government would not be permitted to harm other members of the country through its policies since that citizen is also a member of the whole, and reciprocity would dictate that it would be harmful to the whole if all the members sought such harmful courses of action against each other. Further, despite clear boundaries over jurisdiction, subsidiarity does hold that the higher level can intervene to provide assistance. Thus, rather than viewing the levels as distinct and acting within specified areas of jurisdiction, the principle also validates a cooperative role and argues against policies within the nation that seek to harm the ability of other levels, or citizens in another constituency.

While this principle provides guidance in making the core decisions over the division of powers and establishes some boundaries over behaviour between the levels, it can also be viewed as an efficient principle. Subsidiarity allows for multiple, legitimate majorities to exist within a nation due to the way powers are divided (Cyr 2014). If the central, national level of government held all decision-making power, or had the authority to impose its will across the nation, there would be some issues over which some sub-national levels would be satisfied while others would not. Perhaps a majority was achieved at the national level on some issue, such as the language of instruction, for instance. All schools in the country would then have to comply and adopt that language due to the will of the national majority, even if there was a single small region where few, if anyone, spoke that language. It could be held that satisfying the majority is sufficient. However, if language laws were decided at the sub-national level, all those regions who supported the national language would continue to do so at the local level and they would be at least no worse off. However, the smaller region with the other language would now be better off than before. In this case, more people would be satisfied in the nation with language policy if it were allocated to the sub-national, as opposed to the national level. Subsidiarity, because it favours policy decisions as close to the polity affected as possible, is more likely to result in greater satisfaction for greater numbers of people than if all the decisions were at the national level; it thus maximises social welfare which may or may not be consistent with a strict majority vote ruling. Due to dividing decision-making power the way it does, subsidiarity can be argued to be aligned with the 'greatest happiness principle' since it allows for multiple and legitimate majorities to take place within a nation state (Bentham 1988).

While many of these dimensions of subsidiarity have been adequately explored and helped prepare the way for understanding, one dimension typically left out is the division of fiscal powers. This fiscal dimension of subsidiarity is also crucial, if not of vital importance. If a lower level, such as a province, has specific powers, such as over health, education, local infrastructure, in line with the principle of subsidiarity, that a province is essentially entitled to pursue policies and activities in those areas that best reflect the interests, preferences, and priorities of its constituents. If the power to raise sufficient revenues to cover the costs involved in the provision of these areas is not also at this level, however, the province will find itself less free to pursue the areas within its jurisdiction as it sees fit. This could take place if the province had to rely on conditional transfers from another level of government to finance the decisions it makes within areas of its legitimate jurisdiction.

This dilemma can be seen more clearly by considering the case of a federation where the vast majority of public goods and services are provided at the regional (province, state or territory) level. However, all taxes are collected under the authority of the national government and then transferred to the provinces through some funding formula or with conditions attached. This would mean that the federal government, subject to majority rule at the national level, could in the end dictate to the lower level that they would only receive funds if they made decisions in line with what the majority of the country dictated. The federal level could withhold educational funds unless the lower level adopted, for example, the same language of instruction as the other provinces, territories or states. Thus, despite the fact that the province might have the legal authority to choose another language, or policy reflective of its interests, priorities and preferences, it would in effect be limited to going along with the will of the higher level of government which has the ability to withhold funding. This would render the lower level less able to pursue and use its legal authorities within areas under its jurisdiction.

It does not hold, however, that therefore all taxes should be collected at the lowest level possible and transferred upwards. This would also violate the division of powers. The example of national defence demonstrates the problem with financing from the bottom up. If all taxes were collected at the municipal level and transferred upwards, the municipalities could also hold the federal level hostage and prevent the federal level from delivering and acting in areas where it is expected and efficient to act. If an invasion took place on one side of the country, it would be cumbersome for the federal government to have to request from all the lower levels additional sufficient funding to defeat an invasion. Further, many municipalities, especially those further away from hostilities, might decide that the burden ought to rest with those closest to the conflict and transfer too little upwards in time. If they had the power to tax and decide to transfer, the entire nation would be potentially threatened by expansion of foreign invasion, and by the time the municipalities far away realised it was in their interest to pay more, it would be too late.

As a result, it is argued here that parallel to the discussion on the division of powers across multiple levels of government, the fiscal dimension, revenue raising and spending, must follow this principle. Adequate resources for financing decisions within the jurisdiction of the level of government must be allocated in line with subsidiarity. If a level of government does not have sufficient revenues, it will have to rely on another level of government for finances, and this would in effect violate the very dilemma that the principle of subsidiarity sought to resolve and avoid as far as possible. It also means that in those cases where a level of government is unable to serve its citizens, the national level has greater clarity in terms of providing assistance in addition to the possibility of unconditional and conditional grants to pursue issues of national concern.

To be sure, the principle of subsidiarity will not remove all controversy or disputes over areas of jurisdiction and financing. It will serve to reduce those disputes, however, especially in large diverse countries with multiple levels of governance. Evidence from Canada will help to show that despite being initially designed as a centralised power, there is sufficient diversity that likely explains the decentralised nature of modern Canada and the rationale for adopting the principle of subsidiarity. Further, data shows significant decentralisation of revenues across the country that matches spending, with areas of transfers and co-financing. In many aspects, Canada has embraced the cooperative nature of subsidiarity, the fiscal dimension, yet with significant tax and spending at the national level to pursue common interests.

Fiscal subsidiarity in Canada

According to the preamble of the BNA, the provinces of Canada (Ontario and Quebec), New Brunswick and Nova Scotia, expressed their 'desire to become federally united into one Dominion under the Crown of Great Britain and Ireland, with a Constitution similar in principle to that of the United Kingdom' (British North America Act 1867). Among many reasons for forming this union were the raising of public credit, transportation and defence (Magnet 1978). At that time the former British colonies to the south had already declared independence nearly a century before and had recently concluded a bloody civil war. The remaining British colonies to the north had a scattered, largely rural, population of only 3.5 million with considerable concern over defence since their southern neighbours were beginning to expand westward and northward at a time when Britain did not want to become involved in additional war efforts to defend its remaining claims in North America. The formation of the Dominion government was thought to offer a viable solution to a common set of problems in terms of collective defence, the raising of sufficient funds for transportation and infrastructure to foster growth and development, and an internal common market (Norrie and Owram 1996; Pomfret 1981).

Beyond the BNA outlining a parliamentary system of government, it also divided legislative powers between the new federal government and the provinces. There was, at that time, considerable dispute over transferring power to the new government and a compromise was reached that favoured a strong central government with considerable economic power remaining in the hands of the provinces. In the sixth section of the Act, for example, Article 91 grants the national level with legislative authority over all matters related to peace, order and good government that do not exclusively fall within a list of specific powers granted to the provinces. Article 91 further lists 29 specific issues over which the national government has authority including matters such as defence, weights and measures, navigation and shipping, currency, banking and naturalisation, and ends by granting any residual matters not specifically outlined in the BNA at the time of writing to the national level.

Article 92 outlines the matters falling within provincial jurisdiction which were at that time thought to be less important; the growth of the social welfare state had not yet taken place. This article specifies 16 specific powers followed by additional articles over education (Article 95) and agriculture (Article 93). Most of the enumerated powers were thought to be of a more local nature, such as hospitals, justice administration, and control over municipalities. Further, while the provinces were limited to areas of direct taxation, the federal level had the power to raise funds by any mode or system of taxation, including over customs and excise taxes (Article 122). This latter tax was one of the main sources of government revenue at the time and even during the initial years of the new country, provinces received nearly half of their revenues from the federal government (Magnet 1978).

Canada today, however, stands in stark contrast to these original intentions and designs in 1867. It can be characterised as largely decentralised with considerably more room for tax and spending at the provincial and municipal levels combined than at the federal level (Simeon and Papillon 2006). Further, the country has grown to 36 million people with ten provinces and three territories. Figure 1 shows Canada's population by number and percentage share across the provinces and territories and can help shed light on one of the key challenges the federation faces.

Figure 1: Canadian population, and share of national total, by province and territory, 2015. Source: Statistics Canada (2015).

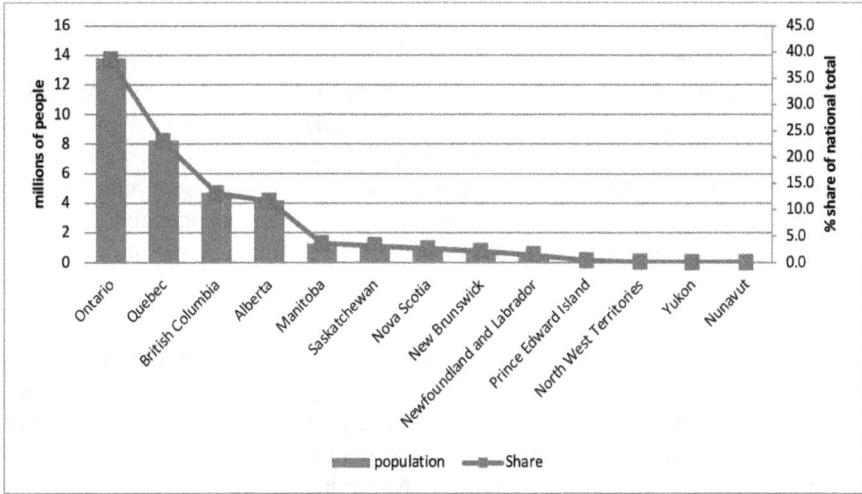

There are several critical observations that can be made from this figure with respect to federalism. First, of the 13 members of the federation, four provinces are large in terms of population while the remaining are small by comparison. In fact, the largest province, Ontario, has nearly 40 per cent of the nation's population and together with the second largest, Quebec, 61.5 per cent. The four largest provinces together have 86.3 per cent of the national population. The rest of the people reside in the remaining six provinces and three territories. In fact, these smaller nine members of the federation have far less than 10 per cent each of the national total.

The distribution of Canada's population across the provinces and territories poses a significant challenge to the governance of the federation. This can be seen more clearly if one were to imagine Canada as a highly centralised country where most decisions were to be made at the national level rather than at lower levels (provincial/territorial, municipal) across the country. If a policy, piece of legislation, or spending proposal satisfied the two largest provinces, or perhaps even all four of the largest together, they could form a majority, democratically, and dominate the national agenda. Even if the remaining nine provinces and territories significantly disagreed or sought a priority that was only in their interests. Even collectively they would not be able to achieve their objectives through a simple majority rule. If Canada, as a nation state, were organised in a centralised fashion, many of the members of the country would find it difficult to find a benefit in remaining within the country when it comes to policy disagreements.

It may be the case, however, that many across the country share much in common. There may even be agreement in many areas, meaning that disputes would be not so common and perhaps majorities of smaller members might be aligned with the larger ones. In a country with such diversity in terms of economic priorities, local infrastructure projects, or the level of prosperity, decentralisation over decision-making would, however, allow for multiple legitimate majorities (Cyr 2014). By having a division of powers between the federal government and provinces and territories, the nation as a whole can avoid dominance by the larger members and allow for divergences in preferences, priorities and views that can accommodate and avoid disputes from arising in those cases where interests diverge, and there is no reason for a higher level to impose its will on the lower level.

Incidentally, and secondly, it is also apparent in Figure 1 that the two largest members of the federation are Ontario and Quebec. Together, these two provinces located in the centre of the country have 61.5 per cent of the total national population, with 38.5 and 23 per cent respectively. While Ontario is an anglophone province, Quebec is francophone. On the one hand, the majority of Canada is in English dominated provinces and territories, and it would be hypothetically possible for a simple majority of the Canadian population to impose its will on Quebec if the country were highly centralised, especially in the area of language laws. A majority of Canadians could simply decide and vote to make the country unilingual, if it so desired. On the other hand, voters in Quebec and Ontario, hypothetically, could also vote together to collectively dominate the national agenda and trade votes strategically, including in areas of language laws. The benefit of dividing powers within the federation can be seen from this hypothetical example more clearly. Lower levels of government can pursue language laws, and the nation as a whole can achieve benefit by adopting and enshrining both English and French, even though Quebec has a sizeable portion, yet minority, of the country's population. Decentralisation allows the members to pursue their own interests, especially where they diverge, yet remain together in a cooperative federal state.

It is also the case that during the past 150 years of Canada's evolution from a centralised to a decentralised nation, many of the matters that were originally considered minor, such as health and education, have become much more important. These matters happen to also fall under provincial jurisdiction and the growth in expenditures to provide health and education in part explains the growth in level of spending at the provincial levels. This trend helps to explain how in Canada the share of public spending at the federal level has declined since the 19th century. Canada's federal level of government spends about 35 per cent of the total public spending. This is similar to comparable data from Switzerland (34 per cent) while it is much lower than other states, such as the USA (61 per cent), Australia (53 per cent), and Germany (41 per cent). Thus, Canada appears by comparison to be one of the most decentralised federations by portion of budgetary spending (Simeon and Papillon 2006).

The share of total public spending could be somewhat misleading. It could be that the federal level of government collects the bulk of revenue and then transfers through some mechanism funds to lower levels of government. This takes place to some degree in Canada, but not to the degree that would take place in nation-states where the division of taxation powers is more centralised and exercised at that level. If this were the case in Canada, it would be possible, hypothetically, for the federal level of government to make decisions over the use of public funds at lower levels and impose conditions on receiving revenues. This would, in effect, leave lower levels with less decision-making authority than what might otherwise appear in terms of a constitutional division as stated on paper. For example, the federal level could withhold funding if it thought the lower level was not going to spend it in a way that the national level thought best, such as on a specific set of educational programs. The federal level could state that it would provide funding for vocational schools, colleges and universities to the sub-national level only if the lower level provided specific training in specific areas and in a specific language. Canada could state that it would provide funding to Quebec for higher education, but only if the language of instruction were in English, otherwise the funding would stop or not be provided. This makes the case clearer for why authority over revenue raising also plays a critical role in the distribution of powers in a federal state; without the ability to adequately raise revenue to spend on areas within an authority's power, it would have potentially less real say in how it exercises its powers to meet local needs, priorities and preferences.

Figure 2 sheds some light on the revenue and expenditures by level of government in Canada's federation. It shows the total in 2015 of revenues and expenditures by the federal level followed by each of the provinces and territories. Municipal and local level spending are included in the provincial and territorial totals. Although four members are too small to show up comparatively in the figure, namely Prince Edward Island, Yukon, the North West Territories and Nunavut, the overall trends remain similar. In Canada, the two levels of government have revenue bases that are similar to their expenditure level. In fact, Canadian provinces and territories have significant access to fiscal resources to cover the areas over which they exercise authority. This helps prevent the possibility that the significantly larger members could overshadow or dominate how smaller members of the federation use their powers. Second, it is evident from the figure that two provinces, Ontario and Quebec, appear on the national scene as being almost as large as the federal government when compared to the size of the other provinces. Third, it appears that Canada's federation has not only significant powers at the principle or territorial level, but also a division of fiscal powers that provides a level of adequacy to hold considerable decision-making authority over the powers they have.

Figure 2: Total government revenues and expenditures in Canada by level of government, 2015. Source: Statistics Canada (2015).

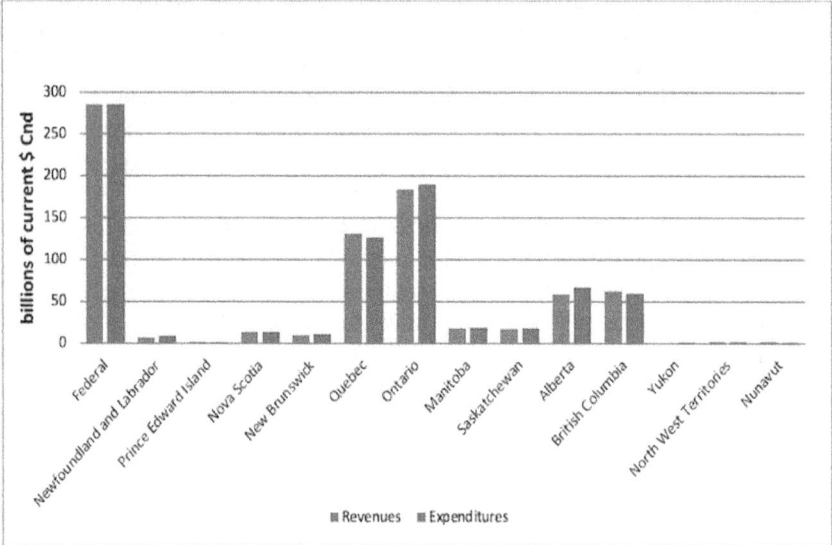

At the same time, for areas of common interest across the country, the national level plays a significant role in terms of tax and spending. The federal level has access to own resources to not be left completely dependent on seeking bilateral and multi-lateral deals constantly in order to access revenues and spend as it sees fit. This point is worth emphasising as well when it comes to decentralisation. It is not as if the country is completely decentralised in the hands of lower levels of government. The principle of subsidiarity holds that the higher level is delegated a subsidiary role and that power should remain at the lower level as far as possible. This does not deny that there are areas of national concern, such as national defence, inter-provincial infrastructure projects, or other policy areas that are in the legitimate sphere of power of the national level. Further, it would be cumbersome to relegate the role of the federal level to only engage in Canada at the consent of lower levels. This would mean that two to four large players would dominate the scene, and the federal government would essentially be the government of Ontario, Quebec, and plausibly Alberta and British Columbia. For the federal level to not be dominated by a small number of large members, and to also avoid the cumbersome process of seeking consent over legitimate national issues, it makes sense to have some power at that level. In fact, the federal level also has fiscal authority to raise and spend funds. It oddly has constitutionally the greatest power to tax, but through cooperation, court decisions, and evolution, does not actually play the role originally intended in 1867 today.

Not apparent in Figure 2 are some worthwhile nuances about the federal system in terms of subsidiarity and fiscal relations. Collecting taxes is not free. Tax administration is costly, and it would pose even more burden per capita on smaller members of the federation than on the larger, at least generally speaking. In areas where both the federal and provincial/territorial levels of government tax the same base, having separate tax administrations at both levels would replicate costs and pose an even greater burden on taxpayers across the country. Further, it could be argued that having provinces and territories carry out all taxation and transfer to the federal level might have some negative consequences, such as the larger members having more effective say in the country since they hold larger purse strings. It would also involve arguably more costs than perhaps having a nation-wide collection agency that transfers to the lower levels.

In Canada, although tax powers are divided in the 1867 BNA, with lower levels having less room to tax than the federal level, the federal level provides for the collection of the bulk of taxes collected in the country. The Canada Revenue Agency (CRA) collects personal income tax across the country, for example, with both provinces and the federal level taxing personal income similarly, but with some room for difference across the provinces. The share of provincial tax collected in a specific province is then transferred back. This is an example of subsidiarity potentially providing a basis for cooperative federalism, especially when it is considered that exceptions have also been tolerated. Within this general system, Quebec collects its own share of the personal income tax in that province. For corporate taxation, Alberta, Ontario and Quebec also collect their own portions separately (withheld at source). These nuanced details not only indicate some areas where there are federal-provincial tensions, but also where there is scope for cooperation and agreement to allow for diversity while remaining a nation state as a whole.

Although there is significant room for members of Canada's federation to tax and spend in areas within its jurisdiction as outlined in the 1867 BNA and the 1982 Constitution, there are areas of national interest and overlap in some program areas. Although there are divisions and tensions, there is considerable room for dual identities. While citizens may view themselves as residents or members of a specific province or territory, and while these identities can remain quite strong even when members of the federation move to another province or territory, they are also citizens of the federation. In areas such as health, education, and other social programs, the provinces and territories would differ to some degree in their ability to raise revenues sufficiently to cover similar levels of these across the country simply because of income inequality and other economic differences, such as stability in regional economies over time.

Due to differences in abilities to pay for social programs across the country, the federal level of government has four major transfers they make to provinces and territories: the Canada Health Transfer (CHT), the Canada Social Transfer (CST), equalisation payments to provinces, and a Territorial Financing Formula (TFF). From 2015 to 2016, the total transferred through all four programs from the federal to the sub-national levels was nearly $ Cnd 68 billion. While the first two are for financing specific programs, equalisation and TFF are considered unconditional grants, with the intention overall to ensure that citizens of the federation enjoy similar levels of what are considered critical social programs regardless of the province or territory in which they happen to reside. Without detailing a history of contentions over these sizeable transfers, such as interference into powers that are technically within the scope or jurisdiction of provinces, in terms of the principle of subsidiarity it could be argued that while the bulk of spending and revenue raising takes place at these lower levels, this overlap and transfer also provides citizens with benefits to being members of a federal state and a large common market.

Overlap also would indicate and be in line with modern interpretations of subsidiarity involving cooperative approaches to achieve equity, solidarity, efficiency and effectiveness in program delivery rather than defending strict divisions of powers as may be outlined in constitutional provisions. For example, education is technically within the scope of provincial jurisdiction, yet it might be nationally desirable to ensure that all Canadian citizens, regardless of where they live, have access to similar levels of educational programs, while at the same time recognising that local economies may have sufficient differences in needs, specialisation to permit some degree of diversity in funding, and programming.

Figure 3 provides an overview of the four major transfer programs in Canada for 2015 to 2016. Due to scaling issues, it is difficult to see the levels of all four across all provinces and territories. In that year, Newfoundland and Labrador, Saskatchewan, Alberta and British Columbia did not receive equalisation payments, but they did receive CHT and CST transfers. All three territories received TFF, and the remaining received a combination of all three (except TFF).

Figure 3: Transfers from federal to sub-national levels of government by province and territory, 2015–2016. Source: Government of Canada, Department of Finance (2017).

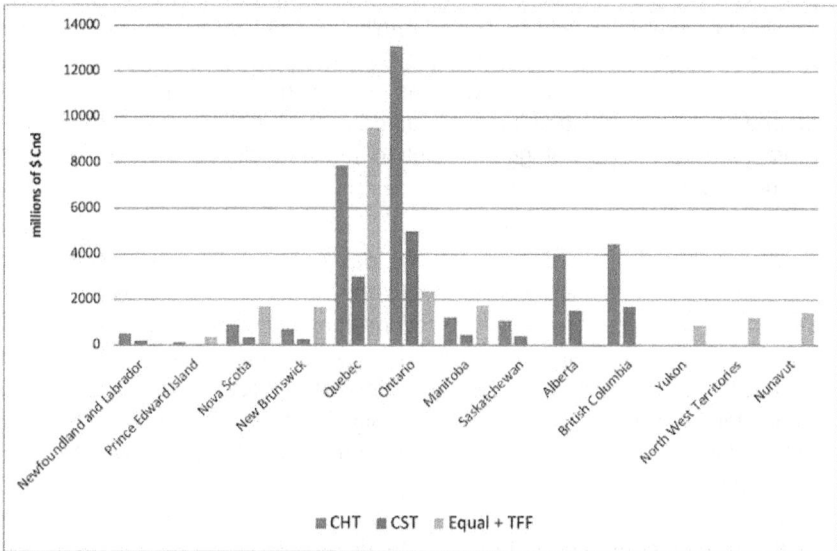

Thus, while Canada can be characterised as having a highly decentralised federation in terms of the share of public spending at the federal level, there is not only considerable room for lower level raising of revenue to act in areas under their jurisdiction, but also general overlap and cost sharing between the two levels to ensure that there is adequacy in terms of local provision of core public goods and services. Canada's decentralised federation has characteristics of federal jurisdiction in some areas, provincial or territorial in others; yet overlap in fiscal terms despite clear legislative boundaries outlined in the original BNA of 1867. These fiscal dimensions indicate considerable evolution from the original intent to the reality of today.

Conclusion

The fiscal dimension of subsidiarity can help to understand how Canada can remain together as a highly decentralised federation. It is not arbitrariness, pure historical luck, or a history of *ad hoc* decisions made on a short-term basis. The country could have been configured, despite the division of powers in 1867, in favour of a strong centralised government that raised the bulk of taxes and found ways to impose its decisions through national majority rule on the provinces and lower levels of government. This would be difficult in a country like Canada due to several key features within the country. There is considerable diversity across the provinces and territories in terms of population, economic interests, culture and preferences. If the country were highly centralised, there would be considerable risk that national decisions would be dominated by a small number, perhaps even just two or three provinces. Economic interests and policy preferences and priorities of the remaining members would be considerably overshadowed with the exception of those few areas where there were coincidentally common views. These key features, when combined with the original division of powers, lends a degree of understanding as to why Canada is decentralised with considerable room for lower levels of government to make decisions that reflect local priorities, preferences and culture.

Further, this evolution of decentralised decision-making and jurisdiction in Canada appears to be consistent with the principle of subsidiarity in the sense that authority is closer to the constituents' concerns with the federal level playing a subsidiary role. This also appears to be the case in the fiscal dimension since each level has considerable access to resources to act within those areas of its jurisdiction. Subsidiary is less meaningful, and potentially violated, if each level is not provided with the power to raise adequate revenues to cover the expenses involved in carrying out the decisions it has the power and authority to make. Subsidiarity, however, is not explicitly adopted in terms of the original division of powers in the 1867 BNA nor in the Constitution of 1982. In Canada's case, the principle of subsidiarity has shown up instead directly and indirectly in modern Supreme Court decisions over jurisdictional disputes between the levels of government. Whether by intentional design, custom or habit, Canada has, effectively in these key ways, adopted the principle of subsidiarity lock, stock and barrel.

References

Bentham, J. (1988). *The Principles of Morals and Legislation*. Amherst, New York: Prometheus Books.

British North America Act (1867) 30-31 Vict., c. 3. Available at: https://www.justice.gc.ca/eng/rp-pr/csj-sjc/constitution/lawreg-loireg/p1t11.html

Broullet, E. (2011). 'Canadian Federalism and the Principle of Subsidiarity: Should we open Pandora's box?'. *The Supreme Court Law Review: Osgoode's Annual Constitutional Cases Conference* 54 (Article 21): 600–32.

Cyr, H. (2014). 'Autonomy, Subsidiarity, Solidarity: Foundations of Cooperative Federalism', *Constitutional Forum* 23(4): 20–40.

Follesdal, A. and V. M. Muñiz Fraticelli (2015). 'The Principle of Subsidiarity as a Constitutional Principle in the EU and Canada'. *The Ethics Forum* 10(2): 89-106. Available at: https://www.erudit.org/en/journals/ateliers/1900-v1-n1-ateliers02386/1035329ar.pdf

Friesen, M. (2003). 'Subsidiarity and Federalism: An Old Concept with Contemporary Relevance for Political Society'. *Federal Governance* 1(2): 1–22.

Government of Canada (2017). *Federal Transfers to Provinces and Territories 2011-2012 to 2015-16.* Department of Finance. Available at: https://www.canada.ca/en/department-finance/programs/federal-transfers/major-federal-transfers.html

Halberstam, D. (2009). 'Federal Powers and the Principle of Subsidiarity'. In V. Amar and M. Tushnet *(eds) Global Perspectives on Constitutional Law,* 34–47. Oxford: Oxford University Press.

Hueglin, T. O. (2013). 'Two (or Three) Tales of Subsidiarity'. Paper Presented at the *Annual Meeting of the Canadian Political Science Association,* June 4–6. Victoria, B.C. Available at: https://www.cpsa-acsp.ca/papers-2013/Hueglin.pdf

Kong, H. L. (2015). 'Subsidiarity, Republicanism and the Division of Powers in Canada', *Revue de Droit de l'Université de Sherbrooke* 45: 13–46.

Magnet, J. E. (1978). 'The Constitutional Distribution of Taxation Powers in Canada', *Ottawa Law Review* 10: 473–534.

Norrie, K. and D. Owram (1996). *A History of the Canadian Economy.* Toronto, Ontario: Harcourt Brace.

Pomfret, R. (1981). *The Economic Development of Canada.* Agincourt, Ontario: Methuen.

Statistics Canada (2015). *Table 10-10-0017-01. Canadian Government Finance Statistics for the Provincial and Territorial Governments.* Available at: https://www23.statcan.gc.ca/imdb/p2SV.pl?Function=getSurvey&Id=298948

Statistics Canada (2015). *Table 17-10-0005-01. Population Estimates on July 1st, by Age and Sex.* Available at: https://www150.statcan.gc.ca/t1/tbl1/en/tv.action?pid=1710000501

Simeon, R. and M. Papillon (2006). 'Canada'. In A. Mujeed, R. L. Watts, D. M. Brown, and J. Kincaid (eds) *Distribution of Powers and Responsibilities in Federal Countries,* 91-122. Montreal: McGill-Queen's University Press.

Note on Indexing

Our publications do not feature indexes. If you are reading this book in paperback and want to find a particular word or phrase you can do so by downloading a free PDF version of this book from the E-International Relations website.

View the e-book in any standard PDF reader such as Adobe Acrobat Reader (pc) or Preview (mac) and enter your search terms in the search box. You can then navigate through the search results and find what you are looking for. In practice, this method can prove much more targeted and effective than consulting an index.

If you are using apps (or devices) to read our e-books, you should also find word search functionality in those.

You can find all of our e-books at: http://www.e-ir.info/publications

www.ingramcontent.com/pod-product-compliance
Lightning Source LLC
Chambersburg PA
CBHW070924030426
42336CB00014BA/2529

9 781910 814574